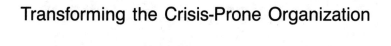

Transforming the Crisis-Prone Organization

**Thierry C. Pauchant
Ian I. Mitroff**

Transforming the Crisis-Prone Organization

PREVENTING INDIVIDUAL, ORGANIZATIONAL, AND ENVIRONMENTAL TRAGEDIES

 Jossey-Bass Publishers
San Francisco

For sales outside the United States contact Maxwell Macmillan International Publishing Group, 866 Third Avenue, New York, New York 10022

Printed on acid-free paper and manufactured in the United States of America

The paper used in this book meets the state of California require-ments for recycled paper (50 percent recycled waste, including 10 percent postconsumer waste), which are the strictest guidelines for recycled paper currently in use in the United States.

Library of Congress Cataloging-in-Publication Data

Pauchant, Thierry C.
    Transforming the crisis-prone organization: preventing individual, organizational, and environmental tragedies / Thierry C. Pauchant, Ian I. Mitroff. — 1st ed.
       p.   cm. — (The Jossey-Bass management series)
    Includes bibliographical references and index.
   ISBN 1-55542-407-4 (acid-free paper)
    1. Crisis management.   I. Mitroff, Ian I.   II. Title.
III. Series.
HD49.P38   1992
658.4—dc20   91-37910
                                                  CIP

FIRST EDITION
HB Printing   10 9 8 7 6 5 4 3 2 1   *Code 9212*

The Jossey-Bass
Management Series

Consulting Editors
Organizations and Management

Warren Bennis
University of Southern California

Richard O. Mason
Southern Methodist University

Ian I. Mitroff
University of Southern California

Contents

ix

Preface

Bhopal, Chernobyl, the Exxon *Valdez* disaster, the Gulf War—these are just a few landmark events that demonstrate a startling point: for the first time in history, human beings have the potential to create catastrophes that rival natural disasters in their scope.

Until recently, the impacts of most human-caused disasters were mainly confined to the relatively intact and isolated communities in which they occurred. Today, however, a chemical or nuclear accident in one part of the world is capable of affecting large regions of the planet, if not the entire globe. This alone has significantly raised the stakes for global safety and makes today's crisis environment very different from the one we knew sixty or seventy years ago.

Natural and human-caused disasters, while similar in many ways, are different nonetheless. While we can predict some natural disasters, we are still largely powerless to prevent them. The best we can do is to prepare for them, mitigate their worst effects, and recover from them as quickly as possible. Human-made crises, on the other hand, are in principle both predictable and preventable. Given this fact, organizations have little choice but to do everything in their power to prevent these crises from ever occurring.

Transforming the Crisis-Prone Organization argues that we have taken decisive steps toward understanding why modern industrial crises happen and learning how to prevent them. The book is based on information gathered through our research and consulting work over a six-year period in the field of crisis management (CM). With the help of our associates at the University of Southern California Center for Crisis Management (CCM), we have conducted more than five hundred personal interviews with managers, professionals, and senior executives responsible for CM in the United States, Canada, and France. The interview results were supplemented by questionnaires sent to Fortune 1000 companies. (See Resource A for further discussion of this material.) We have also presented numerous workshops and training seminars in CM, as well as conducted crisis audits or interventions in several corporations, government agencies, and universities. In addition, we have analyzed the available scientific literature on crises.

We wrote *Transforming the Crisis-Prone Organization* to address a fundamental paradox. On the one hand, the current increase in human crises is one of the most visible signs that our usual ways of conducting business are not only seriously outdated but dangerous as well. On the other hand, despite all the public attention given to disasters, as well as their increase in number, the best available evidence indicates that fewer than 10 to 15 percent of the large corporations in North Amcrica and Europe have currently developed significant crisis management programs.

This book looks at the deeper reasons for the paradox. It explores the gap between our intellectual ability to acknowledge the need for change and our emotional inability to translate that understanding into action.

Overview of the Contents

The first two chapters of *Transforming the Crisis-Prone Organization* deal with the nature of human crises and crisis management. The complexity of these issues is demonstrated through the case of the Bhopal disaster. Chapters Three through Seven present the components of what we call the Onion Model of Crisis Management, which emphasizes the interrelationships between the psyche of individuals, organizational culture, organizational structure, and the strategy of an organization. Chapter Eight presents an ideal crisis management plan drawn from the best examples we have found in the United States, Canada, and France. Finally, in Chapters Nine and Ten we discuss the difficulties of changing the crisis management behaviors of managers and organizations, propose some hypotheses for the future, and place crisis management in the broader context of ethics.

Throughout, we address the dual objectives of better understanding the phenomenon of crises and recognizing the difficulty of change. We also provide a number of tools and practical models to assist managers in accomplishing these objectives: evaluation questionnaires to assess their crisis-preparedness and compute a "crisis profile"; concrete strategies for crisis management; and numerous case studies drawn from our research and consulting experience.

Audience

This book is addressed first to executives, managers, and employees who wish to develop a serious crisis management program in their organization. In particular, we believe that the book will be helpful for managers and executives who are responsible for public relations, government relations, public and environmental affairs, security management, or corporate planning. In addition, organizational development consultants, management training specialists, and change agents who wish to expand their practice to the field of crisis management will find it useful. Furthermore, *Transforming the Crisis-Prone Organization* will be of interest to public officials involved in security and safety planning and regulation; it will help them understand better the issues of crisis management and the realities in which the managers of organizations are often trapped.

The book is also addressed to graduate students in business, public administration, and engineering and those studying the social sciences in general. Professors need to expose their students to the reality of industrial crises and the complexity of crisis management.

Third, we hope that this book will motivate researchers to undertake scientific studies in crisis management. While important strides have already been made, crisis management is still in its infancy, and a general theory of crisis in organizations is badly needed.

Last, *Transforming the Crisis-Prone Organization* is addressed to all those who care about organizations, about the people working in them, and about the art and science of business, since the book is not only about crisis management: it is an in-depth study of the feelings, thoughts, and actions of people in organizations. In a crisis, the behaviors of both individuals and organizations are often more visible and explicit. Thus, to a real extent, the context of crisis is an excellent one in which to study organizations and the people within them.

Acknowledgments

We wish to thank Omar Aktouf, Warren G. Bennis, Dorinda Cavanaugh, Alain Chanlat, Jean-François Chanlat, C. West Churchman, Omar El Sawy, Taleb Hafsi, Richard Mason, Danny Miller, Michel Provost, Warren H. Schmidt, Paul Shrivastava, Firdaus Udwadia, Didier Van Den Hove, and Gerry F. Ventolo. Estelle M. Morin helped tremendously with her expertise in the field of psychology. Similarly, we wish to thank the more than twenty corporate sponsors of CCM for their comments and practical advice. We would also like to thank our editors at Jossey-Bass: William Hicks, editor of the Management Series, for his positive critiques and his patience about a draft that was always "in the mail"; and Marcella Friel, our production editor, who worked diligently to apply the finishing touches.

We owe a tremendous debt to the several research scientists and research assistants in Los Angeles at CCM and at L'École des Hautes Études Commerciales (HEC) in Montreal, who collected diverse material at different stages of the research and enriched our understanding of crisis management. They include Judy Clair, Nathalie Cotard, Roseline Douville, Jean Dupuis, Mike Finney, Isabelle Fortier, Sarah Kovoor, Mireille Lebeau, Maria Nathan, Lucie Poliquin-Zaor, and Christophe Roux-Dufort. Above all, Chris Pearson, associate director of the USC Center for Crisis Management, deserves special mention. Without her, very little of the research described in this book could have become a reality. Special thanks go to Professor Patrick Lagadec from the École Polytechnique, Paris, for sharing the content of his interviews with French organizations, as well as for the many fruitful exchanges we had with him over the years on the subject of crisis management, comparing the issues present in the United States, Canada, and France.

This book would not have been possible without the hundreds of executives, managers, professionals, and other organizational members who gave generously of their time during the interviews. We are grateful as well for the commentaries we received from both the managers attending our workshops and the graduate students in our seminars.

Our research has been supported by several sponsors and foundations. In particular, we wish to thank CCM's corporate sponsors, the Herbert Hoover Foundation, the University of Southern California, AT&T, the Conseil de Recherches en Sciences Humaines du Canada (CRSH) and the Fonds pour la Formation de Chercheurs et l'Aide à la Recherche (FCAR), as well as L'École des Hautes Études Commerciales, for their generosity.

Last but not least, we wish to thank Dorinda Cavanaugh, Diane Losson, and Lucie Pagé for their very professional and cheerful help in typing the many versions of this book.

February 1992

Thierry C. Pauchant
Montreal, Quebec

Ian I. Mitroff
Los Angeles, California

To my parents,
Claude Pauchant and Anne-Françoise Willem,
in appreciation of what you gave me
and the way you did it.

— Thierry

To the memory
of my father-in-law,
George Drevenak.

— Ian

The Authors

Thierry C. Pauchant is assistant professor of management at l'École des Hautes Études Commerciales (HEC) of the University of Montreal. He received his B.S. degree (1977) from the University of Grenoble in marketing; his M.S. degree (1979) from the Pantheon-Sorbonne University (Paris) in planning; his M.B.A. degree (1984) from the University of California, Los Angeles, in strategic and organizational sciences; and his Ph.D. degree (1987) from the University of Southern California in business administration.

Pauchant has been a research associate at the Center for Crisis Management (CCM) at the University of Southern California since 1985, as well as a consultant on industrial and organizational crises for firms located in the United States, Canada, and France. He is currently a member of the American Academy of Management, the Association for Humanistic Psychology, the Strategic Management Society, and the World Future Society.

Pauchant's research interests lie in industrial crisis management, the social and ecological implications of corporate strategies, and the existential dimension of business. Before joining HEC, he taught at the University of San Francisco, UCLA, USC, and Laval University. He has written more than twenty scientific and professional articles and will be the guest editor of the international scientific journal *Industrial Crisis Quarterly* for the year 1993. He is also the author of *We're So Big and Powerful That Nothing Bad Can Happen to Us* (1990, with I. Mitroff).

Ian I. Mitroff is Harold Quinton Distinguished Professor of Business Policy and Strategic Management and director of the Center for Crisis Management at the Graduate School of Business of the University of Southern California. He received his B.S. degree (1961) in engineering physics, his M.S. degree (1963) in structural engineering, and his Ph.D. degree (1967) in engineering psychology, with a minor in the philosophy of social science, all from the University of California, Berkeley.

Mitroff is a well-known consultant to many Fortune 500 companies and government agencies. He is on the editorial board of several management journals and management book series and has written more than two hundred articles in scientific journals and popular magazines. Mitroff's books include *Break-Away Thinking: How to Challenge Your Business Assumptions (and Why You Should)* (1988), *The Unreality Industry: The Deliberate Manufacturing of Falsehood and What It Is Doing to Our Lives* (1989, with W. Bennis), and *We're So Big and Powerful That Nothing Bad Can Happen to Us* (1990, with T. Pauchant).

Mitroff is a member of the American Association for the Advancement of Science, the American Psychological Association, the American Sociological Association, the Institute of Management Science, the Philosophy of Science Association, and the American Academy of Management.

Transforming the Crisis-Prone Organization

Those who flow as life flows know they need no other force: they feel no wear, they feel no tear, they need no mending, no repair.

—Lao Tzu, *The Way of Life*

All is divisible and indivisible . . . they all ignore this. . . . They do not know how being at variance it agrees with itself: there is a connection working in both directions, as in the bow and the lyre.

—Heraclitus of Ephesus, *The Cosmic Fragments*

A Delicate Balancing Act:
People, Organizations, and Technologies

It is in [the] whole process of meeting and solving problems that life has its meaning. . . . Wise people learn not to dread but actually to welcome problems.

—M. Scott Peck, *The Road Less Traveled*

Whoever is educated by possibility remains with anxiety. . . . For him, anxiety becomes a serving spirit that against its will leads him where he wishes to go.

—Søren Kierkegaard, *The Concept of Anxiety*

Each time a major industrial accident happens, our minds are flooded with disturbing thoughts and emotions. Why do such disasters continue to happen? Why have we not learned more from previous crises? How many more have to occur before we finally change our ways of managing large organizations?

Through our research, we have learned that just as some individuals are accident-prone, so are organizations. Some organizations are in fact a crisis of huge proportions just waiting to happen. We call these organizations *crisis-prone*. Others, while not totally immune, have at least done everything possible to prevent major crises from occurring in the first place and to better manage those that do occur. We call these organizations *crisis-prepared*.

Disasters such as Bhopal, *Challenger*, Chernobyl, or the Exxon *Valdez* have fueled our ongoing love/hate relationship with technology in particular and with narrow management perspectives in general. On the positive side, we recognize the necessity for in-depth, specialized competence within a confined area of expertise. However, industrial disasters also remind us strongly of the darker side of restricted perspectives: the tendency toward

1

narrow thinking; the tendency to fragment complex questions into microscopic parts that distort the real issue; the inflated sense of self-importance that some professionals attach to themselves and their narrow concerns; the arrogance that they often exhibit toward other perspectives. We believe that this darker side of professionalism is one of the major causes of many industrial crises.

To be clear, we are not saying that professionalism and specialization should be abolished altogether. We are certainly not saying that our civilization would be better off if we abandoned all technology and retreated to some utopian, pretechnology "golden age." The argument that we need to give up driving our cars and heating our homes with oil if we wish to avoid all accidents is both facetious and fallacious. We reject such either/or solutions, since they themselves are prime examples of narrow thinking. Our argument is that if our society continues to depend on many technologies in order to function, then we need to establish appropriate procedures for managing them. In short, we must create a strong balance between the complexity of modern technologies and the complexity of the human beings who manage them.

We will come back to this theme in different ways through each of the following chapters. We hope to demonstrate, for example, that we can no longer trust the narrow perspective of any one profession to manage large organizations. While we may trust engineers or research and development specialists to invent new products and services, financial and accounting experts to manage the monetary assets, or marketing professionals to develop the sales of new products and services, we can no longer trust any of them to manage all the critical aspects of large organizations that deal in dangerous products and technologies. Professionals may be adept at understanding the complex, technical linkages between the various components of their individual professions, but they are generally ignorant of the even more complex linkages between professions, the multiple divisions of modern organizations, or the diversity of concerns and needs in society as a whole. And they are often ill at ease with the intricacies of human behavior. This gets to the heart of why we are experiencing a drastic outbreak of human-induced crises of all kinds. Humans are now managing technologies that are at the very limit of both their understanding and their ability to control.

We have to realize that reliance on a restricted number of perspectives operates not only at the cognitive or thinking level but at the affective or emotional level as well. The cognitive realm includes the capacity to analyze and conceptualize problems through abstract thinking and the use of language. The emotional realm, on the one hand, includes the raw affective energy literally pushing individuals to diverse interests, such as their professional specialization, their personal life-style, their friends, peers, or spouse. Management texts often emphasize the cognitive limitations of managers and professionals, but that is not sufficient to explain how and why major crises occur.

During our interviews with corporate executives, we encountered a number of attitudes in crisis-prone organizations that cannot be explained by limitations in cognitive ability alone. There was ample evidence that the executives could think well enough when they wanted to. There was also ample evidence that all of them had been exposed, in one way or another, to a number of industrial disasters such as Bhopal, *Challenger,* Chernobyl, Exxon *Valdez,* Perrier, Seveso, and Tylenol. Theoretically, all of them were cognitively aware of the very real disaster potential of companies in their industry. Nonetheless, they were unable to consider the possiblity of similar crises happening in their *own* companies. For example, a director of security at a large food organization considered that the worst crisis for his customers would be to not find the company's products on the shelves. He could not imagine customers being poisoned by his company's products. For another, during a major breakdown in technology, the public relations director of a large telecommunications company relied on TV news for learning how her company's customers were faring. She could not understand the need to speak directly with her customers to understand firsthand the issues they faced. For the director of a large oil refinery plant, the worst crisis he could think of was not meeting his quarterly targets. A major accident that could severely harm the plant's employees and the broader community was beyond his imagination.

In the interviews it also became clear that many managers and professionals in crisis-prone organizations attempted to protect their own individual sense of identity and their perceived sense of the organization's identity. To admit that their organizations could encounter a major crisis meant admitting that the company was not perfect, and that maybe they were not good professionals. Even worse, they might have to admit that the profession to which they had committed their entire lives was partly responsible for widespread injuries or environmental damage.

Because the cognitive approach is so limiting, we take special care in this book to emphasize the existential side of crises. Experiencing a major crisis—even merely thinking about it—unleashes powerful feelings of anxiety. This anxiety is not rational in the traditional sense of the term, but it is very real. In response to the deep existential questions that arise during a crisis or its aftermath, many executives and professionals resort to various defensive strategies. Some explain the crisis away, pointing to factors that make it "different," so that it no longer challenges their overall perspective. Some blame other people, shifting the fault of a crisis to someone else. Others feel an urge to act quickly or to make hard and fast decisions, to keep themselves from reflecting on the crisis's deeper meaning. Still others develop chronic anxieties that paralyze their ability to act. And others seem to shut down completely.

The tragedy is that these defensive mechanisms lead to further crises, setting off the need for more powerful defense mechanisms, triggering even more crises, and so on. We call this circular phenomenon an existentially based vicious circle, with tragic effects on organizations and the environment.

Our inability to handle the severe emotions unleashed by a crisis comes not only from our limited abilities to think and process information. Nor is it strictly due to a quality that March and Simon (1958) have called "bounded rationality," the basic human limitation to apprehend cognitively the many facets of an issue. It has also to do with deep defects in the "feeling" capacity of individuals managing organizations. We call this limitation *bounded emotionality.*

The fundamental difference between a crisis-prone organization and a crisis-prepared one lies in the concept of *responsibility,* in the existential scnse of the term. Individuals who manage crisis-prepared organizations are more able to confront the anxiety triggered by crises and to act decisively. Being less bounded emotionally, they are more able to be ethically, emotionally, and cognitively "responsible" toward themselves, their employees, their business partners, and their surrounding environment.

While we mention the crisis-prone organization in the title of this book, we do not mean to conceptualize the organization as an entity that exists independently of those who manage it. On the contrary, the concept of responsibility serves to reinforce the notion that it is only the individuals present in and out of an organization who can feel, think, and act. As the following chapters will illustrate, to speak of organizations such as Exxon or NASA as entities is itself a powerful mechanism for forgetting the responsibilities of the individuals managing or working in these organizations. While broad terms such as *top management* and *organization* are useful on a day-to-day basis, in crisis situations they have the negative effect of siphoning responsibility away from individual human beings. In this book, we use the term *organization* in a generic sense, as a practical figure of speech. We also deliberately include more cumbersome expressions, such as the "managers' perceived culture of their organization," to reintroduce into our language the centrality of individual responsibility."

It will also be apparent that this book is written from two very distinct moods. The first is anger, disgust, and moral outrage toward some individuals managing crisis-prone companies who consciously engage in practices that result in major crises. In our minds, they are criminals and should be treated as such. Our second mood is empathy for other individuals in these companies. While we may strongly disagree with their practices that result in major crises, we nonetheless understand the emotional underpinnings of their behaviors. It is the only way they know to maintain their sense of personal identity and self-worth in the face of very real emotional pain.

Our anger is especially directed toward a class of crisis-prone organizations that we label "destructive." We describe these organizations in great detail later, and so here only mention some of their more dominant characteristics. People who manage destructive crisis-prone organizations believe it is their fundamental right to exploit any resources — human, financial, or physical — without limitations. They admit no wrongdoing, no necessity for change. If a crisis occurs, they are likely to blame others. They are incapable of empathizing with others, and they exhibit little concern for issues of human dignity or ethics. Examples of the influence of these destructive individuals on the conduct of organizations include managers at ITT during the leadership of Harold Geneen, managers at the Johns Manville Corporation during the asbestos crisis, managers at the Ford Motor Company with the Pinto crisis, or those managing the Firestone Company with the Firestone 500 radial tires crisis (Hills, 1987). While we primarily feel anger toward such individuals, we are also striving to recognize what causes them to behave as they do. In order to prevent the kind of wrongdoing they perpetuate, it is necessary to understand its origins and workings.

Our empathic understanding is directed toward another kind of crisis-prone organization, which we label "tragic." Individuals who manage these organizations at least partly understand the necessity for change, but lack some of the necessary structural, cognitive, or emotional resources to make those changes. They are trapped by the structural and bureaucratic rigidity existing in their organizations, and by their own feelings of boredom and anxiety. They fiercely hold on to the status quo. In other words, they are incapable of managing organizational, industrial, or environmental crises because they are overly absorbed in attempting to manage personal and existential crises such as boredom, depression, rage, drug abuse, and so on. It may be even better to say that the people managing or working in these organizations spend most of their energies avoiding confronting their own existential anxiety.

"Tragic" individuals are, as their very name indicates, like the heroes of Greek tragedies, entrapped in a web of self-destruction. While we strongly disagree with such behavior, merely to condemn such individuals and their firms, or to provide them with a number of conceptual models for crisis management, will be of little help. Instead, such firms and their employees need not only empathy but real tools that will help them break the existential vicious circle in which they find themselves trapped.

This book is not the story of any single crisis, although we use many concrete examples to make general points. Nor is it a definitive plan for crisis management, guaranteeing managers who follow it that their organization will never experience a crisis. While we do propose concrete actions that have proved effective in reducing both the number and the impact of crises, we more pointedly ask a number of difficult questions. This book is an attempt to get beneath the surface of crises. It identifies the factors that lead individuals to trigger major crises and to avoid developing crisis management programs. It examines the individual and organizational factors that make large-scale crises an inherent characteristic of today's world. Most of all, it exhorts us to understand what we inhabitants of an increasingly fragile planet must do if we are to avoid future large-scale crises that threaten our very existence.

ONE

Living in the Age of Mega-Crises:
The Need for a Systemic View

A crisis is exactly what is required to shock people out of unaware
dependence upon external dogma and to force them to unravel
layers of pretense to reveal naked truth about themselves.

—Rollo May, *Existence*

I was determined not to watch this launch, but Bob Ebeling coaxed
me inside the large projection TV room and I sat on the floor in
front of the screen, leaning against Bob's legs. When the Shuttle
[*Challenger*] lifted off, Bob leaned forward and whispered in my
ear: "We just dodged a bullet." Sixty seconds later, he leaned over
again and said he had just completed a prayer of thanks to the
Lord for a successful launch. Just thirteen seconds later, we both
saw the horror of destruction as the vehicle exploded. We all sat
in stunned silence for a short time, then I got up and I went straight
to my office. I sat there, staring at the walls for the rest of the day,
fighting tears. When people would come in and ask me if I was
okay, I couldn't speak; all I could so was nod my head, for fear
of totally breaking down.

—Roger Boisjoly, *Solid Rocket Motor Company*

At four-thirty on a Friday afternoon, a call comes into the headquarters of a large corporation. Panic is on the other end of the
line. "You've got to do something. I've found something terrible-
smelling in the baby food that I just bought from the Jiffy Store
here in Louisiana. My baby is reacting violently. I don't know
what to do." The company operator struggles to get the dis-
traught mother to stay on the line long enough so that he can
get important details. If he is lucky, he will be able to contact
somebody in top management who is still around this late afternoon. If he is even luckier, the company will have on staff
a trained medical specialist who knows the properties of the
products. If he is even luckier still, the operator or person on

the medical staff may be able to contact somebody in top management — that is, if the organization has been prepared for such an eventuality.

A number of critical questions have to be addressed. Is the report trustworthy? Is the mother faking it? Is she trying to extort money from the company? If the complaint is real, is the contamination localized? Have similar reports been coming in from different cities across the country? Is there a problem with a particular batch or shipment of the product? Is there a possibility of sabotage? Have the reports of the contamination been picked up by the local news media? Is the contamination so widespread or sensational that it has made the national news? Are other critical parties already taking action? Have grocers pulled the product off their shelves without contacting the manufacturer? Has the situation gotten so out of hand that even if the manufacturer were to determine that there is nothing wrong with the product, the decision to pull the product has already been exercised by others?

Imagine other scenarios: a chemical fire at sea burns wildly out of control, injuring hundreds of workers trapped on an oil platform; a large tanker collides in the open sea, spilling millions of gallons of oil. These accidents make national and even international news. Public reaction is almost immediate: fear, dismay, shock, anger, moral outrage. How could accidents of such magnitude have happened? Why? Were they deliberate? Were they preventable? Were they the result of gross incompetence, normal human error, or callous indifference? Whatever the cause, we feel betrayed. A basic trust in the institutions that are supposed to manage such things has been shattered.

Increasingly, large-scale crises seem to be built into the very fiber of modern life. They seem to occur almost daily. Their very names have become virtually synonymous with a special type of disaster: Tylenol (the injection of cyanide into capsules caused nine deaths and the recall of hundreds of thousands of bottles from shelves across the United States); Chernobyl (the world's largest nuclear disaster threatened the very existence of the entire nuclear industry); the *Challenger* (the catastrophic explosion of the space shuttle caused a tragic loss of seven lives and threatened the very continuity of the U.S. space program); Bhopal (the release of a deadly gas by a Union Carbide plant in Bhopal, India, killed between two thousand and ten thousand people, injured hundreds of thousands, and wreaked environmental havoc); San Juan Ixhuatepec (the explosion of a gas processing plant in the suburbs of Mexico City killed more than one thousand people, injured five thousand more, and had major effects on the environment); Hinsdale (a fire in a telecommunication hub in the Chicago suburbs cut both telephonic and computerized telecommunications for five hundred thousand subscribers for days, even weeks); Sandoz (the massive chemical pollution of the Rhine River by the Sandoz Corporation in Switzerland); Amoco's *Cadix* or the Exxon *Valdez* (the accidental releases of thousands of gallons of oil in ecologically fragile areas and their impact on the oil industry as a whole). And the list goes on: Three Mile Island; Love Canal; the DC-10 crisis; the Perrier crisis; the Pinto crisis; splinters of glass in Gerber's Baby Food; the Chrysler odometer setbacks; the Audi accelerator pedal problem, the Suzuki Samurai's pronounced tendency to tip over when rounding corners; the poisoning of Chilean grapes (which led to an international incident between U.S. and Chilean officials); the threat of international terrorism directed against Salman Rushdie, the author of *The Satanic Verses.*

We are experiencing a wave of crises on a scale not previously encountered. And they are quite different from past crises such as earthquakes, floods, or tornados — most of them are human caused. Increasingly, modern crises are due to criminal human intervention (such as product tampering), errors in design and systems maintenance, mistakes in operation, or faulty values and culture (as when bad news is deliberately kept from company leaders). In principle, all human-induced crises can be prevented.

When it comes to acts of nature such as a tornado, all we can do is prepare ourselves. But in the case of human-induced crises, we can do more than prepare — we can also attempt to prevent them from happening in the first place.

Definition of Terms

Crisis management is not the same as "crash management" — what to do when everything falls apart. Obviously this is important, but it is only one part of a total crisis management effort. Unfortunately, this confusion is common: 90 percent of the articles written on crisis management are of the "what-to-do-when-the-worst-happens" school (Pauchant, 1988b). Also, most crises management programs in organizations are reactive in nature. Here we focus not only on crash management — what to do in the heat of a crisis — but also on why crises happen in the first place and what can be done to prevent them. This difference in focus requires us to begin by defining precisely what we mean by the terms *crisis* and *crisis management.*

What Is a Crisis?

The concept of crisis is overused and poorly defined. In our interviews, many managers and professionals defined their primary functions as "troubleshooting," "making sure that the operation runs smoothly," or "managing crises." This view is particularly evident in organizations where individuals who are perceived as having resolved a crisis are endowed with an aura of heroism and excellence. However, these managers often confuse a crisis with other concepts such as accident, conflict, technical failure, and other more trivial circumstances. To put it bluntly, finding a last-minute substitute for a key speaker is not the same kind of "crisis" as the disaster at Bhopal.

Over the years, management scholars have battled over the definition of the term *crisis.* Hermann's classic (1963) definition — an event surprising individuals, restricting their time for developing a response, and threatening their high-priority goals — has been criticized by later researchers (see, for example, Billings, Milburn, and Schaalman, 1980). After our interviews, we have found that a combination of two definitions — Perrow (1984) and Habermas (1973) — seems to capture the experiences these managers described.

Following Perrow, we define an *incident* as a disruption of a component, a unit, or a subsystem of a larger system, such as a valve or a system generator in a nuclear plant. The operation of the whole system is not threatened and the defective part merely repaired. We define an *accident* as a disruption that physically affects a system as a whole, such as an entire plant, an organization, or an industry. In this case, the production of a whole operation, such as a nuclear plant, is stopped or needs to be interrupted for repairs. Following Habermas, we distinguish between a disruption occurring at the physical or tangible level, encompassing elements such as the technology used, and a disruption occurring at the social or symbolic level, including the subjective meanings that inform and direct actions, such as the routines of an organization that provide a sense of identity for the members. We propose the term *conflict* to describe those times when the symbolic structure of a system is disturbed, but not to the point of challenging its basic set of assumptions. Finally, we define a *crisis* as a disruption that physically affects a system as a whole and threatens its basic assumptions, its subjective sense of self, its existential core. These four terms are illustrated conceptually in Figure 1.1.

Two Conditions of Crisis

Thus, in our definition, a crisis requires at least two conditions: first, the whole system needs to be affected to the point of being physically disturbed in its entirety; second, the basic assumptions of the members of that system need to be challenged to the point where they are forced either to realize the faulty foundation of these assumptions, or to develop defense mechanisms against these assumptions. These conditions formalize the dimensions emphasized by several scholars, such as Nystrom and Starbuck's notion (1984) of "threat to the organization's own survival"; Fink, Beak, and Taddeo's concept (1971) of "threat to the system in its entirety"; or Tushman, Newman, and Romalli's perception (1986) of crisis as a "frame-breaker."

The first condition of a crisis—its impact on whole systems—is the easier to understand. In essence, this means that

Figure 1.1. Definition of Terms in Crisis Management.

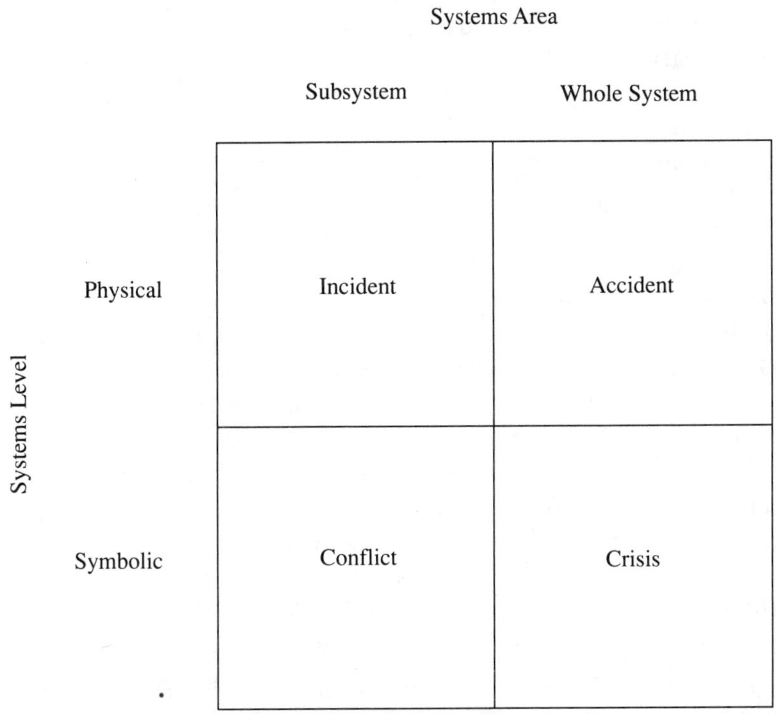

Systems Area

	Subsystem	Whole System
Physical	Incident	Accident
Symbolic	Conflict	Crisis

Systems Level

an event is *not* a crisis if it has affected only a self-contained part of a system; that is an incident. However, this notion is likely to shift depending on the definition of *system:* if we define a system as a company or a manufacturing plant, the disruption of that system will be expressed by the halt of its productive output. This particular perspective seems to follow the view expressed in mainstream management literature, where a crisis is viewed as disrupting the technical core of an organization (Thompson, 1967) or its input-throughput-output process (Katz and Kahn, 1978). However, if we view a system as the totality of similar products in operation, or the entire industry in which a company operates, or even the planet as a whole, the nature of the disturbance is likely to transcend the notions used in management. For example, the problems detected in several DC-10s in the United States have affected not only the entire DC-10 fleet around the world, but also the McDonnell Douglas Company as a whole, the future of other airplanes such as the European Airbus, and the entire airline industry worldwide. As another example, the Chernobyl explosion not only wiped out a particular nuclear plant; it spewed radiation around the entire planet, affecting the fate of the entire nuclear industry (Starke, 1987). Bhopal not only affected a particular region in India, causing the deaths of thousands of people and injuries to hundreds of thousands more, not to mention animals and plants, but it also threatened the chemical industry worldwide and triggered questions about the operations of multinational companies in Third World countries (Shrivastava, 1987).

Frequently, this first condition is perceived in financial terms. From the perspective of a manager, the financial dimension of a major crisis is often the most visible. Most crises exact a tremendous financial cost; for example, Exxon agreed to pay $1 billion in cleanup costs and fines for the *Valdez* oil spill. Even if the organization's managers were not responsible but were themselves victims of the crises, they may still have to suffer tremendous financial losses. For instance, the withdrawals of Tylenol from market shelves and the conversion from capsules to caplets are reputed to have cost Johnson & Johnson nearly half a billion dollars. Few organizations can readily absorb these amounts.

It is easy to understand how a major crisis drains the physical and financial resources of an organization: resources that normally go into the production of products and services have to be diverted to handle the crisis. However, a major crisis also exacts a severe emotional toll, and this can be more difficult to grasp. Often, those who are involved or affected either directly or indirectly suffer from what is known as post-traumatic stress (Lystad, 1988; Raphael, 1986; Slaikeu, 1984). They relive the crisis over and over again in memories, dreams, and nightmares. They exhibit general nervousness, anxiety, loss of sleep, decreased sexual energy and interest, and in many cases noticeable depression. This is one poignant manifestation of the second condition for the development of a crisis—the disturbance of the basic assumptions of the members of a system.

The Three Existential Effects of a Crisis

As we have already suggested, one of the most difficult aspects of a crisis is understanding its existential dimensions. By *existential* we mean something specific and not at all abstract. The existential component has at least three effects.

First, a crisis can threaten the legitimacy of an entire industry. As we have seen, Bhopal, *Challenger,* and Chernobyl affected the future development of their industries — chemicals, space, and nuclear energy, respectively. It is well known that the public's perception of an industry seriously affects how they relate to that industry in the future. As many authors have observed, a crisis often destabilizes or "destructures" this perception (Derrida, 1973; Habermas, 1973; Lagadec, 1991).

Second, a major crisis can reverse the strategic mission of an organization. Consider Tylenol, a product designed to alleviate pain and hence to "do good." Placing cyanide in Tylenol completely reversed the properties of the drug, converting it from an agent for doing good into an agent for accomplishing evil. The basic strategic purpose for both the organization and the product was flipped on its head. Indeed, the incident dramatically demonstrated one of the bizarre aspects of being a market leader: the product can be used as a vehicle to cause the greatest hurt for the greatest number of people. Thus there is a paradoxical side to being a market leader in today's world. As we shall see in Chapter Five, many managers use this to justify not investing in crisis management. Some managers are under the delusion that well-managed companies do not have crises. If anything, the existential component of crises shows that just the reverse is true. This reversal of mission can be observed in virtually all industries, including those not generally thought of as operating in dangerous technologies. In the space industry, for example, NASA's mission as the developer of outer space has been threatened by the *Challenger* crisis. With this event, the space shuttle was suddenly associated with the destruction of human lives. Similarly, in the field of education, the murder of several students at the Montreal Institute of Technology reversed the university's mission: instead of providing a brighter future for young people, this school was the theater of their death. This reversal effect was also observed in the food industry, with the Perrier crisis of 1990: a beverage strongly linked (via the company's advertising strategy) with "nature's purity and goodness" was suddenly associated with poisoning. As a last example, the 1990 crisis at Larousse, a leading French firm producing, among other things, high-quality encyclopedia, showed that even information can be dangerous. A printing error led readers to confuse the description of toxic and edible mushrooms, thus endangering thousands of mushroom gatherers.

The third effect occurs at the individual level. Crises also disturb people's subjective world: the way they perceive the world and themselves; their inner sense of self-worth, power, and identity; their inner cohesion. Human beings use denials and faulty rationalizations to escape the terrifying experience of "existential death" induced by crises. The "death" we are speaking of here is not merely physical; we are also referring to what people experience when their inner cohesion or subjective experience is shattered. In this sense, death is more psychological than physical.

An example will make this clear. After the *Challenger* accident, engineers at NASA experienced such strong psychological trauma that the agency set up a psychological emergency hot line and a counseling program. This trauma was not limited to a few specific domains; it challenged the totality of people's inner experience. Some engineers felt their personal identity as engineers was challenged. Am I a good enough engineer? they wondered. Could I have done anything to prevent the accident? Some engineers wondered whether NASA as an organization was capable of managing advanced technologies, and questioned their prior assumption of excellence (Schwartz, 1987; Starbuck and Milliken, 1988). This disaster also challenged the assumption that the field of engineering itself was "good enough" to manage the complexity of such technologies and to prevent such accidents. Even deeper, some of these engineers questioned their overall adequacy as human beings — Am I a good friend who will not let others down? Some also reevaluated their contribution to humanity as a whole, as they struggled with feelings of responsibility for the death of fellow human beings or their inadequacy in preventing the disaster. At home, some of them were challenged by their own children. "Dad, Mom, are you responsible for the death of the astronauts?" For others, President Kennedy's dream of space colonies, the overall promise of technology in society, and America's adequacy as a nation for fulfilling this promise — all these were challenged (Schwartz, 1989). Studies conducted after the accident found that many who watched the accident on television suffered psychological trauma, including headaches, lack of sleep, and anxiety attacks (Black and Worthington, 1988; Schwartz, 1989).

The *Challenger* tragedy, in other words, threatened people's very sense of being and existence through their different roles: as manager, scientist, employee, engineer, customer, citizen, parent, friend, member of the human race, individual self. An indication of the strength of these existential challenges was the large number of protective strategies that were developed. Partly as an attempt to reduce the issues to two narrow and manageable domains, the disaster has been blamed on a technical failure and on poor communication from NASA management. Engineers who had sounded warnings before the disaster were fired (Boisjoly, 1988; Schwartz, 1987, 1989). Children of the engineers who worked on the shuttle were ridiculed by classmates who labeled their parents "the astronauts' killers." NASA's whistle-blowers, such as the Boisjoly family, were isolated from and blamed by members of their community, leading them to move from the town they had lived in for years (Boisjoly, 1988; Maier, 1988).

It would be a grave mistake to believe that the strength of these existential challenges and defensive mechanisms were motivated only by the international visibility of the shuttle program. A large body of research on natural disasters and industrial crises reports identical existential trauma in other instances (Lystad, 1988; McFarlane, 1985; Raphael, 1986; Weisaeth, 1975; Wilkinson, 1983). During our research we uncovered identical patterns of existential trauma and defense in crises much less "important." We report these findings in later chapters.

For the moment, it is important to emphasize that industrial crises are not only threatening to the "input-throughput-

output" processes that make up the technical core of organizations, as classic management texts simplistically note. They also
threaten the overall system of symbols, beliefs, and feelings that
individuals attribute to industries, organizations, and themselves. This connection between crisis and existence is so profound that the field of existential psychology has given itself the
task of studying how humans experience crises. For example,
Rollo May, one of the fathers of this movement, defines existential psychology as that which seeks to develop "an understanding of the reality underlying all situations of human beings in
crises" (1958, p. 7). We are convinced that it is essential to address this existential domain. Without it, we can neither understand the reality of human beings confronted with crises, nor
manage efforts for change.

To some extent, this is what distinguishes *crisis management,* where both the physical and symbolic dimensions of a crisis
are addressed before and after a crisis, from *security management,*
which is limited to the technical side of safety and *crash management,* which is limited to reactive actions. In contrast, managers
in crisis-prepared organizations take the concept of crisis management seriously. They are proactive as well as reactive, and
they focus not only on the physicality of crises but also on their
symbolic aspects. To understand these differences, we need to
understand how crises develop.

The Origins of Crisis: Multiple Perspectives

Every scientific field of knowledge presents its own definition
of a crisis. An in-depth review of this abundant literature will
lead us too far afield; however, to demonstrate the complexity
of crises, as well as the need for a theory in crisis management
that can address this complexity, we briefly present some of the
perspectives used by different fields.

In economics theory, a crisis situation is often defined by
criteria such as inflation, unemployment, stagnation, government deficit, recession; its causes are often attributed to decisions made by governments or a general failure to follow the rules
of the international economic system (Block, 1979; O'Connor,

1987). Political scientists attribute crises to such phenomena as failures in political leadership, the "ungovernability" of political systems, the inability of diverse political parties to manage social conflicts, or the failure to develop an equitable international political system (Hill-Norton, 1976). Those who draw from marxist political economic theory attribute crises to the contradiction existing between social classes and between the values of the exchange and the use of the production (Aktouf, 1991; Habermas, 1973). Sociologists often attribute crises to social inequalities, decreases in motivation and incentives, challenges toward authority, failures in control mechanisms, increase of "utilitarian individualism," or the decline of family, community, civic and religious heritages (Bellah and others, 1985; O'Connor, 1987). Others see the phenomenon of crisis as a "social fact," akin to mysticism, allowing individuals in a given society to give meaning to events that otherwise would be incomprehensible (Baudrillard, 1983; Jacob and Sabelli, 1984; Morin, 1968). Thus, paradoxically, the concept of crisis not only challenges people's basic assumptions, but enables them to give meaning to their challenged experiences, invoking the presence of a crisis in the absence of another explanation.

Historians often view crises as the result of a cumulative loss of harmony between the elements of a society, such as overexpansion in military power, technology, sexual behaviors, and so on (Kennedy, 1988; Toynbee, 1972). In chaos theory, writers define a crisis as the breakdown of equilibrium, but view the cause of the crisis as itself an attempt to achieve a greater order (Gleick, 1987; Prigogine and Stengers, 1984). Psychologists consider a crisis the breakdown of individuals' identity or their subjective sense of self and meaning and describe many causes: instinctual drives; the influence of "collective unconscious" forces; the effect of traumatic experiences such as birth, illness, or accident; the decline of parental empathy and guidance; the social influences leading individuals to be experienced as objects; the lack of spirituality; the fear and denial of death; and more (Becker, 1973; Bettelheim, 1943; Freud, 1961; Grof and Grof, 1990; Horney, 1937; Kohut, 1984; Kübler-Ross, 1969; Lasch, 1979; May, 1950). Such diversity of thought has led some researchers to quip that the field of crisis theory is itself in crisis! (O'Connor, 1987; Morin, 1976).

The Management Approach

Unfortunately, most writers in management science do not embrace this multifaceted view of crises. They tend to define a crisis in terms of a restricted number of its effects (see for example Hermann, 1963), and they generally advocate security management — attempting to contain the effects of crises by introducing additional mechanisms of control.

Perhaps the most erroneous misconception in management is the refusal to see a crisis as a positive force, as a factor itself contributing to the existence of an enterprise. By stating that a crisis has both a positive and a negative side, we are not only saying that a crisis is both a danger and an opportunity; we are also saying that the destructive side of a crisis is itself a *sine qua non* condition for the development of an organization.

Currently, only a few authors in management have emphasized this critical paradox (Miller, 1990; Pauchant, in press; Schwartz, 1990; Sievers, 1986a; 1986b). In essence, all these authors are pointing to the fact that life and death, order and chaos, construction and destruction, order and disorder, "business as usual" and crisis, should not be seen as opposites but rather as a unified whole. This notion of the complementarity of both life and death is as old as western philosophy itself. It was stressed by Heraclitus of Ephesus, one of the founders of Greek and western philosophy, in 500 B.C. The current misconception about order and crisis is perhaps the single most important factor why so many organizations are not currently crisis-prepared. In this respect, the theory and practice of management seem to lag behind many other disciplines that have already recognized the importance of this paradox, such as the arts (Blake, 1958; Dostoyevsky, 1958; Goethe, 1959; Hesse, 1929; Hofstadter, 1980); biology (Maturana and Varela, 1980; Prigogine and Stengers, 1984); history (Toynbee, 1972); mythology (Campbell, 1949); philosophy (Bergson, 1982; Foucault, 1984; Kierkegaard, 1980; Koestler, 1979; Nietzsche, 1972); physics

(Capra, 1982; Gleick, 1987); psychology (Becker, 1973; Freud, 1961; Jung, 1971; May, 1950); sociology (Cooper and Burell, 1988; Morin, 1976; 1990); spirituality (Grof and Grof, 1990); systems theory (Jantsch, 1980; McWhinney, 1990); or theology (Tillich, 1963; St. John of the Cross, 1959). Three current groups of management scholars, while not totally embracing the Heraclitian view of crises, point nevertheless in that direction. The first tends to embrace a historical and sociological view. They see crises as the result of a cumulative process. Charles Perrow's ground-breaking study of "normal accidents" (1984) is typical. He emphasizes that crises are normal, that they result from the complexity of the technology we now use. In this perspective, crises are not so much caused by faulty human decisions as by the complex interrelationships among the many components constituting modern technology. If a human responsibility can be seen at all, it is in the wish to build large and complex technological systems in the first place, for these systems escape human understanding and control and develop behaviors of their own.

A second group embraces a more sociopsychological and political view. They consider crises the result of faulty decisions, placing the responsibility of individuals and groups at center. Irvin Janis's study of crucial decisions (1989) typifies this perspective. In his view, the purpose of crisis management is to decrease the usual constraints on decision making and thereby avoid policy disasters that could be lethal. We see in the next chapter, with the example of Bhopal, how faulty decisions both triggered this disaster and hindered crisis management interventions.

The third group of management scholars attempts to integrate the previous two perspectives. They stress that crises are normal events triggered both by the complexity of the system itself and by faulty decisions, as well by the interrelationships between technological systems and the humans who attempt to manage them. Paul Shrivastava's ground-breaking study (1987) on Bhopal, in which he documents the inevitability of that disaster, is typical of this perspective.

In this book we adopt this integrated perspective. This

view has both an element of determinism — the fate of a system is influenced by its own total complexity, where each variable bears the force of both order and chaos, and where the influence of human decisions and intervention is only relative at best — and an element of free will, where human decisions are a source of both potential disasters and potential resolutions.

A Heraclitian View of Complexity

It should be emphasized here that, in the Heraclitian view, the phenomenon of complexity not only includes the interrelationships between the number of variables existing in a system, but also embraces the paradoxical nature of each variable, bearing in itself both the sources of order and chaos. From this perspective, a systemic view precludes a focus on one or two major causes of crises. Instead, the focus is on how one or several events can trigger certain patterns of energy, movement, or interactions in a system. We use the word *trigger* rather than the more traditional word *cause* because in the heraclitian view it becomes absurd to speak of one variable causing change in another. To give some concrete examples, it is absurd to state that the drunkenness of a tanker's captain "caused" the Exxon *Valdez* disaster; or that a terrorist's sabotage "caused" the Bhopal disaster; or that a defect in an O ring "caused" the *Challenger* disaster — even though managers at Exxon, Union Carbide, and NASA used these simplistic explanations to escape their responsibilities.

A systemic view of crises urges us to understand as much as possible what would be the effect of a change in one variable on the total system, considering that this variation will itself be amplified by other variables in the system.

Instead, taking a systems perspective, we can see that some managers at Exxon were at fault for not noting the seriousness of the potential drunkenness of its captains, considering how that variable could be amplified by others, such as the lack of safety devices on tankers; the lack of technical preparations in Alaska if such accidents happened; the lack of effective communication networks between the tanker, Exxon's executives, the coast guards, the Alaskan emergency services, the local population; or the lack of psychological training of the diverse intervening individuals. Similarly, as we see in the next chapter, some managers at Union Carbide were at fault for not considering the seriousness of a sabotage act (if the cause was in fact sabotage, as representatives of the firm claimed) on the total system, considering the amplifying effect of other variables: the technical deficiency of the plant in India; the lack of preparation and knowledge of the local management team, the local population, the local emergency teams and facilities, and the Indian government. And some NASA managers were at fault for not considering the seriousness of potential problems with O rings, considering other amplifying variables such as the tendency of NASA managers to downplay potential problems; the communication problems existing between NASA's hierarchy and its partners; the technical fragility of space shuttles; and the crucial visiblity of that launch in particular.

A word of caution: the source of all these disasters is not to be found only in "wrong" human decisions. Accidents do happen, even with the best preparations; in fact, they are a condition for the very existence of these living systems. However, the managers of these three crisis-prone companies *are* responsible for their lack of effort to reduce the risk of these disasters or, at minimum, to be prepared for their occurrence.

Vicious Circles

A crisis is a self-feeding phenomenon, what many have called a vicious circle. To use Merton's example (1957), imagine that a bank is experiencing a problem in liquidity. The withdrawal of money from that bank by nervous customers will further endanger its liquidity, leading more customers to withdraw money, leading to further problems of liquidity, and so on, until bankruptcy.

Vicious circles have two main origins: they can be introduced through human intervention, or they are an inherent characteristic of complex sociotechnical systems. NASA provides a recent example of the first. To lower product defects on the space shuttle, NASA developed a bonus program designed to encourage employees to report such defects. Result: the number of product defects *increased,* leading NASA management to suspect that some employees had deliberately tampered with their products to collect the bonus (*New York Times,* August 26, 1988). NASA's actions not only failed to solve the original problem, but actually resulted in another, perhaps even worse, problem. This case illustrates a vicious circle in policy action. Such circles are a feature of crisis-prone organizations, where managers are much more likely to create vicious circles through the wrong kind of interventions.

Vicious circles also originate from the systems themselves. These systems are so complicated, complex, and interrelated that they develop a dynamic of their own, making human corrective actions extremely difficult (Durkheim, 1982; Forrester, 1971). Large bureaucracies are a case in point (Argyris, 1957; March and Simon, 1958; Crozier, 1963). Often they are so complex and formalized that attempts to correct them fail miserably, often increasing their overall rigidity.

Currently, only a few authors in the field of crisis management have taken note of these vicious circles. Perrow (1984), in his landmark study of high-risk technologies, for example, has argued that two characteristics of a sociotechnical system — its overall complexity and its degree of tight coupling, that is, the degree to which a change in one variable affects changes in another — increase the likelihood of industrial accidents. For example, he argued that technological fixes in marine transport had not made a great difference in its safety, and had even in some cases increased the likelihood of accidents. Similarly, he stressed that even the best talents, the most advanced technology, and the best resources could not overcome the accident potentials of dangerous industries. As he stated, "We have produced designs so complicated that we cannot anticipate all the possible interactions of the inevitable failures; we add safety devices that are deceived or avoided or defeated by hidden paths in the systems. . . . In the past, designers could learn from the collapse of a medieval cathedral . . . or the collision of railroad trains. . . . But we seem to be unable to learn from chemical plant explosions or nuclear plant accidents. We may have reached a plateau where our learning curve is nearly flat" (pp. 11–12).

The Amplifying Power of Small Variables

This systemic view of crises emphasizes another dimension: the potential result of changes in small parts of a system when amplified by other variables. Earlier we distinguished between an incident, an accident, and a crisis (see Figure 1.1.) From a systems perspective, many incidents (at the level of a part) can turn into accidents (at the level of an entire system) and then into crises (challenging basic assumptions) if they are amplified by other variables.

Table 1.1 lists potential incidents that can turn into accidents or crises. Notice that the full progression into a crisis is rare. For example, out of the 3,000 incidents encountered in 1987 by the U.S. nuclear industry, 430 of them, or 14.33 percent, led to a temporary shutdown of the facility — "accidents" (Public Citizen, 1988). And the nuclear industry as a whole has officially encountered only two major crises to date — Three Mile Island and Chernobyl — bringing the crises-incidents ratio to .000666. A small percentage, to be sure, but these events can have enormous impact.

The potential effect of small variables on total systems was first emphasized in the field of atmospheric research. It has been called the "butterfly effect" — suggesting that the flap of a butterfly wing in one corner of the world can trigger a large atmospheric change such as a cyclone in another (Lorenz, Malkus, Spiegel, and Farmer, 1963). Similarly, writers in management science (Weick, 1979; Perrow, 1984) have stressed the dangers of tight coupling for large systems, where the amount of slack or buffer between variables is limited. While tightly coupled systems can be more efficient and respond more rapidly to change, they are also particularly prone to disasters because of the many complex interactions and feedback loops. A change in one variable can trigger changes in other variables, leading, in the absence of regulation, to the breakdown of the entire system.

Examples of this effect in crisis management are numerous; many major crises have been triggered by seemingly insignificant disruptions — what Perrow calls "trivial events in nontrivial systems" (1984, p. 43). The Chernobyl catastrophe, for

Table 1.1. Incidents That Can Turn Into Accidents or Crises.

Abortion	Divestiture	Mergers
Accidents	Downsizing	Multiple-use issues
Acquisitions	Drug and chemical abuse	New-product failures
Activist action	Embezzlement	New-product introductions
Acts of God	Employee injury	No comment
Adverse government action	EPA hearings	Noise
AIDS	Equipment malfunction	Nuclear emissions
Aircraft crashes	Exposure as a source	Odor emissions
Aircraft safety	Extortion	OSHA
Airport safety	Falling reputation	Political problems
Airport security	False accusations	Premature disclosure
Ambush interviews	Falsification	Product recalls
Analyst presentations	Federal investigations	Product tampering
Annual meetings	Fiberglass	Proxy contests
Anonymous accusers	Fire	Public testimony
Asbestos	Foreclosure	Quote in context
Bad debts	Government intervention	Quote out of context
Bankruptcy	Government spending cuts	Rationalization
Chapter 11	Grand jury investigations	Reclamation
Chapter 7	Grassroots demonstration	Rumors
Chemical abuse	Hazardous-material accidents	Sabotage
Chemical dependency	Hostage taking	Scandal
Chemical spills	Hostile takeovers	Security leaks
Civil unrest	Image distortion	Seepage
Competitive misinformation	Inaccessibility	Sexual addiction
Congressional testimony	Inconsistency	Sexual harassment
Contamination	Indictments	Shifts in value
Corporate campaigns	Insider activities	Special interest group attacks
Corporate control	International accidents	Strikes
Corporate governance	International competition	Takeovers
Cost overruns	International issues	Tax shifts
Counterespionage	Irradiation	Technology transfer
Crashes	Irritated reporters	Television interviews
Customer misuse	Judicial conduct	Terrorism
Death, customer	Labor problems	Traffic
Death, employee	Landfill siting	Transplants
Death, key executive	Lawsuits	Transportation accidents
Demographic changes	Layoffs	Uncontrolled exposure
Depositions	Leaks	Unethical behavior
Deregulation	Leveraged buyouts	Vandalism
Discrimination	Liquidation	Visual pollution
Disparagement	Lying	Whistleblowers

example, was triggered by a standard security procedure; the *Challenger* accident by a technical break in a ring of the shuttle; the 1984 Tokyo telecommunications outage by a regular maintenance effort. In another example, a plant of the Virginia Electric and Power Company was shut down for four days in 1980, costing the company and customers several hundred thousand dollars, after an employee's shirt pocket caught on a handle of a circuit breaker.

These small events triggered (not "caused") crises because they were amplified through their tight interrelationships with a great number of other variables constituting the total system. Depending on when they occur in the total process of a crisis, incidents such as an operator error or a rumor can be both triggers *and* effects, amplifying the crisis further.

Clusters of Crises

In one of our research projects, conducted under the auspices of the National Association of Manufacturers, we found that crises cluster together into just a few groupings (Mitroff, Pauchant, and Shrivastava, 1988a, 1988b). In 1986 we sent questionnaires to managers of Fortune 1000 organizations. Respondents were asked to indicate, out of a list of twenty-three possible crisis scenarios (see Resource A), how many their organizations had experienced in the previous three years. Results indicated that, statistically, crises cluster together. Furthermore the clusters were relatively distinct from one another, with little overlap.

The clusters are displayed in Figure 1.2. For the most part, the groupings and their labels are self-explanatory. For example, the "External Information Attacks" cluster contains all those attacks on an organization that emanate mainly from outside the organization and attack its proprietary, confidential information. The "Breaks" cluster is exactly what its name implies — a breakdown in plants, equipment, or in human operators themselves through stress or normal human error. "External Economic Attacks" represent attacks emanating from outside the organization that directly threaten its economic well-being. "Megadamage" includes catastrophes of the magnitude of a Bhopal, Chernobyl, or Exxon *Valdez*. The "Psycho" category consists of psychopathic and sociopathic attacks that are connected statistically and conceptually. The "Occupational Health Diseases" cluster includes such things as worker fatalities due to occupational hazards such as asbestos poisoning, as well as nonoccupational threats such as AIDS.

Figure 1.2 also shows two dimensions that differentiate the groupings. In the vertical dimension, groupings near the

Figure 1.2. Crisis Clusters.

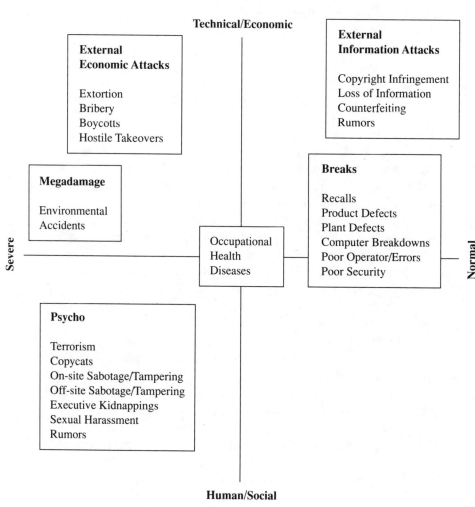

top are more technical or economic in nature; those at the bottom of the figure are due more to human or social actions. Of course, these dimensions are not absolute. The technical and social factors are so intertwined it is usually extremely difficult, if not impossible, to say exactly whether the trigger of a major crisis was technical or social in nature. When we take a detailed look at most crises, we generally find that if the trigger was a technical break in the system (the infamous O ring, for example), the underlying cause was almost always a breakdown in some human or social system.

It bears repeating that one of the other findings that emerged from our research is that any member of any of the clusters can be either the cause *or* the effect of any other crisis. To get a better sense of these interdependent relationships, we provide in Resource A the correlation coefficients between the types of crises and a graphical representation of these relationships. These results indicate very clearly the futility of defining strict cause and effect relationships in the area of crisis management. It is impossible, for example, to determine whether environmental accidents are "caused" by on-site tampering, or whether the accidents themselves are "causing" additional on-site tampering by disturbed employees, thus amplifying the original accident.

It is clear that the phenomenon of crises behaves in a circular and amplifying way. A crisis is ill structured, systemic, and messy. No wonder then that the tendency of managers in crisis-prone organizations to focus on one narrow outlook, such as engineering or finance, has such a dreadful effect on their vulnerability to crises. These managers have not yet learned to take a systemic view.

The ends of the horizontal dimension of Figure 1.2 overlap as well. On the right-hand side are clusters whose underlying cause can be explained more easily in terms of everyday or "normal" human behavior. It does not take in-depth psychology to explain how an operator may misread a dial in a nuclear power plant. On the other hand, the crises at the extreme left-hand side, particularly the group labeled "Psycho," are generally far removed from the ordinary, everyday experience in business. It takes a great deal of psychological sophistication to understand the motivations of a person who would engage in wide-scale product tampering or sabotage. Managers of crisis-prepared organizations fundamentally understand the systemic nature of crises and crisis management; they also recognize the bizarre interrelationships that sometimes occur between technology and humans.

Clusters of Prevention Strategies

In the same study, we also established that, just as crises tend to cluster, so do preventive actions in crisis management. The same set of managers were asked to select from a list of possible preventive actions the ones they had adopted in the previous years. The results are displayed in Figure 1.3. Again, the labels are descriptive. The category labeled "Audits" is exactly what its name implies: a series of operations that attempt to assess how well the organization's legal and financial systems are operating, whether hazardous materials are present, or whether toxic chemicals could be brought in by a terrorist using the organization as a staging ground for hostile action.

In our research we found that the preventive actions grouped under "Internal Emotional Preparation" are the least often undertaken by organizations — *two hundred times* less developed than efforts targeted to the "Internal Repair/Design" group. Emotional preparation efforts were the last domain on which Fortune 1000 companies had focused. This denial of the emotional aspects of crises is very distressing, for it means that companies fail to protect one of their most critical assets, their employees. But this lack of awareness is not only apparent in corporations. It is also amplified by scholars and management consultants working in the field. For example, we conducted a content analysis of the 281 articles published on the specific subject of crisis management up to mid-1988 (Pauchant, 1988b), and found that only 16 percent *even mentioned* the emotional realm.

In interview after interview, the executives who recognized the emotional burden of crises spoke of the tremendous forces pushing for denial of the emotional aspects. An executive in a major U.S. airline stated, "In this company, we're sup-

Figure 1.3. Preventive Action Clusters.

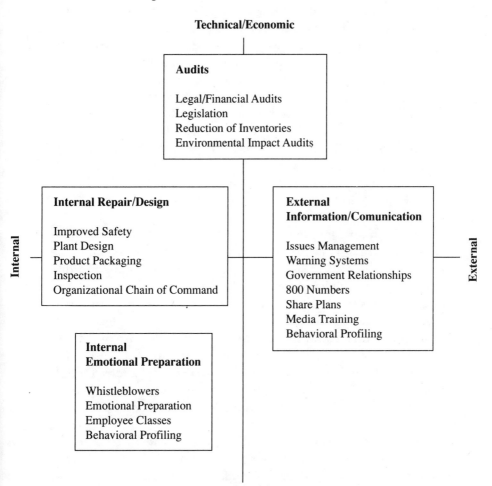

Technical/Economic

Audits

Legal/Financial Audits
Legislation
Reduction of Inventories
Environmental Impact Audits

Internal

Internal Repair/Design

Improved Safety
Plant Design
Product Packaging
Inspection
Organizational Chain of Command

**External
Information/Comunication**

Issues Management
Warning Systems
Government Relationships
800 Numbers
Share Plans
Media Training
Behavioral Profiling

External

**Internal
Emotional Preparation**

Whistleblowers
Emotional Preparation
Employee Classes
Behavioral Profiling

Human/Social/Organizational

posed to be macho enough to take it . . . it is impossible to get approval on a seminar if the word 'stress' is in it." An executive in a large consumer goods company: "This company does not understand how stress is related to bodies and actions. . . . There has never been a formal workshop on stress management in this company."

These results are sad. They are also extremely dangerous. They indicate that the vast majority of individuals in organizations still do not understand the crucial linkages needed
between technology, people, and organizations if crisis management is to be successful in today's complex world.

Sadly, corporations are learning these lessons the hard
way. The most convincing factor that leads managers to begin
a program of crisis management is the direct, personal experience of a repeated series of major crises. This means that both
employees and stakeholders suffered tremendous pain needlessly.
It also means that we will likely have to endure in the future
even more disasters of the extent of a Bhopal, a Chernobyl
or a *Valdez* before wide-ranging proactive measures will be developed.

The familiar reactive "try-and-fail" method, the "muddling-
through" strategy, is ill suited to the present situation. Considering the dangerous technologies used nowadays, industrial disasters now have global impacts. In the past, a boat accident at
sea could result in the loss of its crew; today a marine accident
can devastate an entire region. In the past, the explosion of a
powder factory could kill or injure some of its employees and
have a limited impact on its community; today, disasters of the
extent of Bhopal are occurring. We can no longer afford to mud-
dle through. We need to become proactive and anticipate as
thoroughly as possible the lessons for the future.

Concluding Remarks: A Heraclitian View of Crises

An organized living system, such as an organization, needs both
integrative and destructive forces to be alive or functioning. The
life of a system is sustained by the paradoxical interplay of order
and chaos, being at the same time complementary, competitive and antagonistic. Paul Tillich, for example, writes that all
high achievements include "an inseparable mixture of good and
evil, of creative and destructive forces, both individual and social . . . there is nothing unambiguously creative and nothing
unambiguously destructive. They accompany each other in-
separably" (1963, p. 58).

From this perspective, the presence of destructive forces, made more visible through crises, is both a prerequisite for the life of a system and, at the same time, its doom. Thus, to label a particular organization as crisis-prone can be misleading, for all organizations are potentially crisis-prone. However, we do wish to point out that managers of crisis-prone organizations do not recognize the fundamental dialectic of life and death, creation and destruction, present in all actions, whereas managers of crisis-prepared organizations attempt to do so. In other words, the psychological bedrock of crisis management is the existential, intellectual, and emotional recognition of the fragility of life and its paradoxical nature.

We are not saying that because crises are "normal" nothing should be done about them. Crisis-prepared managers, or Heraclitian managers, do their best to reduce the likelihood of crises and their effects when they do happen. Crisis-prone managers, on the other hand, completely deny the possibility of crises; they believe they can manage them perfectly through an increase of control and technology or else invoke fate as an excuse for doing nothing about them.

A Heraclitian view of crises is paradoxical; it maintains that crises are not only normal but life-enhancing. At the same time, it demands that individuals do their best to reduce the effects of the crises, even though available knowledge and action may be incomplete or even ill suited to the situation. Therefore, dealing with crises means more than trying to prevent them or diminish their impact. It also means fundamentally appreciating that they are necessary for life itself.

TWO

When People and Systems Fail:
Lessons from Bhopal

A community may clear the timber from a hillside in order to have
more cultivable land, but this end may be submerged and over-
whelmed in the floods and erosion resulting from the absence of
trees.

— Jean-Paul Sartre, *Search for a Method*

This chapter tells the devastating story of Bhopal. It is a concrete example of the systemic issues present in both accidents
and crises. We selected Bhopal for several reasons. For one, this
accidental release of deadly poison is considered to be among
the very worst industrial crises in human history. For another,
managers are often aware of at least some of the dimensions
of that disaster. Also, it has been studied and documented extensively (see, for example, Ayres and Rohatgi, 1987; Bowman
and Kunreuther, 1988; Bowonder and Linstone, 1987; Marcus,
Bromiley, and Goodman, 1987; Pauchant and Mitroff, 1990;
Shrivastava, 1987; Weick, 1988; Weir, 1987).

Using the definitions presented in Chapter One, Bhopal
first began as an *incident* at the plant level and then quickly de-
generated into an *accident* that affected the total system of the
plant as well as its community, finally turning into a full-blown,
multifaceted, international *crisis*. Note that in this chapter we
distinguish between the Bhopal *accident* and the Bhopal *crisis*.

Background

In 1984, the world chemical industry was highly competitive.
Although Union Carbide was an important company, with
almost one hundred thousand employees in forty countries, its
managers were under strong pressure to increase profitability

and reduce costs. In 1984, the company's after-tax profit was only about 60 percent that of its major competitors. Also, as part of a major strategic shift, in the late 1970s Union Carbide divested about forty business units and was considering selling its 50.9 percent controlling interest in Union Carbide of India, Ltd. (UCIL).

Like its parent company, UCIL faced difficulties. Although the twenty-first largest company in India, employing more than ten thousand people at the time of the accident, the plant operated at less than half of total capacity. Faced with a highly competitive Indian pesticide market, which was itself in decline, and the strong pressures of its parent company, UCIL tried to take advantage of economies of scale. It especially increased its production of MIC, a highly toxic gas used in the manufacture of pesticides.

Demoralized partly by the potential divestiture of UCIL, many top managers left. Many of the managers hired in their *TRAINING* place lacked expertise in the chemical industry. UCIL had to cut personnel, lowering morale even further and compromising security and emergency procedures.

Meanwhile, the Indian government had for a long time encouraged the widespread use and the large-scale production of pesticides as part of its "green revolution" campaign and its efforts to develop a stronger national industrial basis. The government was reluctant to place a heavy safety burden on industries, fearing a decrease in job opportunities. The government had also encouraged the industrial development of Bhopal and the surrounding area. Almost overnight, Bhopal was transformed from a feudal community to a large industrial city in 1959. Attracted by jobs, people moved to the area, and Bhopal's population grew from about one hundred thousand in 1961 to six hundred and seventy thousand in 1981, a growth rate 300 percent higher than the national average. The exponential growth in population resulted in a severe lack of housing facilities and a declining city infrastructure, notably poor water supply, inadequate transportation, communication, education, health facilities, and so on. For example, at the time of the accident, there were only thirty-seven public telephones, eighteen hundred

SPILL REPORTING

Figure 2.1. A Model of the Factors Related to Bhopal as an *Accident*.

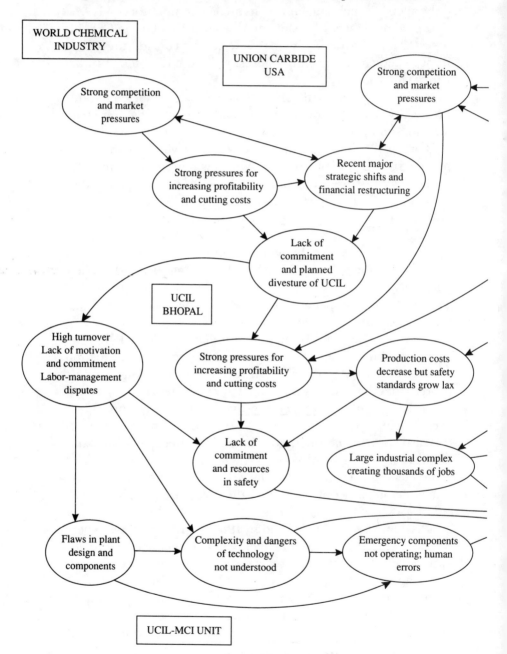

Figure 2.1. A Model of the Factors Related to Bhopal as an *Accident*, Cont'd.

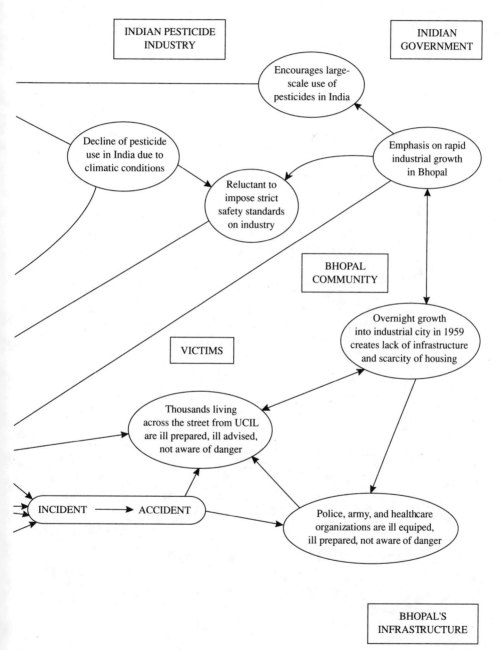

hospital beds, and three hundred doctors for a population of six hundred and seventy thousand. A severe housing shortage led to the development of concentrated slums in the area; thousands of people lived literally across the street from the UCIL plant.

The Accident

On December 2, 1984, the Bhopal "accident" occurred. The precipitating incident was a leak of the highly toxic MIC. This incident was contextually related with a number of different factors, and escalated into an accident. Figure 2.1 presents a model of the many factors associated with the "accident" and the wide variety and complexity of the relationships between the nine principal stakeholders. (Since this figure is so complex, we also present a much simpler version in Figure 2.2.) For the sake of simplicity, we discuss here only five of the most important factors.

First, neither top management nor employees were knowledgeable about the potential dangers of MIC production. For example, storage of MIC and other hazardous materials was inadequate and an emergency plan was nonexistent. Second, several technical malfunctions and human errors were confounded:

Figure 2.2. A Simplified Model of the Systems
Dynamics of the Bhopal Accident.

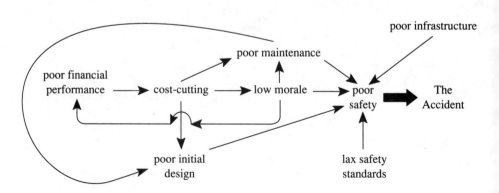

a number of safety valves in the MIC unit were missing or failed to operate during the incident; an emergency refrigeration unit was under repair and thus not available for use; an audio emergency signal to warn the outside population had been turned off. Third, the immediate population of Bhopal had no awareness of danger; the general impression was that the plant produced "plant medicine." The thousands of people living directly across the street received the full impact of the toxic gas. Fourth, local authorities, also ignorant of the nature of the danger, commanded the population to flee the city. A better strategy would have been to direct people to lie on the ground and breathe through a damp cloth, thus alleviating the effects of the gas. Similarly, the health community, ill prepared for such an emergency, treated only symptoms, lacking adequate equipment and resources to treat the full health consequences that developed. Fifth, the city's inadequate infrastructure contributed to the poor level of emergency response.

All these factors taken together created a total context that contributed to the death of between eighteen hundred and ten thousand people and the injury of between two hundred thousand and three hundred thousand, depending on which sources of information are used. The effects on animals and the total environment are incalculable.

It is impossible to pinpoint specifically what "caused" the accident or what "caused" the death and the injuries of so many victims. Certain things stand out: Union Carbide's lack of commitment to UCIL; the general lack of knowledge and preparation of UCIL's management and employees; the technical failures and human errors; the push by the Indian government to develop Bhopal as an industrial area, with its resulting lack of infrastructure and safety procedures; the fact that thousands of people were living directly across from the plant and were unaware of its potential danger; the lack of knowledge and preparation of the local authorities and health specialists. These contextually related factors were associated with Bhopal as an *accident*. Another set, adding to the complexity of the case, were associated with Bhopal as a *crisis*.

The Crisis

Figure 2.3 is a model of the contextual relations associated with the Bhopal "crisis." It is organized around four major stakeholders: the Indian government, Union Carbide, the local population, and other stakeholders. The Bhopal crisis emerged from and was played out in various domains in which the key stakeholders interacted.

In the first domain, several controversies developed between various stakeholders: the exact nature of the gas released (the presence of cyanide was suspected by some and denied by others); the nature of the long-term effect of the injuries, varying from no effects to long-term and even intergenerational effects; and the exact death toll, the number fluctuating between eighteen hundred and ten thousand. These controversies were themselves related to other issues. For example, there was debate over the appropriate treatment (treatment for MIC and for cyanide poisoning are quite different). There was controversy over legal issues such as Union Carbide's financial responsibility, which depended on the number of dead and injured as well as the emergency planning procedure. The Indian government's role in the cause and alleviation of the crisis was debated. These controversies were also related to the population's general mistrust of both the Indian government and Union Carbide. Because of this mistrust, thousands of people fled the city, which contributed even further to severe economic, social, and psychological difficulties.

Many lawsuits were entered: by the victims against the Indian government and Union Carbide, by the Indian government against Union Carbide, and by the firm's shareholders against the company. The total dollar amount of these suits was evaluated in 1985 at between $350 million and $4 billion. Union Carbide's stock was undervalued for several months, and the firm had to defend itself against a takeover attack, divesting 20 percent of its most valuable assets. The media coverage of the crisis was also extensive; the crisis occupied the front page of the *New York Times* for two weeks. The issues debated in the press ranged from the ethical role of U.S. corporations in foreign countries and the Third World in particular, the safety of complex technologies, to the legal issues related to compensation. In turn, these questions triggered threats to the social identity of Union Carbide (what we have referred to as one of the existential components of a major crisis), the chemical industry in general, and U.S. business as a whole operating in Third World countries. Bhopal as a crisis also involved a number of other stakeholders: different countries with similar technologies, several activist groups, the U.S. Congress, and the chemical industry as a whole.

The issues related to the Bhopal crisis are inordinately complex; they involve a web of financial, legal, medical, technical, managerial, political, communicational, and therapeutic factors. Since 1987, however, press coverage of the crisis has focused mostly on the issue of litigation. In 1990, after six years of legal battle, the Indian government accepted $470 million in damages from Union Carbide. At this writing, the Indian government has appealed this decision and is again suing the company.

Vicious Circles at Bhopal

As we have seen in the last chapter, vicious circles are generated by the forces existing in a total context and by the interventions of stakeholders, both sources being themselves in interrelation. For example, a contextual vicious circle can be seen in the Indian government's encouragement of industrial development in Bhopal, which influenced the government's reluctance to impose strict safety standards, which contributed to the increase of production by UCIL and its attraction of new workers, which further influenced the Indian government to maintain its initial encouragement.

Other vicious circles were introduced through incomplete, faulty, or poorly thought-out interventions. Union Carbide's original desire to divest UCIL, which put pressure on the Indian company to lower its operating costs, was partly the result of an earlier attempt by Union Carbide to avoid a crisis with its shareholders. Thus, a proactive crisis management effort that focused primarily in the financial domain also fueled the context of Bhopal as a crisis.

Similarly, the various strategies used by different stakeholders to provide scientific analyses validating their particular point of view contributed to further problems. The lack of reliable data added to the decrease of trust. These were associated with other problems such as uncertainties about which medical treatment to provide and the Indian government's difficulties in making equitable financial compensations.

Pseudosolutions and Risky Interventions

Many observers have criticized Union Carbide for its lack of emergency plans at UCIL, the poor state of its emergency procedures, the lack of proper operator training, the cuts in emergency staff, the limited resources allocated to emergency procedures, and the low compensation scheme offered and its slowness in settling claims (see, for example, Ayres and Rohatgi, 1987; Sehti, 1985; Shrivastava, 1987). While these factors are important and deserve emphasis, they are not our principal focus. From our experience, one of the major differences between crisis-prone and crisis-prepared organizations comes down to this: managers in crisis-prepared organizations attempt to understand the total context of their actions in order to act effectively; managers in crisis-prone organizations do not.

If Bhopal as an accident has anything to teach us, it is this: the financial decision by Union Carbide to divest itself of UCIL was a pseudosolution. It did not take into account the negative effects that a planned divestiture could have on the UCIL system as a whole, including its safety. The strategic decision made to solve a potential financial problem instead helped spread the problem wider, to an issue of safety. Of course, the great irony is that, with the accident, they had far more serious financial loss. A systemic view of the problem would not have been guided by financial considerations only, but would have considered UCIL's overall performance, culture, and motivation, including its degree of reliability.

Reducing vicious circles that are embedded in the total context of a system, as in the case of Bhopal, presents a great challenge. We have to reduce the coupling between components to a level where they can be dealt with by ordinary human beings.

Examples of tightly coupled events that have defeated emergency procedures and scientific understanding are numerous in Bhopal. Here we mention four.

1. The chemical reaction between MIC and water was increased by small amounts of contaminants and impurities that were in the tank but not anticipated in emergency plans, triggering a number of secondary chemical transformations that were themselves not anticipated.
2. Particular safety features (such as a scrubber) could not operate; they had been designed to act on gas alone, not on the unexpected mixture of gas and liquid.
3. Because of the complex chemistry developed in the tank, a number of intermediate compounds were released into the environment in addition to the MIC, making it impossible for scientists to diagnose with certainty their content; this decreased the effectiveness of emergency procedures.
4. Union Carbide was unable to give the emergency teams precise information, as an accident of this size with this particular gas had never occurred before and was beyond scientific understanding.

With all the complexities and uncertainties, it is apparent that any intervention had the potential for creating other major problems. As one observer has noted about crisis situations, "Our actions are always a little further along than is our understanding of those situations, which means we can intensify crises literally before we know what we are doing" (Weick, 1988, p. 308).

In the case of Bhopal, even interventions at the level of the whole system would have been different, depending on who is defining the "system." From the perspective of Union Carbide, managing the system would have led to questioning the overall efficiency of the large-scale production of hazardous products, not to mention the company's basic purpose. From the perspective of the Indian government, to intervene at the system level would have led to questioning the large-scale production of pesticides, which was itself embedded in the "green revolution," and the rapid development of industrial complexes.

Figure 2.3. A Model of the Factors Related to Bhopal as a *Crisis*.

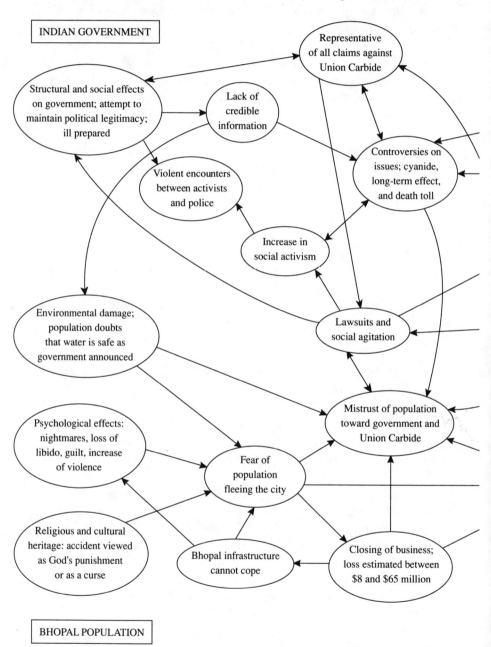

Figure 2.3. A Model of the Factors Related to Bhopal as a *Crisis,* Cont'd.

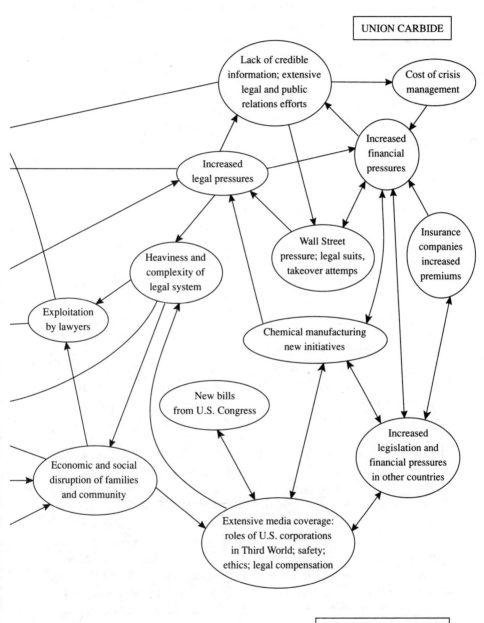

Complex systems render obsolete traditional strategies that have worked in simple systems. For example, while Union Carbide did notify the Indian government that it was risky to have people living across the street from the UCIL plant, thus protecting its legal liability, the company did not explore possibilities for resolving the issue. A more humane, more ethical approach would have considered not only the legal aspects of the situation but also the issue of human dignity involved in the event of a major accident. All the stakeholders — Union Carbide, UCIL, the Indian government, the local government, and the local population — could have participated in seeking a broader solution.

Emotional Side

The emotional and existential aspects of major crises raise even greater challenges. Before a crisis, anxiety can have perverse effects: people often deny that a crisis could happen or that it could be serious. After a crisis, they can deny that it happened or that they might be responsible. On one hand, these are healthy defense mechanisms through which human beings can assure their psychological survival in the face of adversity. On the other hand, they enhance the likelihood of large-scale accidents. At the very moment when an individual needs most to embrace a systems perspective, these mechanisms close off this option.

In the Bhopal disaster, denial was immense. For example, leaders of both Union Carbide and the Indian government had stated before the accident that such an event at the UCIL plant was impossible and would not happen. Furthermore, Union Carbide had failed to act on several warning signals from similar incidents that fortunately did not develop into systems accidents.

A broadly based program of crisis management would have attempted to understand the emotional need for protective denial while at the same time moving beyond it. At the even broader level of national and international affairs, a truly effective effort would have attempted to reconcile the conflicting purposes of different stakeholders. In Bhopal, such conflicts involved the issues of cost efficiencies versus overall production safety; the economic efficiency of large-scale production systems versus the accident potential of such systems; and the Indian government's strategy of massive and rapid economic development versus the necessity of limited growth considering the inadequate infrastructure.

It is becoming clear that many crises are caused by overly simplified conceptions and fragmented perspectives in complex systems. As virtually all large-scale disasters remind us, broadening both our thinking and our feeling is no longer a luxury but a necessity.

THREE

Crisis-Prone or Crisis-Prepared: A Diagnostic Model of Crisis Management

> Since life poses an endless series of problems, life is always difficult and it is full of pain as well as joy.
>
> —M. Scott Peck, *The Road Less Traveled*

In the next five chapters we address the factors that make an organization either crisis-prone, at the "bad" end of the spectrum, or crisis-prepared, at the "good" end. Remember, though, our belief that an organization, per se, cannot be either crisis-prone or crisis-prepared, but only the individuals within it, those who influence the organization's perspective on crises and foster — or resist — crisis management efforts. Also, an organization's crisis orientation has to be seen on a continuum, with many shades of gray. Finally, while an organization can be said to be dangerously crisis-prone at a given time, this is not to say that this cannot be changed. Making change in this area is difficult, but indeed possible — except, that is, for the special category of firms we have labeled "destructive." They are managed by individuals suffering from such serious pathologies that treatment can be effectively prohibited.

Through our research we have found that four key factors make an organization crisis-prone or crisis-prepared (Mitroff, Pauchant, Finney, and Pearson, 1990). Evaluating the degree to which an organization is prepared for, or prone to, a crisis means looking at each factor in turn. Because these factors are uncovered sequentially, like the layers of an onion, we developed what we call the Onion Model of Crisis Management (see Figure 3.1). All these layers are so important that we devote a separate chapter to each one.

48

Figure 3.1. The Onion Model of Crisis Management.

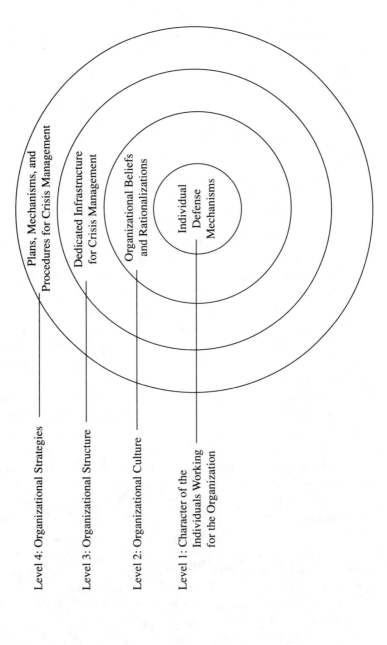

Level 4: Organizational Strategies — Plans, Mechanisms, and Procedures for Crisis Management

Level 3: Organizational Structure — Dedicated Infrastructure for Crisis Management

Level 2: Organizational Culture — Organizational Beliefs and Rationalizations

Level 1: Character of the Individuals Working for the Organization — Individual Defense Mechanisms

The outer layer (layer 4) comprises an organization's strategies for crisis management — existing programs, procedures, and mechanisms specifically developed to deal with crises. This surface layer is the one most easily seen, even by the untrained observer. Consider the case of Exxon *Valdez*. Here examining the outermost layer would involve determining whether Exxon had in place the appropriate, fully tested mechanisms and procedures to handle a crisis of the magnitude that occurred. If the answer is no, then Exxon would be rated in the danger zone for this layer.

Layer 3 of the model evaluates how well the everyday operating structure of an organization either contributes to or inhibits crises. In the case of Exxon, each operating division was supposed to have its own crisis management plan. But the crisis was of such magnitude that it crossed divisional lines and affected the company as a whole. Precious time was lost getting accurate information on the spill to headquarters, so that a proper response from the corporation as a whole could be mounted.

Layer 3 (structure) is placed below layer 4 (strategy) in the model because it is just beneath the surface of what can easily be seen by an outsider. (Ironically, layer 3 is often equally invisible to those who work *inside* an organization. They are frequently unaware of how the structure of their own organization affects their way of working and interacting in general and crisis management efforts in particular.) This layering relationship is not meant to imply that the structure of an organization strictly determines its strategies. While this view was strongly held in the 1960s (Chandler, 1962), it is now admitted that both structures and strategies influence each other in an interactive process (see, for example, Burgelman, 1983). Further, we have found that an organization's structure is much more than tangible elements such as established norms, rules about authority and power, and the formal hierarchy. We also include in the Onion Model *symbolic* functions, that is, how the formal structure of an organization reveals the perceptions of its members (Eraly, 1988). For example, the degree of formalization in control mechanisms (quantity of reports, control agents, procedures and so on) can tell us much about the degree of trust that exists in an organization.

Layers 2 and 1 are the most fascinating of all, for they tap into the largely unconscious invisible aspects of an organization. For precisely this reason, they are the hardest to see — and often the most important.

Layer 2 addresses an organization's cultural aspect: its unwritten and unspoken rules, codes of conduct, belief systems, what can be said or not said, what can be done and what cannot. We found that one effective way of differentiating a crisis-prone organization from a crisis-prepared one was to study how managers and employees spoke about crises and crisis management. As we see in Chapter Five, managers in crisis-prone organizations use many more rationalizations.

Layer 1 addresses the subjective experiences of the individuals who form an organization. Factors such as their propensity to use different defense mechanisms in relation to crises, or the degree of their existential anxiety, exert a central influence of the kind of crisis management efforts developed in an organization.

In summary, each layer in the Onion Model refers to a different level of reality. Level 1 refers to phenomena captured by existential psychology. Level 2 refers to phenomena addressed in the fields of sociology and anthropology. Level 3 incorporates phenomena that are dealt with in organization theory. Level 4 incorporates phenomena from the general fields of business policy and strategic management. Actually, all four layers involve a complex mixture of the individual, organizational, professional, and technological factors. No wonder, then, that companies with a strong technical or professional orientation experience great difficulty with crisis management; they may do well on the technical or professional factors (layers 3 and 4), but they tend to do poorly on the human factors (layers 1 and 2). As a general rule, most organizations in our society are generally insensitive — if not disdainful — toward levels 1 and 2, and yet these are precisely some of the most important factors that actually run any organization.

We address the issues related to the character of the individuals working for the organization (layer 1) in Chapter Four and the cultural issues (layer 2) in Chapter Five. The structural issues (layer 3) are discussed in Chapter Six, the strategic issues (layer 4) in Chapter Seven. However, although we present these layers in different chapters, it is important to remember that each layer influences the others. The strategies implemented in an organization influence, and are influenced by, the organization's structure and culture and the psyche of individuals.

One last qualification before we begin. Because the vast majority of the information we obtained was collected under strict promises of confidentiality, in no case can we mention either the names of the individuals or the organizations that were involved in our interviews. The only organizations we mention by name are those that have already been examined publicly in the media, such as Johnson & Johnson, Union Carbide, NASA, and Exxon.

FOUR

Searching for Individual Meaning: The Existential Nature of Organizational Crises

> They are playing a game. They are playing at not playing a game.
> If I show them I see they are, I shall break the rules and they will
> punish me. I must play their game, of not seeing I see the game.
>
> —R. D. Laing, *Knots*

In this chapter we explore layer 1 of the Onion Model: the individual level. One of the least acknowledged aspects of crisis management is its existential component, particularly the experience of death. Findings in modern psychology can help us understand better the meaning of this experience.

Writers in several schools of psychology emphasize that the central most fundamental motivation for humans in Western societies is to preserve at all cost their sense of personal feelings, their inner view of themselves and of the world, their self-concept, and to be able to affirm this self, being able "to do," to create; to be self-actualized, to feel alive (Becker, 1973; Fromm, 1973; Kohut, 1984, 1985; Maslow, 1968; May, 1975; Miller, 1981; Rogers, 1980). These scholars distinguish between physical death, when the body biologically dies, and psychological death, when the inner structure of an individual's experience is shattered, destroyed, or challenged in a traumatic way. Both types of death are so terrifying that individuals will resist them with all their strength.

Industrial crises can trigger both deaths. Victims can be physically injured or even killed, as in Bhopal. Other individuals—rescuers, eyewitnesses, bystanders, managers and employees of the firm involved, families of the victims, community members—are victims of psychological trauma. Many of those involved with the *Challenger* disaster, as you may remember from Chapter One, found that their entire structure of self — inner feelings about being a good parent, a good engineer, a good member of the human race — had been challenged. These feelings of disintegration or fragmentation of self are so painful that they are often accompanied with physical and somatic trauma: nightmares, headaches, sexual impairment, physical illness, nervousness, stress, or anxiety.

The challenges presented by crises are very personal and it is difficult to know precisely which of these feelings and symptoms a crisis will trigger. It does seem, however, that crisis situations affect basic assumptions: one's sense of certainty about issues and about the future; a sense of perfection and therefore invulnerability; a sense of connection with others, that one has "a place in the world"; the sense of "righthood," that one is involved in a worthwhile cause (Becker, 1973; Bettelheim, 1943; Frankl, 1959). In Western societies, the challenge to our feelings of competence and effectiveness is especially important, for this sense that we are producing something valuable is one of the most powerful means for giving meaning to our lives. As Eric Fromm points out (1973, p. 235), "To be able to effect something is the assertion that one is not impotent, but that one is an alive, functioning, human being."

The Search for Existential Meaning

It would be a great mistake to believe that existential questions come only from obscure philosophers or from disturbed or depressed individuals, or that they are a pathological side effect of the experience of a crisis. While it is true that a crisis tends to make these issues more visible, the search for existential meaning is very much present in today's corporations for many managers and employees alike — even though it is often disguised as something less threatening.

The Search for Excellence

Perhaps the most visible sign of these issues in corporations is the emphasis on the "search for excellence." The book *In Search of Excellence* (Peters and Waterman, 1982) sold more than five million copies and has been translated into fifteen languages. Indeed, the "search for excellence" has become the buzzword for the 1980s; most corporations, most universities, most governmental agencies, and most other organizations proclaim it as their company self-concept and philosophy and as their strategic means for competing successfully. For our part, we see this trend as an expression of the existential tradition; we believe it shows that existential concerns are very much at the heart of the fundamental purpose of an organization in today's world.

To grip these existential issues, we need to give the book *In Search of Excellence* a more careful reading. At a superficial level, it appears that Peters and Waterman define an excellent company through financial criteria. Most of the criticisms of Peters and Waterman's arguments have addressed only these financial ratios or their famous eight criteria of excellence. This misses the deeper existential message of the book. A more careful reading shows that Peters and Waterman attempted to address "existential despair." Indeed, they say in their introduction that the "magic" of excellent companies resides in the theory advanced by Ernest Becker, one of the most influential of the existential writers, who won the Pulitzer Prize in 1973 for his book *The Denial of Death*.

> Discussions of management psychology have long focused on theory X or theory Y, the value of job enrichment, and, now, quality circles. They don't go far toward explaining the magic of the turned-on work force in Japan or in the American excellent company, but useful theory does exist. The psychologist Ernest Becker, for example, has staked out a major supporting theoretical position, albeit one ignored by most management analysts. . . . About the winning team, Becker notes, "Society . . . is a vehicle for earthly heroism. . . . *Man transcends death by finding meaning for his life*. . . . It is the burning desire for the creature to count. . . . What man really fears is not so much extinction, but extinction with insignificance [Peters and Waterman, 1982, pp. xxii–xxiii; emphasis added].

Indeed it is clear that Peters and Waterman believe that addressing existential issues is essential for corporate excellence. At the end of the book, they conclude, "The skill with which the excellent companies develop their people recalls that grim conflict . . . our basic need for security versus the need to stick out, the 'essential tension' that the psychoanalyst Ernest Becker described" (p. 323). Unfortunately, while Peters and Waterman claim to have based their principles on Ernest Becker's work, they only partially presented his argument; they shied away from his in-depth analysis of the inescapable issue of death. It is not our intent to critique Peters and Waterman's work. Rather, we hope to illuminate the existential issues present in business and point to the inadequate answers proposed in most organizations.

First, Peters and Waterman proposed throughout their book that the search for "heroship," both at the individual and organizational levels, can answer the existential search. Quoting parts of Becker's work, they proposed that individuals will be willing to commit or "surrender" themselves to the purpose of an organization if it provides them with a sense of greater meaning; at the same time, they will wish to stand out by themselves in these organizations, striving to accomplish their own ambition. "So we observed, time and again, extraordinary energy exerted above and beyond the call of duty when the worker . . . is given even a modicum of apparent control over his or her own destiny" (p. xxiii).

While it is true that Becker spoke of the quasinecessity for human beings to engage in "earthy heroism" (springing from the culture in which individuals are immersed) and "personal heroism" (a creative act separated out of the common pool of shared meanings), he spoke also of these heroisms as an *escape* from human "authenticity." As a true existentialist, Becker situated the human condition squarely within the context of the struggle with the issue of death. For him the realization that it takes sixty years or so of tremendous effort to make an individual, and then that this individual is "only good for dying," is the basic paradox to be dealt with (Becker, 1973, p. 69). Arguing that a function of a societal culture is to forget the reality of death, he stressed that the task of "authentic" individuals is to challenge the sources

and the validity of these heroisms and to realize their dangerous illusions. "Human heroics is a blind driveness that burns
people up; in passionate people, a screaming for glory as un-
critical and reflexive as the howling of a dog. In the more passive masses of mediocre men it is disguised as they humbly and
complainingly follow out the roles that society provides for their
heroics and try to earn their promotions within the system" (p. 6).

Second, while Peters and Waterman stated that organizations could make "meaning for people," turning "the average
Joe and the average Jane into winners" (p. 239), Becker's own
argument is much different. Throughout his book, he argues
that the search for and discovery of meaning is a personal experience; individuals have to feel and to believe *by themselves* that
what they are doing is "truly heroic, timeless and supremely
meaningful" (p. 6). He describes "unauthentic" individuals: people who "do not belong to themselves, are not 'their own persons,' do not act from their own center, do not see reality on
its terms" (p. 73). He gives examples of unauthentic individuals who did not create meaning from themselves, such as "the
corporation man in the West or the bureaucrat in the East."
He describes a continuum of "unauthenticity," starting at one
extreme from the "depressive psychosis" (individuals who are
afraid of being themselves and fearful of exerting their individu-
ality) and, at the other extreme, "schizophrenic psychosis," where
individuals experience a sense of inflation of inner fantasy and
symbolic possibility (pp. 77–79). We shall come back in more
detail to this continuum in the next section. For the moment,
it is important to note that Becker did not argue that the resolution of the existential despair of death is for a person to be
"made heroic" by an organization, as Peters and Waterman advocate. Rather, he emphasized that healthy, "true," "real" individuals have transcended themselves by realizing the truth of
their fragile situation, by dispelling the lies that make them believe
that they are immortal, by embracing the precarious human condition, by assuming and "integrating their anxiety" (p. 86).

Third, it also seems that Peters and Waterman have simplistically operationalized their version of Becker's work by stressing the importance of ceremonies and rituals for developing this

sense of "heroship." "Ritual is the technique for giving life," they
state. "Man's natural yearning can be fed limitlessly in the domain
of symbols" (p. xxiii). As an example of this "symbolic management," unfortunately much in vogue today, Peters and Waterman
pointed to a team of IBM salesmen emerging from the players'
tunnel of a stadium, being applauded by executives, colleagues,
family members, and friends. Contrary to this view, Becker
warned of the dangers of building a "compulsive character," building extra-thick defenses against existential despair and anxiety.
Quoting Kierkegaard and echoing Sartre's concept of "bad faith,"
he argued that "for a partisan of this most rigid orthodoxy, truth
is an ensemble of ceremonies" (p. 71). Instead, Becker urged human beings to question the artifacts by which they live their lives
and to derive by themselves their sense of meaning.

Finally, it seems that their overall purposes were fundamentally different. While Peters and Waterman were concerned with increasing efficiency, productivity, and competitiveness for organizations, Becker wanted to explore how human
beings deny "death," including compulsive drives toward efficiency, productivity, and competitiveness. Rather than efficiency,
Becker emphasized the need for effectiveness in the full sense
of "accomplishing" and *including* the need to be "authentic," to
accept one's own anxiety in the face of the precariousness of the
human condition.

Thus the search for excellence, so much developed in today's organizations, is an attempt to address the tangible, familiar, widespread experience of existential issues. At the same
time, this search, while presented as a comprehensive answer,
is itself an escape. In the same vein, we discuss in the next chapter the many rationalizations that managers use for not facing
the issues raised by crises—an attempt to escape their own
anxiety.

However, while Peters and Waterman have denatured
Becker's work, the success of *In Search of Excellence* is a vivid dem-
onstration of the exactitude of Becker's argument: that individuals
in organizations can precipitate themselves with great energy
into all sorts of techniques and realities for denying the ines-

capability of "death." As Becker stated, "The defenses that form
a person's character support a grand illusion, and when we grasp
this we can understand the full driveness of man. He is driven
away from himself, from self-knowledge, self-reflection. . . .
Anxiety lures us on . . . we flirt with our own growth, but also
dishonestly. . . . We seek stress, we push our own limits, but
we do it with our screen against despair. . . . We do it with
the stock market, with sports cars, with atomic missiles, with the
success ladder in the corporation or the competition in the university" (p. 56).

Existential Questions in Modern Corporations

To be crisis-prepared requires at the very least an attempt to
answer some of the questions posed by existentialists. To do
this requires not only intellectual exertion, but the emotional
robustness to wrestle with these issues in the first place. In other
words, managers *should not be too "emotionally bounded."* Managers'
reluctance to face the reality of crises is not an isolated phenomenon: rather, it is itself part of the tremendous difficulty of facing existential issues in general. This makes changes much more
difficult: it is no longer a matter of providing quick technological fixes.

 We human beings often close ourselves off to painful experiences such as crises, yet it is from these experiences that
we are able to address meaningful questions and to grow. We
have some empirical data to validate this in the area of crisis
management. In a survey of thirty or so organizations, we asked
executives to indicate the effectiveness of various strategies for
convincing top management to adopt a program in crisis management. Table 4.1 summarizes the results; note that the number-
one "strategy" is the direct personal experience of a repeated series
of major crises. One could interpret this as "proof" that humans
do not change if they are not *obliged* to do so. There is certainly
much truth in this assertion, but it does not fully explain the
subjective side of these traumatic experiences and their effects
on individuals.

Table 4.1. Strategies for Convincing Top Management to
Adopt a Program in Crisis Management.

	Strategy	Effectiveness
1.	Direct personal experience of a repeated series of major crises	6.7*
2.	Direct personal experience of a single major crisis	6.5
3.	Strong insistence by your organization's board of directors that you need to adopt a broad program of crisis management	6.4
4.	The recommendation by a top executive from another corporation within your industry that a member of your top management personally knows and respects	5.4
5.	Strong recommendation by a respected member of your corporate staff	5.1
6.	Extensive news coverage of a major crisis that another organization within your industry has experienced	5.1
7.	Recommendation by a top executive from another corporation external to your industry that a member of your top management personally knows and respects	5.0
8.	Extensive news coverage of a major crisis that another organization outside of your industry has experienced	4.5
9.	Following the trend set by other organizations	4.3
10.	Recommendation by a major trade association within your industry	4.3
11.	Reading an article in a major business publication on what other firms are doing in crisis management	4.3
12.	Attendance at a seminar or conference on crisis management	4.0

*7 = highly effective; 4 = neither effective nor ineffective; 1 = highly ineffective

During our interviews, we found many individuals who had difficulty talking about crises affecting their organization. In several cases, they attempted to protect their image of their organization, and of themselves, with rationalizations: "We're prepared." "Nothing bad can happen to us; we are not producing dangerous products." "We are an excellent company. Only bad companies need crisis management." After studying the organizations in depth, we found that, more often than not, these statements were mostly a cover-up. We also realized that the overall tone of the interviews, while courteous, was somewhat formal and stiff, often preventing a real discussion of the issues between the executives and ourselves and with no mention of personal experiences.

This was not the case with managers who had a greater understanding of crisis management issues and who had at least attempted to develop some efforts in the area. With them we were often able to establish a dialogue, exchanging views and experiences on the subject, rather than simply meeting for an interview. They more freely discussed the difficulties they encountered in developing a crisis management program, and many shared personal experiences: an illness, a car accident, the death of a close friend or a family member. Most believed that the pain of these experiences helped them understand the suffering of others, both inside and outside their organizations, when confronted with crises. These executives and managers were more able to acknowledge the truth of their conditions, as pointed to by existentialists such as Becker, as a requirement for existential authenticity; they acknowledged some of the pains and difficulties in their lives; they discussed their relative lack of control over events or situations; they implicitly acknowledged the finitude of life. To put it bluntly, these managers were more able than the others to discuss the human condition.

We strongly believe that to view these individuals as too emotional would be a grave mistake. In fact, these managers exemplified through their thoughts and actions what existential psychologists and philosophers have emphasized. Rollo May, for example, one of the fathers of existential psychology, argued that a crisis is exactly what human beings need in order to challenge their basic assumptions (1950). Kierkegaard ([1844] 1980) emphasized that the most important lesson human beings can learn is how to be rightly anxious, to acknowledge the precariousness and fragility of the human condition without succumbing to dread.

Self-Interest and Compassion

For many months, we puzzled over one of the results of our studies. One of the characteristics of crisis-prepared organizations is that their managers do not define a crisis as an event that could happen only to *them*. We found that managers who were instrumental in developing some of the most systemic efforts in crisis management were very much aware that crises had negative effects on their organization, on multiple stakeholders, and on the broader environment. This finding contradicts the traditional view of human motivation, which focuses on self-interest, and it challenged our previous hypothesis that we would find the best crisis management efforts in organizations where managers were attempting to protect their own interests.

Our research has confirmed this hypothesis, but only partially: we found that the most systemic efforts in crisis management are springing not from self-interest alone but also from human compassion. Managers who only attempted to protect their self-interests were too "emotionally bounded" to address the full human issues present in relation to crises. On the other hand, the managers who were less emotionally bounded, who could acknowledge the tremendous human suffering present in crises, as well as the propensity of human beings to defend themselves with all their might from these painful feelings, were more able to do so. *Compassion* is not synonymous with *altruism: Altruism* (from the Latin *alter,* meaning "the other") emphasizes a person's concern with others; *compassion* (from the Latin *cum,* meaning "to be with," and *passio,* "experiencing a strong emotion") means acknowledging one's own pain *and* being empathetic with the pain of others. It seems that these managers, being more aware of their own precariousness and fragility as human beings, were also keenly aware of the human condition of others.

To state it again, crisis management is not primarily a set of tools and mechanisms to be implemented in organizations. It is rather a general mood and a set of actions by managers who are not too "emotionally bounded." We are not saying that managers who take crisis management seriously do so because they are "nice to people." That would denature the issue and would be in itself a dangerous defense mechanism. Rather, we have found that to develop an effective crisis management effort requires much more than the search for self-interest. The defect in emotionality we have called being "emotionally bounded" is found both at the origin of crises and the lack of systemic efforts in crisis management. For example, emotionally bounded managers cannot sustain the bringing of bad news by whistleblowers, as seen with NASA; emotionally bounded managers cannot fundamentally question their organizational culture, structure, or strategies to understand how they were in part responsible for a crisis, as seen with Exxon; emotionally bounded managers cannot put themselves in the shoes of victims of a crisis, as seen with Union Carbide; emotionally bounded managers cannot fully realize the impact of their actions on the lives of their employees or customers, as seen with the Johns Manville Corporation during the asbestos crisis or Ford during the Pinto crisis.

Now that we have presented the existential bedrock of crisis management, we can attempt to answer two important questions: Why is it that some people are either paralyzed or destroyed by crises, while others seem to grow from them? What are the basic types of defense mechanisms that emotionally bounded individuals use to protect themselves from these painful feelings?

Relation of Personality Types to Crises

One of the most important studies in psychology was undertaken by Rollo May in the 1940s (May, 1950). In a series of studies May and his colleagues interviewed young adults who had suffered traumatic experiences in childhood. The purpose was to understand why some individuals were crushed by these experiences and could not function normally in life, while others could function well, sometimes even better than the average person. Their findings challenged several notions held by common sense. For example, the studies established that the nature and intensity of the crisis did not determine future behavior. Some people who had experienced traumatic crises were found to behave normally; others, even those who had experienced milder events, did not. May and his colleagues established that the key was how well these individuals had integrated these traumatic experiences. They found that "neurotic" people could not fully integrate and use these traumatic experiences, while "non-neurotic" people could. They also found that non-neurotic people had integrated their traumatic experiences by, for example, forgiving the persons responsible or forgiving themselves for their own actions at the time. Today the beneficial effect of the integration of traumatic events is more commonly accepted, but the basic principle is still implemented rather rarely.

Another finding was even more important: these researchers found that people who had integrated their traumatic events did not experience *less* anxiety than those who did not: in fact, people with higher intelligence, greater originality, or greater level of creativity experienced *more* anxiety. Conversely, individuals who did not experience feelings of anxiety were found to have an impoverished personality. As May stated, "The more creative and productive the personality, the more anxiety-creating situations it confronts. . . . This capacity to experience a gap between expectations and reality and, with it, the capacity to bring one's expectations into reality, is the characteristic of all creative endeavor" (1950, pp. 352–353).

In effect, these findings validate the claim made by existential philosophers such as Kierkegaard: that the most important lesson for human beings is to learn "rightly" to be anxious. We do not imply that all creativity or "genius" springs from very disturbed individuals, a thesis that seems to have been somewhat romanticized in our current society. It seems rather more correct to say that creative individuals have a greater capacity to confront anxiety, emerging either from the depth of their own healthy personality or from their traumatic experiences. We can thus say that a creative individual is less emotionally bounded—he or she has the capacity to deal with the occurrence of traumatic issues such as industrial crises. This is not to say that a creative individual does not suffer from neurotic tendencies, but that these individuals can use their neurosis to create something worthwhile.

Personality Disorders and Mental Health

To understand why people are affected differently by crisis, we need to understand more fully the difference between an "authentic" person and one who is "bounded emotionally." This takes us into the realm of psychology, and immediately into the problem of vocabulary. To use labels for individuals or organizations such as "paranoid," "compulsive," "depressive," or "schizoid" runs the risk that these individuals or organizations stay stuck in their labels, preventing us from seeing behind the stereotypes. We prefer to differentiate between individuals' character by using a few general tendencies, and so we have developed a simplified representation of mental health and pathology (see Figure 4.1). Without doubt, it does not do justice to the complexity of defining health and pathology. However, it will help us understand better the differences between creative or more authentic individuals, and less creative or more bounded ones.

In our representation, mental health is determined by two poles: a pole (or tendency) toward "inflation," and a tendency toward "deflation." Briefly, self-inflated individuals tend to de-

Figure 4.1. A Simplified Representation of Mental Health and Pathology.

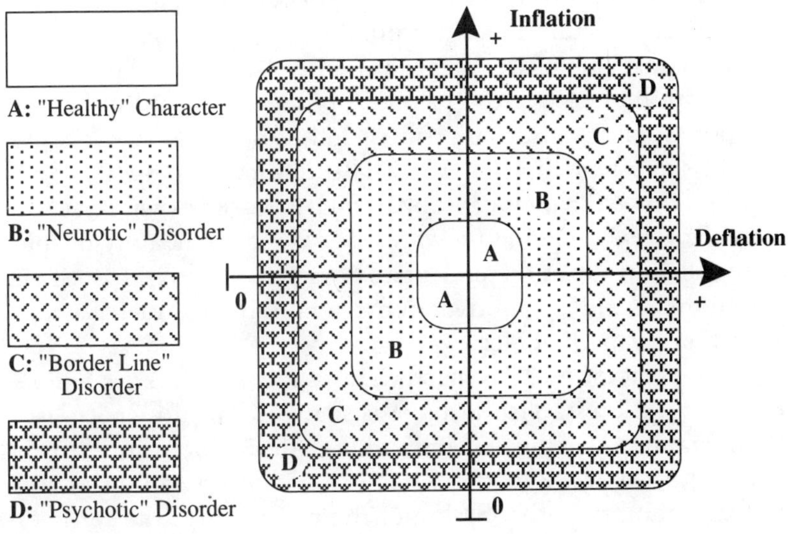
A: "Healthy" Character
B: "Neurotic" Disorder
C: "Border Line" Disorder
D: "Psychotic" Disorder
Inflation
+
Deflation
+
0
0
A
A
B
B
C
C
D
D

velop an unrealistic view of themselves; self-deflated individuals tend to not believe in themselves enough. Note that we have placed these two tendencies orthogonally, as they are often combined: people suffering from inflation often experience, at an even deeper level, a sense of deflation. Thus, the poles of inflation and deflation are not opposed tendencies set up on a continuum; rather, they are tendencies that often reinforce each other.

Four zones are apparent in Figure 4.1. Zone D includes the two extremes pointed out by Becker (1973), the schizophrenic psychosis and the depressive psychosis, reflecting an extreme sense of inflation or deflation, respectively. Notice that both extremes can be expressed when an experience of inflation or deflation is either maximal *or* leading toward zero. In general, psychotic individuals (zone D) experience a global breakup of their personality and completely lose touch with external reality. This zone represents a minority of individuals. Zone C — borderline disorders — is much more common. Borderline disorders are important personality defects that do not result in a total breakup (Kernberg, 1979; Kohut, 1984). Zone B is even more common than borderline disorders, and thus more frequent in organizations. These neurotic disorders or pathologies do not affect basic personality structure in a substantial way. Neurotic individuals remain conscious of the external reality but their pathologies hinder optimal functioning. Zone A points to a healthy character, potentially leading to positive self-regard. Zone A people exhibit some tendencies toward self-inflation or deflation, but in a healthy way: they can appreciate themselves while at the same time realizing that they are not perfect. In healthy people these inflation-deflation tendencies do not interfere with optimal functioning, and are motivated more by basic character structure than by pathologies.

A pathology is thus mostly a question of degree, as Figure 4.1 shows. To establish a diagnosis, mental health specialists often evaluate whether an individual can distinguish between "self" and "non-self," between what he can and cannot affect, and the stability and cohesion of the personality, the sense of being whole. Thus we come to a key definition: the condition

of "bounded emotionality" includes mostly the neurotic and borderline disorders: individuals suffering from psychoses are much
less frequent in organizations.

Positive self-regard. Carl Rogers (1980) proposed the term *positive
self-regard* to typify healthy individuals. His description of this
structure of self echoes existentialists such as Martin Buber,
Søren Kierkegaard, and Rollo May, as well as Maslow's "self-
actualization" (1968). People with positive self-regard tend toward
"authenticity": they are more able to fully realize the precariousness and the fragility of human life but do not succumb to
dread. They are more able to realize their own distinctiveness
and thus to actualize or fulfill it. They are also—and this is a
crucial point—more able to recognize it in others, and thus more
inclined to accept and encourage in others different views or
perspectives. They are less inclined to close themselves off from
challenges to their own basic assumptions. Their personality is
more integrated, unified, and stable, and so they have a greater
capacity to accept both the joys and pains in life, including crises.
Behaviorally, they exhibit some of the characteristics that Maslow has attributed to self-actualized individuals—use of humor,
congruence, an expression of joy and relative serenity, a better
mood stability, creativity, a greater acceptance of others, a sense
of relative autonomy, a greater capacity to handle uncertainty
and anxiety, and a sense of purpose or potential involvement
in a cause outside oneself (Pauchant and Dumas, 1991).

Of course, we are not implying that crisis-prepared organizations contain only positive self-regard individuals while
crisis-prone organizations have none. We have met a number
of people with positive self-regard in crisis-prone organizations,
people who were involved in implementing diverse crisis management efforts in their organizations. However, they often
stressed that they had to work underground, that their top management did not consider these issues crucial, or that often they
were not understood by their colleagues. They mentioned that
they often used their own departmental resources, when possible, to develop some crisis management efforts. Sometimes these
efforts were, on the surface, tolerated by top management, but

limited strictly to specific areas or narrow concerns. Often top management used these narrow actions as a token, as a reason for not implementing a systemic and cross-organizational strategy of crisis management. But even if some of these efforts are used for the wrong reasons, to cover up an overall crisis-prone mentality, they are, nevertheless, positive examples of what an individual can do.

Self-Inflated Disorder. The behaviors of self-inflated individuals are described precisely in the *Diagnostic and Statistical Manual of Mental Disorders,* where they are labeled as "histrionic" and "narcissistic personality disorders" (American Psychiatric Association, 1987, pp. 348–351). Some individuals, in an attempt to cover up their inner defects and their profound sense of emptiness, have developed patterns of behavior that are dramatic, authoritarian, and grandiose. They are often interpersonally exploitive, taking advantage of others, developing a sense of entitlement or unreasonable expectations from others; they have developed a grandiose sense of self-importance, exaggerating their achievements and talents, being preoccupied with fantasies of unlimited success, power, or brilliance, and requiring constant attention and admiration from others. They lack empathy, often being unable to recognize or experience the feelings of others, and they have no tolerance for the frustration of delayed gratification.

It is easy to understand why people suffering from this personality disorder of self-inflation react very strongly to crises, often with rage, shame, or humiliation. And it is alarming to realize that the description of this personality disorder coincides rather nicely with what is required nowadays to get ahead in many major corporations: a great sense of entitlement; expectations of dramatic results; a sense of self-importance or a callous sense of self-worth; a wish for fame, success, and power, associated with a lack of empathy, feelings, and emotions; and a focus on fragmented and narrow issues with a reliance on the short term. Some corporate leaders and management writers (Bennis, 1989; Kets de Vries and Miller, 1985; Zaleznik, 1989) have denounced these characteristics, arguing that over the long run they lead to disaster, but in our interviews we found that

many managers in crisis-prone organizations still honor and reward these characteristics. Self-inflated individuals are instrumental in creating in their organization a self-inflated culture, a set of norms, values, behaviors, ways of doing things
that reward this behavior and penalize individuals who do not
play this self-inflated game. This reminds us again that self-
inflation and self-deflation do not exist independently of each
other; rather, they are complementary tendencies.

To make matters worse, the "normality" of self-inflated
culture, and especially its encouragement, effectively silence
managers who would change toward a less self-inflated culture
that would be more crisis-prepared. Indeed, any such attempt
would be tragic for self-inflated individuals, threatening the
strategies they have developed to cover up their inner deficien-
cies. So attempting to develop crisis management programs for
the sake of the organization and its stakeholders is likely to result
in an existential crisis for these self-inflated managers and executives.

Have self-inflated character disorders increased in Western
societies? It is a matter of some controversy, but we tend to agree
with Lasch, who concluded in his study of narcissism in our
current society (1979) that the number of these individuals has
not necessarily increased, but rather they have attained positions with legitimate or informal power in corporations, thus
reinforcing their self-inflated cultures. The problem seems thus
more related to their growing weight in the control of large,
powerful, and potentially dangerous corporations around the
planet.

Self-Deflated Disorder. The *self-deflation* personality disorder represents the mirror image of the self-inflation disorder. Both have
the inner experience of fragmentation and alienation. When
describing their inner feelings, both groups could mention their
"vague sense of not being real," a lack of purpose and direction, a sense of falling apart, a lack of zest or joy for life, the
experience of endless futility and boredom, a sense of separa-
tion from society and community, a sense of alienation from
life and work, or a sense of fear and anxiety about the future.

However, the two groups differ in what they do on a day-to-day basis for covering up or coping with these painful feelings. Self-inflated individuals have developed fantasy of omnipotence and grandiosity, and engage in dramatic behaviors; self-deflated individuals are more likely to stay behind the scenes, afraid of not measuring up to the task at hand, believing that they are not good enough for guiding their own life. Self-deflated individuals will be likely to idealize self-inflated people, who project an image of self-esteem, courage, heroship, and strength. People suffering from a self-deflated borderline disorder could even go to the extreme of idealizing an omnipotent and grandiose leader, even a cruel and destructive one like Adolf Hitler or Jim Jones. When the disorder is less pronounced, as in the case of a neurotic disorder, people can be very much aware of the destructive outcomes triggered by their organization or their leader, but they will often lack the existential courage to confront the issues and stand up for change. Some of them are also likely to take refuge in a corporation that has developed a self-inflated culture, drawing from this culture the inner strength they cannot derive from themselves.

It is, as we have seen, currently unclear whether the number of self-inflated individuals has increased in our society, but it seems evident that the number of self-deflated individuals is rising. One of the most obvious signs is the infatuation with the search for excellence. There are other signs: many mental health professionals have stressed that the vast majority of their patients are no longer experiencing the classic psychological trauma of fixation and phobias but very painful and real alienation from life—in other words, self-deflation. Multiple signs in our society seem to also confirm that many people feel that their soul has gone stale—the nice but terrifying expression proposed by Nietzsche. For example, when asked if they would like to change something about their physical appearance, 96 percent of Americans answered positively, leading the researchers to state that "a solid majority of the American people are close to being obsessed with their physical appearance" (Harris, 1987, p. 3). These people are alienated from their own body. As another, more dramatic sign, suicides of young American men (ages fourteen to twenty-five) increased by 243 percent from 1960 to 1985, while this number has increased by 280 percent in Canada and 242 percent in France (U.S. Bureau of the Census, 1986). Currently, for all age categories, it is estimated that suicide attempts have doubled or tripled in most industrial countries in the past twenty years. And recent polls indicate that about 60 percent of the population in the United States feels alienated from the power structure, experiencing a basic sense of powerlessness (Harris, 1987, p. 33).

This trend is also present in modern corporations. For example, a plethora of books have recently been published in America and in Europe on the psychological disorders and biases experienced by managers and employees alike, and the effects these disorders have on whole organizations. The titles are poignant: *Le Coût de l'Excellence* [*The Cost of Excellence*] (Aubert and de Gaulejac, 1990); *Why Leaders Can't Lead* (Bennis, 1989); *Le Mal de l'Ame* [*The Suffering of the Soul*] (Bombardier and Saint-Laurent, 1989); *Quiet Desperation* (Halper, 1988); *The Neurotic Organization* (Kets de Vries and Miller, 1985). While the number of these books is an indication that diverse disorders affect managers and organizations alike, it also suggests that the current focus is on pathology rather than on the "positive self-regard" dimension.

Perhaps one of the most convincing examples that, increasingly, the soul of some managers and employees has gone stale is the current fascination with flamboyant leaders. As an indication of the strength of these idealizations, recent biographies of leaders such as Lee Iacocca, Donald Trump, and James Goldsmith have remained on the *New York Times* best-seller lists for many months. According to *Fortune* (February 13, 1989, p. 103), it is estimated that more than 2.5 million copies of Iacocca's autobiography were sold in 1984 and 1985, while Trump's autobiography sold close to 1 million copies in 1988 alone. It seems that a large part of the public has fallen in love with these "leaders," no longer focusing, as in the past, on their moral qualities or on the characteristics of their products, but on the image of power, wealth, and success these leaders project (Bennis, 1989). James Goldsmith's biographer expressed this idealization well: "[Goldsmith] lives out the fantasies of others with a flamboyance that is unmistakable" (Wansell, 1987, p. 11).

Self-Inflated Cultures. Notice, then, that to speak of a "self-inflated" corporation focuses on only one side of the issue, emphasizing the dramatic behaviors of a few individuals. It would be more exact to say that these corporations suffer from a self-deflated or stale culture, with a minority of corporate members with positions of power exhibiting some self-inflated behaviors, while the great number of managers and employees, suffering from self-deflated tendencies, follow these flamboyant individuals. The point is that self-inflation cannot exist without self-deflation. They feed and reinforce each other. Self-inflated individuals require from self-deflated ones the adulation and admiration that they need to give. In this exchange, the "I want you to admire me" of the self-inflated leaders is complementary to the "I want to idealize you" of the self-deflated followers (Pauchant, in press). It is through this complementarity that a self-inflated culture can develop in a group, society, or corporation (Becker, 1973; Kohut, 1985).

Thus, both types of individuals will defend with all their strength their self-inflated corporate culture: self-inflated individuals in order to preserve the context in which they can feel all-powerful and "perfect"; self-deflated individuals in order to preserve the protective cocoon in which they have surrounded themselves. Because of this mutual addiction of self-inflated individuals to self-deflated ones, it is not enough to blame industrial crises and the present lack of preparation in crisis management on a few self-inflated individuals. Efforts at change have to go much deeper. Self-inflated corporate cultures, influencing corporations to become crisis-prone, will not disappear overnight. While we can blame the behaviors of a flamboyant few, their behaviors are both wished and encouraged by thousands of individuals who crave this type of leadership and who existentially need it in order to feel alive. To put it bluntly, the problem is not so much with self-inflated individuals, for they are a minority. Most of the problem seems to be with *us,* for we allow self-inflated individuals to control our lives.

As an additional argument for the powerful links between crises, self-deflation, and self-inflation, research in "accident proneness" indicates very clearly that these two character types are strongly associated with the occurrence of accidents (Pauchant, 1988a). For example, road-accident studies indicate that people with self-deflated or self-inflated personalities are more prone to accidents than other personality types (Shaw and Sichel, 1971). We present in Table 4.2 some of the personality traits associated with risk of a serious road accident (correlation coefficients range from .60 to .30). Note the similarity to our earlier description of the personality characteristics of self-deflated and self-inflated individuals.

Table 4.2. Personality Types Correlated with Serious Accidents.

Self-Deflated Personality	Self-Inflated Personality
Helpless and inadequate	Emotionally unstable and extremist
Constantly in need of guidance	Uncontrolled aggression
Chronically indecisive	Selfish, self-centered
Difficulty in concentrating	Highly competitive
Easily influenced	Overconfident, overassertive
Easily intimidated	Blame-avoidance
Fatalistic	Intolerant
	Resistance against authority
	Driving need to prove oneself
	Unduly sensitive to criticism
	Lacking appreciation of own limitation
	Addiction to alcohol or drugs

Source: Adapted from Shaw and Sichel, 1971.

Defense Mechanisms

Considering the extent of signs of character defects in organizations and in society at large, it is not surprising that many managers are disinclined to develop a systemic crisis management effort in their organization. In the next chapter we discuss the reasons they invoke for not making these changes. Here we describe the mechanisms of defense that people use to protect themselves from painful feelings and their existential implications. We emphasize that these defense mechanisms are not, by themselves, pathological. Indeed, they are often the source of very creative actions, allowing people to survive psychologically traumatic events. However, if they are used extensively, they can also have a negative effect on life and on efforts in crisis management, which is our concern here. Using the terms from the previous section, we can say that people with positive self-regard will use these defenses much less often; self-inflated and self-deflated people suffering from borderline or neurotic disorders will use them extensively.

Common Types of Defense Mechanisms

One of the earliest and most significant discoveries of Freud and other pioneers of psychoanalysis was the mechanisms by which the human mind distorts external reality as a way of coping with trauma. With very, very rare exceptions, most humans suffer tremendously while facing psychologically painful events. The technical literature on the subject of defense mechanisms describes eight basic devices (S. Freud, 1926; A. Freud, 1966; Hampden-Turner, 1981; Klein, 1937; Kohut, 1977, 1984):

1. *Denial* — the expressed refusal to acknowledge a threatening reality or realities.
2. *Disavowal* — acknowledging a threatening reality but downplaying its importance.
3. *Fixation* — the rigid commitment to a particular course of action or attitude in dealing with a threatening situation.
4. *Grandiosity* — the feeling of omnipotence.
5. *Idealization* — ascribing omnipotence to another person, object, or organization.
6. *Intellectualization* — the elaborate rationalization of an action or thought.
7. *Projection* — attributing unacceptable actions or thoughts to others.
8. *Splitting* — the extreme isolation of different elements, extreme dichotomization, or fragmentation.

The main purpose of these mechanisms, singly and in combination, is to help people avoid having to deal with complex, potentially threatening situations that, if acknowledged, would overwhelm their ability to cope.

A Simple Example

Suppose you go outside your house one morning to pick up the daily newspaper and encounter an enormous, threatening tiger. The sudden sense of panic is so great that your mind shuts down to protect you from having to acknowledge and hence to deal with the life-threatening situation in front of you. Each of the eight mechanisms can be explained in terms of this simple example.

If the sense of panic is great enough, your psyche will send a signal to the part of the brain that controls vision and you will literally not see the tiger at all. This is denial in its purest and fullest sense. The mind refuses to see a danger directly in front of it. Disavowal is less radical than denial. It is the mechanism by which the mind sees the danger in front of it but downgrades its importance. You would tell yourself that the tiger is really only a small pussy cat and hence not a very important threat.

To appreciate these mechanisms more fully, it is helpful to consider examples that are not hypothetical. The stress of battle can be so great that some soldiers react by behaving as if there were no war at all, or believing that they are immortal, blessed by a special grace. Their minds shut down, literally go blank, by closing off all contact with the outside world (Bettelheim, 1943; Kohut, 1985; May, 1950). Victims of childhood sexual abuse sometimes describe how they distanced themselves from their bodies so that they would not have to feel the psychological pain that was being inflicted upon them. Some talk of their minds "going into the wall" so that even though they were physically present they were not psychologically present (May, 1958).

Fixation is the mechanism by which individuals become rigidly attached to a particular course of action for dealing with the threatening reality, so attached that they cannot change to a more appropriate course of action as the situation demands. To arm yourself against the threatening tiger, you might fixate on the nearby lawn rake and completely rule out other courses of action, such as shutting the door or picking up a rifle.

Grandiosity — an overinflated sense of power and importance—might lead you to imagine that you are Superman and can wrestle the tiger to the ground. Self-inflated individuals would likely choose such a strategy. At times grandiosity can seem ridiculous, but it can also lead to incredible acts of heroism.

If you waited for Batman to descend from the sky and zap the tiger out of existence, you would be using the defense of idealization. You believe your own actions would be ineffective, so you idealize someone else as the protector of the family. Idealization is present in many authoritarian and dictatorial regimes. In Nazi Germany, for example, we find the complementarity between a self-inflated leader and his self-deflated public.

Of all the defense mechanisms, intellectualization is perhaps the most familiar. It is most easily seen in people who pride themselves on being "rational." This particular defense mechanism is so widespread in organizations that we devote the entire next chapter to it. Intellectualizations often involve distorted schemes of reasoning to rationalize or justify a particular course of action. Confronted with the tiger, you might sit down and do a detailed calculation of the best way to raise a five-hundred-pound weight above the house in order to drop it on the tiger.

Projection occurs when we attribute a traumatic situation to the inherent evil of others. You convince yourself that the tiger would not be there if it were not for the crazy neighbor down the block who is responsible for all the problems in the neighborhood. An interesting thing about projection is that it often involves attributing to others aspects of our own personality that we do not like. This mechanism is often responsible for the conflict between nations; each one perceives itself the savior of the world and the other as the devil incarnate.

Splitting is one of the most tragic mechanisms. It is likely to be used by people suffering from borderline and psychotic disorders. It occurs when the situation is so traumatic that the individual's personality actually splits into different parts or sub-personalities in the attempt to handle the initial event. The most dramatic cases are those involving multiple personalities, each of which is extreme or one-sided. One character may represent the angry part of the person; another, the loving or tender part. Each will be charged with dealing with a different part of the person's total problem. If the splitting is extreme enough, the various personalities will be only dimly aware of the others. Faced with a threatening tiger, the person would probably use the different subpersonalities to adopt several different defense mechanisms, such as projection, grandiosity, and idealization. However, it is very likely that the use of mini-strategies is likely to end up in a mega-banquet for the tiger.

Examples from Crisis-Prone Organizations

Let us turn now to some examples of these mechanisms in operation. All are drawn from real companies, through our interviews with the managers charged with overseeing crisis management for a particular organization. However, because of the sensitive nature of the topic, neither the particular individuals nor their institutions will be named.

Our research indicates that managers in crisis-prone organizations use these mechanisms approximately *seven times* as much as crisis-prepared organizations (Pauchant, 1988a). The comments in this section came from managers in those organizations we have labeled crisis-prone. In several cases, however, they were expressing the sentiments of their superiors; they themselves disagreed sharply. Also, even crisis-prepared managers are not entirely free from these same mechanisms. All individuals in all organizations make use of them from time to time. The difference is in the degree, the extent, and the frequency with which they use them. The examples here are only a tiny fraction of the overall sentiments we have heard expressed.

An executive in a top consulting firm said that his superiors "believed in magic." His sense was that they felt they did not need to do anything about a problem "until it leaked out." In the course of his interview, he commented that "our organization considers a 70 percent yearly turnover of employees as normal." This is a classic example of disavowal: the company acknowledges that there is a problem (high turnover) but downgrades its seriousness by classifying it as normal. "Belief in magic," on the other hand, is an example of grandiosity. The expressed policy of doing nothing about a problem until it leaks out is an example of denial. The same executive also acknowledged that the main concern of his top management was "staying current" — managing the flow of new information — with no awareness of the necessity for crisis management, suggesting once again the presence of denial.

An executive in a finance company told us his top superiors believed that "nothing big can hurt us" and "no matter what the crisis, it will not happen to us." Here we see both denial and grandiosity at the same time.

An executive in a top health company put it this way: "Our top management really believe that they are bigger than life." This is, to put it mildly, an example of grandiosity. He went on to say, "The only thing that motivates our top management is their preoccupation with the bottom line." This is an example of fixation, especially when it dominates all other concerns, as it does in too many organizations.

An executive in a food company remarked, "Our top management took no action whatsoever even when the FBI explicitly warned them about a threat to the physical security of both our CEO and chairman. Their response was, 'This won't happen to us.'" On another occasion, they said: "Terrorist action in our international facilities is not our problem. It is the problem of our international partners." Again, a strong case of denial, disavowal, projection, and splitting.

An executive in a top insurance company commented, "There is a real refusal around here to acknowledge that there is ugliness in the world. At the same time, this company is also run with a police atmosphere. Our president also truly believes he can predict the future. There is the strong belief that crises just cannot happen to us. The only area in which we put any effort into crisis management is in protecting our information system." Here we find the simultaneous use of grandiosity (the president's statement that he can predict the future), denial ("no crisis can derail the company"), and fixation (using a single course of action, practicing crisis management in a highly selective area).

An executive in an oil company remarked, "I believe that our CEO can handle any crisis." This is a classic expression of idealization. The same executive went on to reveal the presence of grandiosity when he uttered, "Nothing can really hurt our company."

An executive in a leisure company said, "My top management has really no awareness of their need for crisis management; their only motivation is to add to the bottom line. They believe that crises just cannot happen to us!" Another example of blanket denial, fixation, and grandiosity.

An executive in a top defense firm noted that his senior management denied characteristically the need for crisis management. He also revealed the use of intellectualization when he noted that the senior executive staff denied the need for crisis management because of "the high cost of training and drills."

An executive in an important food company revealed projection and idealization when he said, "Only bad companies need crisis management. We are an excellent company; therefore we have no need of it." He added, "Crises are part of the normal risk of doing business. No one can predict everything that can happen, so why even bother?" More intellectualization.

An executive in another utility company revealed another rationalization, one that is common in public organizations whose explicit mission is to provide for the public welfare. "We cannot imagine in this company that any employee would want to tamper with our products or our facilities. After all, we do good for society. Who would want to hurt us?"

Concluding Remarks: The Ostrich Complex

The poet T. S. Eliot once wrote, "Humankind cannot bear much reality." It turns out that managers and employees in crisis-prone organizations can bear even less. Surveys indicate that only half of the Fortune 500 companies have anything even approaching a minimum plan for crisis management (Fink, 1986). This means that about half the largest, most powerful companies in the United States have no basic plans in the area of crisis management, nor even the basic structure of a crisis management unit. Another survey, from a sample of seventy organizations, found that generally these firms were only slightly prepared for a crisis and that their managers complained about their lack of information in the domain (Reilly, 1987). The situation seems to be identical in other industrial nations, such as Canada or France (Lagadec, 1991; Smart and Vertinsky, 1984). In another study on Fortune 1000 companies, we ourselves found that more than six firms out of ten, roughly 62 percent, had not yet formed a crisis management unit (Mitroff, Pauchant, and Shrivastava, 1988a, 1988b).

Rate Your Organization

In order to help you rate your organization, we have developed for each layer of the Onion Model a brief questionnaire that we advise you to answer and to share with your employees. You will find in Resource B a questionnaire titled "Personality Issues That Affect Crisis Management," which relates to this layer of the Onion Model.

FIVE

The Culture of Faulty Rationalizations: Thirty-One Ways to Destroy Organizations and the Environment

> To say that we invent values means nothing else but this: life has no meaning *a priori.* Before you come alive, life is nothing: it's up to you to give it meaning, and value is nothing else but the meaning that you choose. In that way, there is a possibility of creating a human community.
>
> —Jean-Paul Sartre, *Existentialism*

> Arguments are the arenas in which educated men establish their right to imagine themselves alive.
>
> —James March, *Academic Notes*

In recent years, those who study, guide, and help organizations change have come to appreciate, and to explore systematically, the forces that guide the behavior of organizations. Of course, many observable factors — the environment in which a firm competes, the structure of its industry, its financial status, its capital and plant requirements — influence the behavior of managers in organizations. However, we also know that other, less observable factors exert a strong effect. These additional factors are collectively referred to as the culture of an organization.

While an organizational culture includes a number of visible items, such as technologies, products, and services, we emphasize in this book the less visible part of this culture: the basic assumptions held by its members about themselves and their organization, their environment, or the nature of people or life in general (Schein, 1985). These beliefs are largely unconscious and rarely articulated. In effect, culture is the set of unwritten rules that govern acceptable behavior within an organization.

81

"If you want to succeed around here, do not disagree with the boss." "Do not be the bearer of bad news." "Do not share information with rival groups within the organization; your first loyalty is to your own immediate work group, not to others."

Corporate culture is the second layer of the Onion Model. Like the first layer, it is mostly invisible. Just as the deep motivations explaining an individual's behavior are often not directly observable, the same is true of behaviors at the organizational level. The concept of corporate culture is relatively new, largely because it is invisible and intangible and thus most management scholars were unaware of it until recently. Because it is new, it is often misunderstood. Management writers, consultants, and managers often view culture as one variable to be manipulated in order to achieve competitive advantage (Chanlat, 1991). They forget, however, that the pursuit of competitive advantage is itself the product of wider cultural values, present in a specific geographic location at a given time. Considering the present confusion on the subject, we need to specify some basic notions on corporate culture before discussing it in relation to crisis management.

First, a corporate culture is a *sub*culture at best, for it is part of a larger societal culture. This means that the rationalizations we will be describing exist not only within organizations but also within society as a whole.

Second, organizational culture has an *existential function.* We do not dispute here that one of the fundamental functions of organizations is to produce goods and services; indeed, an organization is commonly defined as a grouping of individuals who cooperate with each other with the common purpose or the politically defined goal of accomplishing something that they could not do individually. But allowing individuals to produce some goods and services is not the *only* function of organizations. Another is providing people with an escape from their anxiety. This existential function explains why some people will embrace and protect the norms developed in an organization, even if they lead to crises: defending these dangerous values is the "cost" of not confronting their own anxiety.

From Individual to Cultural Rationalization

In this view, in crisis-prone organizations managers and employees alike are very skilled at developing rationalizations that will validate their day-to-day actions, disregarding the fact that these actions can lead, after a while, to crises. So the "psychic glue" that holds these organizations together, that forms the culture of such organizations, that is at the basis of decisions and actions, is the set of sometimes faulty assumptions or rationalizations that the members of the organization have developed. In this chapter we describe the content of these rationalizations. In Chapter Nine we discuss the extent to which they block attempts at change; in Chapter Ten we show that these defense mechanisms, developed in the attempt to "save the self," actually depersonalize people as they lose their sense of responsibility and ethics.

In a ground-breaking book on the affective life of groups, Pagés (1984) proposed that individuals who hold themselves in positive self-regard were able to transcend the "infernal dialectic" of the individual versus the group. These individuals were not joining organizations in the mostly unconscious hope of finding a defense against their own anxiety, but rather joined these organizations because they acknowledged their anxiety. Echoing authors such as Fromm, Jung, or Watts, Pagés argued that, "It is at the very moment when loneliness is experienced as an obligatory state that the other is discovered in his or her loneliness, and that we feel connected to this other" (p. 104, translation ours). Thus, while maintaining that the "psychic glue" of an organization is first affective and then utilitarian, Pagés does not posit that this glue is only applied to support the individual's neurotic desire to hide with others. Rather, he proposes that the cohesive force in a less emotionally bounded corporate culture is the accommodation of normal human anxiety and crises.

This description confirms what we have observed in crisis-prepared organizations in the last chapter, as well as points to a Heraclitian view of organizations, as discussed in previous chapters. Individuals in these organizations could recognize their natural defense mechanisms without holding on tightly to their corporate values, beliefs, and ideals. They viewed the coexistence of life and death, creation and destruction, and order and chaos as relative factors that needed to be acknowledged in order to allow for healthy defense mechanisms against anxiety, both for the members of their organization and their stakeholders.

Managers in crisis-prone organizations are very far from understanding the need to be "rightly" anxious. They are too busy developing and actively sustaining their rationalizations for holding onto the dogma of their corporate culture. They are too emotionally bounded for considering the necessity of rightful anxiety, let alone for discussing it.

Dangerous Fallacies

The series of rationalizations that compose layer 2 of the Onion Model are more than "just" rationalizations. They are symptoms of the general tone, smell, or feel — in short, the mindset — of an organization. More than the surface layers of the Onion Model, this general tone often reveals how seriously managers in an organization take crisis preparedness. Far too many managers kid themselves and their stakeholders that they are crisis-prepared by having tons of equipment that sit in yards and volumes of manuals that sit on shelves, rule after rule, thousands of regulations and procedures. To an outsider, the organization could seem well prepared. However, those on the inside know that this surface is all sham.

Of course, the culture of an organization is more than a set of rationalizations. To get a complete picture, one should carefully study a great number of variables, such as the myths and the stories developed in the firm, the kinds of ceremonies or ritualized events individuals subscribe to, the anecdotes and jokes passed around in the organization, the political games played, the motivations behind rewards and punishment, and so on. Still, studying the rationalizations expressed by managers, and their mindset, captures a significant part of corporate culture (Chanlat and Bédard, 1990; Moscovici, 1984).

In our research we encountered thirty-one different rationalizations. They fall broadly into four groups (see Table 5.1): (1) the special properties or characteristics of an organization that supposedly make it immune to crises; (2) the special properties of the environment that supposedly will protect the organization; (3) the special properties of crises themselves that will not affect the organization; and (4) the organization's history with past crises that supposedly makes it immune from future crises. Note that there is a great deal of overlap between the four groups. Also, while we have numbered these rationalizations from 1 to 31 for convenience, we do not imply any ranking of importance.

No organization that we have encountered appears to subscribe to all thirty-one rationalizations at once. It does appear, however, that some are more common than others: in particular, rationalizations 1 and 11: size and protection. Because these two are so central to the kind of crisis preparedness managers will develop in their organization, we consider them first.

Size

Looks are almost always deceiving. It would be nice if we could spot a crisis-prone organization just by walking in the front door and noting its appearance. True, there are some tipoffs, but so many organizations nowadays project such a grandiose image that it is impossible to spot a crisis-prone organization by looks alone.

For our purposes, the real proof is in the words and symbols, especially if they are widely voiced or shared throughout an organization. However expressed, the belief that an organization is immune to a major crisis because of its size is one of the cornerstones of a crisis-prone organization. In nearly every organization we have been able to diagnose as crisis-prone, this belief is present in one form or another.

At its root, this belief is a crude, blunt expression of the arrogance of power. Alternate expressions, collected during our interviews, reveal this sentiment even more strongly: "Our sheer size will shield us from a major crisis." "We're so big and powerful

Table 5.1. Faulty Rationalizations That Hinder Crisis Management Efforts.

Group 1 Properties of the Organization	Group 2 Properties of the Environment	Group 3 Properties of Crises Themselves	Group 4 Properties of Prior Crisis Management Efforts
1. Our size will protect us.	11. If a major crisis happens, someone else will rescue us.	17. Most crises turn out not to be very important.	24. Crisis management is like an insurance policy; you only need so much.
2. Excellent, well-managed companies do not have crises.	12. The environment is benign; or, we can effectively buffer ourselves from the environment.	18. Each crisis is so unique that it is impossible to prepare for all crises.	25. In a crisis situation, we just need to refer to the emergency procedures we've laid out in our crisis manuals.
3. Our special location will protect us.	13. Nothing new has really occured that warrants change.	19. Crises are isolated incidents.	26. We are a team that will function well during a crisis.
4. Certain crises only happen to others.	14. Crisis management is someone else's responsibility.	20. Most crises resolve themselves; therefore time is our best ally.	27. Only executives need to be aware of our crisis plans; why scare employees or members of the community?
5. Crises do not require special procedures.	15. It's not a crisis if it doesn't happen to or hurt us.	21. Most (if not all) crises have a technical solution.	28. We are tough enough to react to a crisis in an objective and rational manner.
6. It is enough to react to a crisis once it has happened.	16. Accidents are just a cost of doing business.	22. It's enough to throw technical and financial quick-fixes at a problem.	29. We know how to manipulate the media.
7. Crisis management or crisis prevention is a luxury.		23. Crises are solely negative in their impact. We cannot learn anything from them.	30. The most important thing in crisis management is to protect the good image of the organization.
8. Employees who bring bad news deserve to be punished.			31. The only important thing in crisis management is to ensure that our internal operations stay intact.
9. Our employees are so dedicated that we can trust them without question.			
10. Desirable business ends justify the taking of high-risk means.			

that in reality nothing could actually bring us down." In fact, the beliefs that "bigger is better" and "bigger is stronger" are so omnipresent in current American society that we have devoted an entire book to this subject (Mitroff and Pauchant, 1990).

It is amazing to witness these beliefs in action. Senior executives who have sat through detailed discussions of the Onion Model, repeatedly nodding their heads in agreement about the extreme danger in believing in any of the rationalizations that are discussed in this chapter, have nonetheless approached us and remarked, "But really, you know, in actuality there is very little that could bring down an organization of our size." What they fail to comprehend is that while this may be true *of them* — there may well be no crisis big or critical enough to bring them down — their organization's beliefs can help to cause a crisis that will bring down those around them. Consider the Exxon *Valdez*. Exxon is indeed so big, so powerful, that little, if anything, may be able to bring this organization down. However, as we have witnessed recently, this attitude is enough to cause extreme damage to the environment. Notice that, furthermore, this argument is only partially true; even giants such as Ford, General Motors, NASA, E. F. Hutton, and Chrysler have experienced significant troubles.

Notice, too, that what we are saying challenges strongly the perspective of orthodox economists who maintain that the only responsibility of a corporation is to its major shareholders (Friedman, 1970). In fact, industrial disasters are the most terrifying proof that an organization has a responsibility to *all* its stakeholders — employees, customers, and all members of the surrounding community. Furthermore, industrial crises also demonstrate very painfully that organizations have a tremendous responsibility toward innocent bystanders — the millions of people in Europe who were affected by the Chernobyl disaster but had never even heard of Chernobyl before, or the countless animals and vegetation in Valdez, Alaska, for whom Exxon is not even a name.

Protection

Rationalization 1 is characteristic of managers in large and self-inflated organizations; rationalization 11 is its converse. Here, self-deflating managers depend, childlike, on someone bigger, more powerful, more prestigious to protect them. "If something bad happens, someone else will come to our rescue, absorb our losses, bail us out."

It is vital that we appreciate the psychological hold that rationalizations 1 and 11 have on the people who work for the organizations that espouse them. People who work for organizations characterized by their allegiance to rationalization 1 have a strong but unconscious need to be associated with power, greatness, and success. This need goes far beyond mere association. The bigness of the organization substitutes for the general feeling of powerlessness, even emptiness, of many of those, especially at the top, who work within such organizations. Organizations that espouse rationalization 1 are often the very ones whose employees clamor the loudest for empowerment. These people are both sucked into the organization's relentless obsession with power and at the same time repelled by it, since their association with the organization can never fully fill up the internal holes within their personalities.

Often the managers in these organizations treat their employees much like they treat those on the outside—with ruthless indifference, callousness, even malicious political games. However, people with self-inflated personalities do not always fit our image of "bad guys." Very often—and this is precisely one of their most dangerous characteristics—they are particularly attractive, especially to people suffering from self-deflation. They can be charming, witty, clever, and gifted in quick analysis. Their attractiveness makes it difficult to diagnose these individuals. For this reason, we strongly believe that the current emphasis in business schools and executive seminars on strong pathological tendencies, such as the paranoid or schizoid styles, can weaken the issue: by discussing extreme cases in this neat way, students and managers alike have the tendency to forget the day-to-day pathological signs present in their organizations.

Those who work for organizations that espouse rationalization 11 are primarily seeking refuge and protection from what they perceive as a complex, harsh world. Unspoken anxiety drives such organizations and their members. There is the deep fear of abandonment by those bigger than they are, upon whom they depend for basic life support. There is a deep feeling of never being fully in control of one's own destiny. And they are right: they have traded self-control for protection.

Both self-inflated and self-deflated managers deceive themselves and the outside world by producing reams of crisis management manuals, documents, orders, rules, and memos. But the documents are nearly always a sham, because the managers' real energies are invested elsewhere, and everyone connected with the organization knows it. Self-inflated managers are obsessed by the never-ending pursuit of power and prestige. Self-deflated managers are obsessed by the need to stay in the good graces of their superiors and preserve their lifeline of support.

Both rationalizations 1 and 11 can operate within the same company. For instance, those at corporate headquarters may well believe in rationalization 1; from their perspective they are the big powerful organization. At the same time, rationalization 11 can operate in the subdivisions of the company, since they are protected by headquarters. Companies that at the top operate by rationalization 1 often send a signal to those below that rationalization 11 is expected, in the form of continued deference. Many individuals, especially self-deflated ones, live in continuous fear: while they are protected by the organization, that protection has to be won continuously. Little wonder, then, that so many of the subdivisions under self-inflated managers spend an incredible amount of time lobbying for support as well as accepting the orders given from above.

Excellence
Location
Immunity/Limited Vulnerability

These three rationalizations, while not identical with rationalization 1, are offshoots of it. In each case, the ardent desire is to find a special property of an organization that will guarantee protection from a major crisis. Thus, the fallacy of excellence expresses the misguided notion that excellent or self-inflated companies do not have crises; the fallacy of location invokes the illusion that the geographical area in which the firm operates is immune from crises; the fallacy of limited vulnerability suggests that one does not have to worry about special kinds of crises, such as product tampering, because one is not in the kind of business that would be affected. All these rationalizations are quite divorced from reality.

The Tylenol case is enough to dispel the notion that only poorly managed companies have major crises. Johnson & Johnson (J&J), the parent company of McNeil Pharmaceuticals, the makers of Tylenol, has long been regarded as an enlightened, ethical, well-managed, and respected company. Unfortunately, this was no protection against a major crisis. Indeed, as we noted earlier, one of the paradoxes that every successful company has to face in today's world is that its very success makes it a more tempting target.

The Salman Rushdie case — threats of terrorism directed against the author and publisher of *The Satanic Verses* — is enough to dispel the notion that certain geographical locations make one exempt. The company that published this controversial book is headquartered in New York City — the largest city in a highly civilized country. Imagine the reaction if you had approached this prestigious publisher with the warning that they should prepare themselves against terrorism because of a book they were about to publish.

Virtually all organizations are now subject to every kind of crisis imaginable. Over and over again, our research shows that one of the greatest sins in the area of crisis management is narrow, literal thinking, or conditions of bounded rationality and bounded emotionality. Managers in every organization have to ask themselves, What is the *special form* of product tampering that could happen to us? Try to argue with the publishers of *Encyclopedia Brittanica* that they were not subject to product tampering when someone broke into their computer networks and dumped phony information into the system, which was then printed out in the pages of the volumes. Try to convince the organizers of the Miss America Pageant that Vanessa Williams's sexually explicit photos were not a form of product tampering, which "tampered" with the pageant's wholesome image.

"Business as Usual"
Reactiveness

Even the best organizations have not learned all the necessary
lessons. J&J has been rightly and legitimately proclaimed a corporate role model for dealing with a major crisis. In a 1987 poll,
91 percent of the respondents admitted that J&J had "behaved
in an admirable way" during the two Tylenol crises (Harris, 1987,
p. 241). Its CEO, James Burke, did not dodge the press, react
with anger, or stonewall the issues. J&J managers faithfully kept
a log of press inquiries so they could get back with information
when they had it. They responded quickly and effectively to the
general public. They even withdrew the product from the market when the FBI advised them not to, thus earning the trust and
confidence of the American public. With these actions, they re-
stored confidence both in J&J as a company and in Tylenol as
a product, eventually bringing it successfully back to the market.

However, no organization, not even J&J, is currently a
role model for *all* that we have learned about crisis management.
J&J's top management has stated that, prior to the two Tylenol
crises, no special training would have helped it through the situation. Apparently the company believes even today that no
special skills or training either can be given or need to be given
to a team of managers before a crisis, that there is no way to
prepare for the worst. We disagree strongly.

There are two myths that arise perpetually in human
affairs and constantly need to be beaten back. The first is that
perfect or complete control of complex human situations is possible;
this extreme belief in free will emerges from a sense of self-
inflation. The second is that *no control is possible;* this extreme
belief in determinism emerges from a sense of self-deflation. It
is true that every crisis involves an element of uniqueness (see
rationalization 18), but this does not mean that there are no
generic features or no effective procedures for handling them.
Indeed, all human situations involve an element of uniqueness.
No two football players are exactly alike, but this does not keep
coaches from practicing constantly so that their players can learn
how to respond to generic situations.

However, the refusal of J&J's managers to become more proactive involves more than philosophical differences. There are serious emotional issues as well. It is generally not known that a number of the executives associated with Tylenol continue to experience nightmares on the anniversary of the attacks (Collins, 1987). The emotional trauma that accompanies any major crisis leaves our psyche with scars. This is one of the biggest reasons why it is difficult for managers to go back and instigate a successful program of crisis management after they have experienced a major crisis: the training that would prepare them for a new crisis will open old traumatic wounds. Managers who have experienced a crisis prefer to avoid any serious debriefing of how they handled it financially, physically, and emotionally. This is true of J&J, and of countless other organizations with which we are familiar.

Luxury

One of the most difficult issues is the amount of money that should be allocated to crisis preparation. If there is any area in which the field of crisis management is weak, this is certainly it. We simply do not have the data that would allow systematic and thorough cost-benefit analyses. However, some general indications are emerging. For instance, before the fire that disrupted a major telephone switching station of Illinois Bell in the Chicago area, one company spent $600,000 backing up its extensive telecommunications and computer facilities in the case of such an eventuality. Six hundred thousand dollars is certainly a good deal of money. However, with this backup the company was able to operate during the crisis instead of being shut down, and avoided a potential loss of $20 million. From this perspective, $600,000 (3 percent of $20 million) is a wise investment. Further, the company was also able to increase its market share since they were able to conduct business while their competitors were not.

Where crises affect computer systems, or any other advanced technology, the issue of cost takes on broader scope: for many companies, it becomes the very real cost of survival. It is currently estimated that some 85 percent of U.S. corporations are heavily dependent on computer and telecommunication technologies, so much so that on average a company will lose 25 percent of its daily revenues after the sixth day of system breakdown, up to 40 percent for the financial, banking, and utility industries (Christensen and Schkabe, 1988). So the true cost of computers is not simply their initial purchase or maintenance costs but rather the *cost of going out of business if they are unable to function.* Indeed, we have found that some crisis-prepared companies calculate a new kind of cost when deciding whether to purchase a new kind of equipment: they evaluate a "dependency cost," the total cost incurred in lost business if those technologies were to fail (Pauchant and Mitroff, in press).

One of the most disastrous ways of thinking we have found in crisis-prone organizations is the use of traditional probability theory in crisis management. According to this theory (see, for example, Brealey and Myers, 1981), potential cash flows or costs are compared in relation to their probability of occurrence. For example, suppose that a company needs to choose between three different business ventures with potential cash flows of $100,000 (project 1), $200,000 (project 2), and $300,000 (project 3), and respective occurrence probabilities of 50 percent, 20 percent, and 10 percent. Probability-theory analysis involves multiplying cash flow by probability. In this case the managers would choose project 1, because it has the highest expected cash flow ($100,000 × .50 = $50,000). Of course in reality these strategic decisions involve other factors: market opportunities, competition, lines of products and expertise, cost considerations, elaborate calculations of discounted cash flows, political coalitions inside the firm, and so on. However, the principle is the same at the core, for probability theory is used to evaluate the expected return or cost of different scenarios.

In essence this is precisely what distinguishes risk management from crisis management. Risk management involves evaluating the cost of a risk after multiplying by its probability of occurrence. A disaster with a high cost but a low probability of occurrence will not be taken into consideration. In contrast, *crisis* management involves focusing not only on the most probable events but also on the event with the greatest impact on its environment regardless of its probability of occurrence. Traditional probability theory explains one reason why Exxon was not prepared for a disaster such as the *Valdez*. Before the crisis, Exxon's top management had evaluated the probability of such a disaster at one chance out of one million (Stevens, 1989). So the probabilistic cost of a disaster such as *Valdez,* considering nothing more than cleanup costs, reported at $1 billion, could have been evaluated at the ridiculous amount of $1,000 ($1 billion × 1/1,000,000). But even the strictly financial effects spread far beyond cleanup costs: a disaster such as *Valdez* tarnishes the company's image for many years to come, with significant impacts on market share and business effectiveness — not to mention the cost of lawsuits. And of course such an event involves far, far more than cost considerations: there is the emotional effect on the populations involved, the immense damage to the environment, and the disastrous effect on the quality of life of the affected communities.

Crisis management is not a luxury to be indulged in whenever there is sufficient time and money. Crisis management is central to the conduct of *everyday business* of companies competing in a global economy.

Punishing Whistleblowers
"Everybody Loves Us"

Managers of crisis-prone organizations seem to hold onto the unconscious belief that to kill the messenger is to kill the problem. This faulty rationalization is common in organizations; it is also used by people in general in an attempt to preserve their illusion of safety. The example of Roger Boisjoly at NASA after the *Challenger* disaster is a case in point: not only was Boisjoly disregarded by NASA, but also he and his family were harassed and isolated by their community, forcing them to leave their home town (Boisjoly, 1988). Notice also that this strategy can backfire: as of this writing, Boisjoly is lecturing across the world on ethics and management and the necessity for a social system to respect and learn from whistleblowers (Boisjoly, 1988; Maier, 1988).

Rationalization 9 — "everybody loves us" — expresses the

other side of the issue. Crisis-prone managers have the tendency to "kill" the most visible dissidents; they also tend to rely on the benevolence and dedication of their employees. During our interviews we encountered several motivations that underlie this faulty rationalization: some are connected to the belief that nothing bad can actually happen to the firm considering its size and overall power (rationalization 1); others are connected to strict beliefs in economics theory, arguing that employees will not act against their self-interest and jeopardize their employment: still others are connected to beliefs that the firm is technically prepared to handle all crisis situations (rationalizations 21, 22, and 25). Further, and even more perplexing, some underlying beliefs are associated with the illusion that employees will be eternally grateful to these managers and the firm in general for providing them with important and valuable work or for allowing them to be associated with such a prestigious firm.

In crisis after crisis these rationalizations have been proved faulty. Consider, for example, the disgruntled employee who shot his boss a few years ago during a PSA flight and, in so doing, destroyed the plane with hundreds of passengers; consider the attack by a deranged former employee of a Louisville firm who killed seven workers and wounded thirteen others (*Newsweek,* Sept. 25, 1989, p. 22).

The point is that the sociotechnical systems that we call "corporations" are so complex and interdependent that they have become extremely fragile. Considering this fragility and the lack of crisis management preparations, a minor event, even a single individual, can now have a drastic effect on an organization as a whole and on its community and environment. These events will not diminish in this century; they are, in fact, increasing rapidly. It is estimated that two-thirds of employees in some organizations have developed counterproductive behaviors such as drug or alcohol consumption, falsification of hours worked, tampering, and sabotage (Bartol and Bartol, 1986; Clark and Hollinger, 1983). These findings also point once again to this vital fact: a non-authentic culture not only prevents a firm from developing an integrated effort in crisis management, *it also generates crises.* These studies found that counterproductive behaviors such as tampering are strongly associated with the dissatisfaction employees experience with their management. The problem seems thus to be located both in the personality makeup of these individuals *and* the corporate culture developed in the firm, each factor amplifying the other.

"The Razor's Edge"
Fate

Many business organizations believe that they have to assume risks to be able to compete in the global marketplace, and that these risks are just a normal cost of doing business. Both these rationalizations are associated to some extent with a belief in fate. Etymologically, the word *disaster* is formed from the Latin *dis,* expressing negativity, and *astrum,* meaning "star." The occurrence of a disaster is thus, in the structure of our language, connected to a "bad star," fate, or destiny (Baum, 1988). Holding strictly to this thesis of fatality removes us from any responsibility for crises; it allows us to blame crises on events outside our control (Jacob and Sabelli, 1984). As we saw in Chapter One, one of the social functions of the concept of "crisis" is to provide people with some meaning in the midst of turbulence; the concept of "fate" exercises a similar social function. In particular, by invoking fate, self-inflated individuals can still believe in their omnipotence, even though it is at the moment limited by divine providence, and self-deflated individuals can explain why they have abdicated their power in the first place.

An excellent example on the subject has been proposed by Hardin (1971). Analyzing the case of five hundred thousand people killed in 1970 in East Bengal by a cyclone, Hardin disagreed that the cause of these deaths was the cyclone. Instead, he proposed that the real cause was overpopulation. Studying the area of the catastrophe, he realized that it was barely above sea level and positioned on a delta, making it very vulnerable to even ordinary storms. He thus concluded the "cause" of this tragedy was the foolishness of choosing such an area for living, combined with the condition of overpopulation. Thus, Hardin argued, blaming the cyclone was the easiest answer. To see overpopulation as one of the causes brings too many embarrassing questions.

More recently, William D. Stevens, president of Exxon USA, has insisted that the *Valdez* accident was an "act of God that could not have been prevented" (Stevens, 1989). Notice that Mr. Stevens does not acknowledge the twenty-nine oil spills similar to and even larger than the *Valdez* accident, such as the Amoco *Cadix* spill, that have taken place in the past in other waters, according to J. D. Sipes, chief of marine safety for the U.S. Coast Guard (Sipes, 1989). Notice also that, in addition to invoking fate, Mr. Stevens blamed the captain's alcohol problems. As we have seen, the systemic nature of crises renders ludicrous any attempt to point to one or two causes of a crisis. However, the appeal of the "disaster" theory is apparent: on a pragmatic level it could diminish notably the amount of the lawsuits against Exxon; it also allows Exxon's executives to reduce their guilt and lets them continue believing in their self-inflated culture. Notice also that discounting the twenty-nine similar events that happened outside U.S. waters — organizational narcissism at its highest — is an expression of both bounded rationality and bounded emotionality.

As for the fallacy of the razor's edge, the rationalization that to compete successfully in the global marketplace requires taking tremendous risks, let us remember that Mister Duen, director of safety, reliability, and quality assurance at NASA, warned, six years before the *Challenger* disaster, that competitive and cost pressures would bring "some difficult times ahead in the safety world at NASA" (Cohen, 1980). This brings us back to the issues discussed in relation to rationalization 7, viewing crisis management as a luxury.

We should be careful, however, not to limit ourselves to questions of classical economics and strategic theories. It is true that cost and competitive pressures influence crisis-prone companies to cut corners in the area of safety. It is also true that "living on the razor's edge" by taking great risks gives executives the emotional thrills they need. Self-inflated individuals and cultures are particularly prone to flirting with danger; these situations give them a feeling of being alive and decrease their inner sense of boredom and anxiety. We believe that the major scandals in the financial industry during the past years are strongly related to these emotional and existential issues — in addition, of course, to greed and power.

The Garden of Eden
The Past

Both these rationalizations exemplify again the extent of fragmentation present in crisis-prone organizations. In these cases, the fragmentation is directed to the notion of time, focusing on the past (rationalization 13), and to a set of "perfect" social, economic, or political trends (rationalization 12). However, the world is not the same as twenty years ago, and we are not living in a Garden of Eden.

Responsibility
Narcissus

Paradoxically, these two rationalizations are contradictory in nature and yet linked. On the one hand, managers in crisis-prone organizations claim that crisis management responsibility is not theirs; on the other hand, they also state that a crisis is something that happens to *them* in particular. Self-inflated individuals, believing in their uniqueness, will recognize the importance of a crisis only when it concerns them directly; at the same time, they lack the moral strength to recognize their role in the making of an event that has affected others.

Both rationalizations are false — and extremely dangerous. In an interdependent world, anyone's crisis is everyone's crisis. To put the case mildly, industrial crises and pollution threaten not simply a particular organization but the planet as a whole. Try to convince the families living in Bhopal that the gas leak "happened" only to Union Carbide!

Downplaying
Uniqueness
Fragmentation
Luck

The fallacy of downplaying is but a variation of rationalization 1; the fallacies of uniqueness and fragmentation deny the existence of systemic factors, and the fallacy of luck is still another variation of the "disaster" thesis, this time seeing the stars in a more positive light.

Technology
Quick Fixes

Engineers are particularly prone to the fallacy of technology. For example, radar, designed to increase marine safety, actually triggered an increase of accidents; now with the illusion of safety, captains went faster when radar was on board (Perrow, 1984). Similarly, the introduction of DDT, offered as a miracle solution for eliminating devastations caused by insects, had in fact an even more devastating effect (Carson, 1962). Asbestos is another case in point. Obviously, we are not saying that humanity should go back to a technology-free society. However, we are saying that to use technology from a self-inflated and omnipotent point of view often leads to disasters.

The quick-fix fallacy is in many ways similar to the disease of "technophilia," to use Roszak's term (1986). It consists of applying to a problem a limited and fragmented number of solutions that all too often only make things worse. To appreciate the disastrous effect of quick-fix solutions, turn to Chapter Two and examine some of the actions posed by Union Carbide's managers.

Negativity

Given the financial, physical, emotional, and existential burden of crises, we can well understand why many people believe that a crisis is only negative and that nothing good can be learned from it. Indeed, for the most part the impacts *are* negative. However, some aspects of crises turn out, strangely enough, to be positive, although one wishes that there were other ways of reaping such benefits. In fact, crises are often what a human system needs for learning and changing. They allow the "opportunity space" of the actors to broaden (Bryson, 1981). If one talks to enough top executives and CEOs, strange and unexpected benefits sometimes emerge. In our interviews we met a number of executives who actually relished some aspects of their experience during a past crisis, considering the energy developed at the time and the atmosphere of cooperation between employees and even, in some cases, competitors. The more positive self-regard an individual has, the more that person realizes *both* the positive and the negative sides of an issue, viewing all phenomena, including crises, as both an act of destruction and creation.

Insurance
Plans

These two rationalizations, when taken together, create a paradox. Those who compare crisis management to an insurance policy firmly believe in crash management. Unfortunately, buying an insurance policy has no effect whatsoever on the odds of a crisis occurring; it only protects financial interests when something does occur. In contrast, other people believe that they can anticipate every conceivable variable in a crisis and thus idealize their contingency planning. This is associated with the technical and quick-fix rationalizations. To some extent, it is a belief in magic. As many experiences have indicated, a crisis never evolves as previously planned. As we shall see in Chapter Seven, the focus should be not on the plans themselves but on the activities and process of planning.

Teamwork
Secrecy
Toughness

Increased cohesion of a group during a crisis often leads to the reinforcement of the group's previous assumptions and rationalizations. Besides such cognitive limitations as time and space distortions, fragmentation of issues, lack of systemic thinking, or increased feeling of invulnerability, groups under the stress of a crisis also tend to regress emotionally to a relatively primitive state (Bion, 1959; Freud, 1921; Kets de Vries and Miller, 1985; Kohut, 1984, 1985). These mechanisms, both cognitive and emotional, demonstrate the fallacy of believing that an unprepared or untrained group will function effectively during a crisis, and in particular that it will not react defensively.

The fallacy of secrecy demonstrates also, one more time, the narcissistic and self-centered tendencies of crisis-prone organizations (see rationalization 15) as well as their tendencies to think that defusing bad news is the same as resolving problems (see rationalization 8).

Manipulation
Image Making
The Mirror

These last three rationalizations have a common theme: reliance on unreality. The first, focusing on the manipulation of the media, makes the false assumption that good crisis management is primarily a public relations exercise. The priority, then, is to get good press from a bad situation (see Garden, 1979) rather than to reduce the impact of the crisis on the stakeholders and on the environment. Notice also the strong dichotomous tendencies often expressed by self-inflated cultures. Self-inflated individuals, concerned excessively with being admired, cherished, or loved, often condemn individuals or groups that will not cater to their existential needs. Often, these managers divide the world into dichotomized entities: "us" and "them"; "the ones who like us, the ones who do not"; "the ones who are for us, the ones who are against us"; the "good ones" and the "bad ones" (Klein, 1937).

Many of the managers in crisis-prone organizations view the media as evil, as the ones that bring the bad news (Pauchant and Mitroff, 1988). Cut off from reality and unable to empathize with their stakeholders, they focus on the impact the crisis could have on their personal image and credibility. A number of observers have documented, for example, that after Watergate, Nixon considered the crisis to be primarily a "credibility gap" and believed that a good TV appearance could resolve the issues (Lasch, 1979; Zaleznik and Kets de Vries, 1975). Another example of acting on image rather than substance occurred in the late 1980s at General Motors, where managers refused to replace a transmission that was too small for the car it had been inserted in. These managers opted instead to settle the class action suit brought against them on this issue, for a total cost of $19.2 million. A few days later, however, these same managers repurchased up to 20 percent of GM's common stock for an amount over $5 billion, in an attempt to artificially drive up prices, even though it lost market shares (Zaleznik, 1989).

To focus on unreality is to believe in the fallacy of the mirror—the belief that the surrounding environment is a reflection of oneself or one's organization (Mitroff and Bennis, 1989). Thus, for Nixon, driven by his view of his personal image, the world became a stage where magician's tricks and a good line will settle things. For GM, a financial ethos drives the company to the point where corporate strategies are believed to be financial in nature. Crisis-prone organizations and crisis-prone individuals seem to have this characteristic in common: the inability to imagine and feel that the world is different from themselves.

Crisis-prone managers confuse their own internal corporate structure with the structure of the environment in which they operate. More often than not, in their organizations they engage in long and bloody political competition for resources, power, or status. Similarly, they see the world as a battlefield, where every inch is gained through sheer power and survival is the only thing that counts. People so conditioned by the endless search for power consider that those who are lacking in power have no rights. Powerless individuals are to be used, literally, as a resource, like a piece of land or a gallon of oil. In the case of Bhopal, the local population living around the plant had been mostly forgotten, becoming "important" only when it started to sue the company after the tragedy. Destructive crisis-prone organizations not only deserve the same contempt in which they regard others, but they deserve to be strongly regulated and their top executives punished by law.

Concluding Remarks: The Protective Side of Rationalizations

While we have emphasized that rationalizations described in this chapter are faulty, we also need to stress their very important purpose: they allow individuals to function in their daily activities without feeling crushed by the world. Thus, while they are faulty from a crisis management point of view, they are also protective for the individual in an existential sense. They allow us to function and, quite literally, to exist. However, even though these protective mechanisms are essential for the functioning of some individuals, we must not let that blind us to the fact that they are also extremely dangerous for organizations and their environments because they hamper effective actions that could prevent many crises from occurring.

Rate Your Organization

As with the previous chapter, you will find in Resource B a questionnaire designed for rating your organization on this layer of the Onion Model. We strongly recommend that you answer this questionnaire and share it with several colleagues.

SIX

Form Follows Function: Redesigning Organizations to Prevent Crises

The pairs of opposites, of which *freedom* and *order* and *growth* and *decay* are the most basic, put tension into the world. . . . No real understanding is possible without awareness of these pairs of opposites which permeate everything man does.

— E. F. Schumacher, *A Guide for the Perplexed*

Let us summarize the presentation of the Onion Model thus far. In Chapter Four we delved into the subconscious of individuals by discussing the existential side of crises and the defense mechanisms that managers use in traumatic events such as crises. In Chapter Five we explored the set of faulty beliefs or rationalizations that can constitute the culture of an organization and that, if endorsed, constitute a "culture of crisis." In other words, crises do not "just happen." They are rooted deeply in the general mindset of individuals and their organization. This means that from an organizational standpoint, crises are almost never caused by one or two "rotten apples"; they are a reflection of the total organization. This chapter focuses on the *structural* level of organizations, and Chapter Seven on *strategic* and business policy issues. We conclude our discussion of the Onion Model in Chapter Eight, proposing an ideal plan of crisis management.

The Voice of Reality

This chapter treats an important question: what organizational design will permit organizations to minimize the possibility of a major crisis occurring in the first place and to better manage those that result despite our best efforts?

104

To answer this question, we are going to shift moods. In effect, the last two chapters have constituted a one-sided conversation. Up to now, we have heard only the voice of denial, the defensive mechanisms of crisis-prone organizations. That same voice, when applied to layers 3 and 4 of the Onion Model, allows managers and employees in organizations with a "culture of crisis" continually to fool themselves into believing that they are performing well on the outer layers of the model when in fact they are not. They can even pour considerable sums of time, money, and effort into maintaining the illusion of preparedness.

Instead of listening further to the exclusive voice of defense, in this and the next chapter we want to listen instead to an opposite voice, the voice of reality. This is the voice of those who can no longer deny the fact that the world is sometimes a terrifying place to live. Two things in particular characterize this voice: a major charge, or indictment; and an idealized organizational design for crisis management.

The Indictment

The voice of reality is anything but neutral. It is not content merely to describe the facts. It starts instead by making its *value commitments* as explicit as possible so that others can see the underlying premises from which it draws its conclusions.

Its opening thrust is an indictment based on moral outrage: that we are managing twenty-first-century technologies of incredible complexity with nineteenth-century thinking. The charge, in short, is that one of the main reasons we are experiencing a rash of mega-crises is that the managers of institutions that are supposed to develop and control such technologies are hopelessly out of date and hence inadequate to the task.

In the nineteenth century, the dominant concept of the world was that of a machine; literally everything governing the design, the operation, and even the measurement of performance of organizations was viewed in machinelike terms. Since by definition a machine is decomposable into separate, autonomous parts, each of which can function independently of all the other parts, this meant that organizations were divided into separate units, with the functions of production, accounting, finance, and so forth organized into separate departments. Furthermore, following the advice of "machine-oriented" thinkers such as Adam Smith or Frederick Taylor, people and departments were treated as interchangeable parts. If one part of the machine — or one person — broke down, then in principle it could be replaced by another without having to repair the rest of the machine.

The amazing thing about metaphors is not that ultimately they fail, as they must, but rather that they hold for as long as they do. For its times, the "world as machine" metaphor was appropriate. Since areas of the world were still largely separated from one another in space and time, problems could be confined to particular communities. Today, all this has changed drastically. Our planet is now so thoroughly interconnected along every conceivable dimension that anything anywhere is not only local news but can affect everything everywhere almost instantaneously. Technologies such as nuclear power are capable of affecting the entire planet. When the nuclear reactor at Chernobyl exploded, it took only two weeks for the cloud of radiation to circle the globe and contaminate salmon off the coast of the state of Washington (Starke, 1987). It took only a half a day for the world's grain markets to react with fluctuating prices. When the oil rigs in Kuwait were destroyed during the 1991 war in the Persian Gulf, the eternal snow of the Himalayas was polluted.

The consequence of all this is that the organizations that were appropriate for a much simpler world are totally inappropriate for today's. What is worse, they are fundamentally part of the problems we face. That is one reason why organizational redesign and renewal so preoccupies present-day corporations (see, for example, Mitroff, 1987, 1988; Kanter, 1989; Peters, 1988; Zaleznik, 1989). Little by little, the recognition is dawning that Machine Age organizations are totally inappropriate for dealing with Systems Age problems and concerns.

The Prescription

At present there is no organization that can serve as a model for a Systems Age organization, especially a model for exemplary crisis management, so we shall have to talk about an "idealized" one. By *idealized* we do not mean a utopian design, but an organization design that can be a *standard* for evaluating the performance of actual organizations. We also mean a design that is eminently capable of being realized, since it is not beyond the pale of human capabilities. Indeed, many of its aspects are already beginning to emerge. The ideal merely assembles in one concentrated place many of the innovations that organizations are currently exploring in order to cope with all kinds of crises.

A Classic View of Organizations

To start our discussion, we have used Galbraith's classic model of organizational design (Galbraith, 1977). While other models exist, this one presents the advantage of using a systems perspective.

Figure 6.1 shows five of the key variables that influence the design of organizations. Notice the interrelationships: each variable is connected to all the others. This means that, in general, it is not possible to make a change or an intervention in a complex organization without affecting all its aspects.

Let us look briefly at each of the variables. The box labeled *People* refers to the personnel of the organization. However, it encompasses much more than the current cast of characters that the organization employs. It also means the general set of skills and educational requirements that are necessary to perform the tasks of the organization. The box labeled *Tasks* refers not only to those tasks the organization needs to have accomplished, but the way they are grouped together to form relatively self-contained, autonomous jobs. That is, the Tasks box contains the full set of skills that are assembled into freestanding jobs. The box labeled *Structure* refers to the number of worker and executive layers that the organization has — who reports to

Figure 6.1. Variables That Influence
Organizational Design and Behavior.

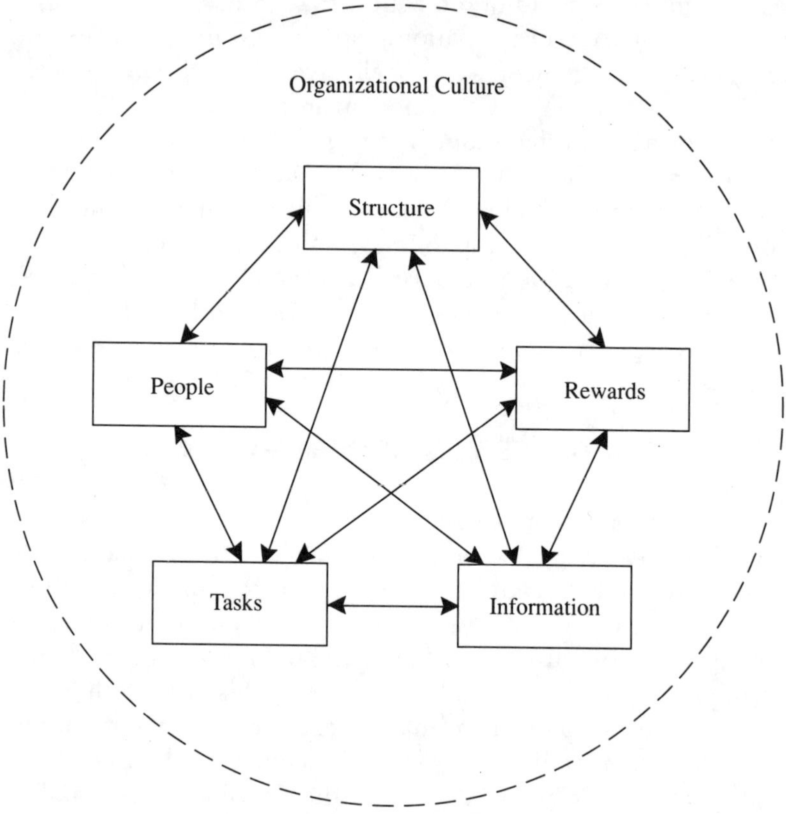

Source: Adapted from J. K. Galbraith, 1977.

whom, who communicates with whom — and how power and
authority are delegated or invested in various jobs. Structure
also refers to the independent subunits or operating divisions
of the organization. In everyday terms, the general notion of
structure is embodied not only in an organization chart but also
in the general day-to-day routines. So the structure of an organization has much in common with its overall culture.

The box labeled *Information* refers to the kind and quality
of communication channels the organization uses to gather and

to disseminate knowledge—not only scientific and technical (quantitative) knowledge but verbal (qualitative) information as well. It also refers to the kind of knowledge that is preferred in the organization; for example, some cultures rely on hunches and intuitive tips, where others are sticklers for quantitative data. The box labeled *Rewards* refers to the full set of mechanisms by which the organization rewards acceptable behavior or hopes to extinguish inappropriate behavior—symbolic, intangible rewards as well as material, physical, and monetary entities.

Forming and Operating a Crisis Management Unit

One of the first ways to evaluate the crisis-preparedness of a firm is to evaluate its Crisis Management Unit (CMU). The function of such a unit is to organize the total crisis management effort of the organization, and as such is helpful in addressing design issues in crisis management. It is important to note, however, that only four out of ten firms have developed CMUs for their organization, and that the mere existence of a CMU is not a reliable sign that an organization is indeed crisis-prepared; we found that many crisis-prone organizations had formed "pseudo" CMUs to make the firm appear as if it were taking crisis management seriously. In the next sections we will discuss the nature of a CMU in an ideal crisis-prepared firm.

Staffing the CMU

As part of the National Association of Manufacturers study described in Chapter One, we have collected some data on crisis management units in organizations (Mitroff, Pauchant, and Shrivastava, 1988a, 1988b). Table 6.1 shows the types of professional roles that are most likely to be represented on an organization's CMU. One of the most disconcerting findings was that, at the time of the survey (early 1987), 62 percent of the respondent organizations did not have a CMU in place. However, of those that did, the chief legal counsel was the person (or function) most likely to be represented, followed closely by the director of public affairs and the director of security.

Table 6.1. Professional Roles Represented
on Crisis Management Units.

Role/Function	Percentage of Occurrence on CMUs
Chief Legal Counsel	90%
Director of Public Affairs	87
Director of Security	83
Chief Operating Officer	82
Director of Environmental Affairs	80
Director of Engineering	78
Chief Executive Officer	68
Director of Personnel	68
Director of Safety	67
Chief Financial Officer	60
Director of Marketing	50
Chairman of the Board	46
Director of Research	42
Outsiders	5

Having these three functions represented certainly make sense. A major crisis is likely to raise all kinds of legal ramifications and liabilities, so having the chief legal counsel on a CMU is essential. The participation of the director of public affairs is also desirable since a major crisis is also likely to involve communication with multiple stakeholders both inside and outside the corporation. The presence of the security officer is logical, since many crises result from the breakdown of a technological system or a security process. The presence of the chief operating officer on a CMU (ranked fourth) also makes sense, since a major crisis certainly disrupts day-to-day operations.

We were troubled to find that other organizational functions, while not entirely absent, did not receive the same generally high levels of visibility. The fact that the personnel function is ranked eighth and the marketing function is ranked eleventh is cause for concern. While the appearance of the chief legal counsel is absolutely paramount, it has been found from previous experience and resarch that no one function must be allowed to dominate if an organization is to be truly effective in responding to all the concerns that a major crisis raises (Janis, 1989; Smart and Vertinsky, 1977; Lagadec, 1981; Starbuck and Milliken, 1988). In fact, it is not clear that the primary concern should be to avoid legal liability at all costs. Although Union Carbide fulfilled its legal obligation of warning the local government of the proximity of the population to its Bhopal plant (see Chapter Two), its subsequent lack of actions contributed strongly to the impact of that disaster. As another example, the primary legal focus developed by the Johns Manville Corporation during the long asbestos crisis had a perverse effect not only on the lives of thousands of individuals, but also on the company itself and on the industry as a whole (Hills, 1987). To capture the systemic issues imbedded in a crisis, the composition of a CMU must be as broad as possible.

Considering the strength of the defense mechanisms discussed in the two previous chapters, we were not surprised to discover that only 5 percent of all CMUs include outsiders. Only a minority of managers have understood the need to listen to their various stakeholders, including those located outside their organizational boundaries, as well as integrate their views into the organizational culture.

Tasks

From our interviews we have found that one of the key tasks that members of the CMU must perform is to facilitate exchanges and understanding among the organization's diverse departments. Central to this task is the role of the facilitators in the CMU. Fundamentally, the facilitators must be able to mediate effectively the various interpersonal and professional conflicts between the CMU members. The facilitators must understand and respect the full range of functions and issues that must be attended to in the heat of a crisis. Thus, they must recognize the importance of legal concerns (or financial, or technical, and so forth) but must not allow them to dominate other equally important concerns. Otherwise, the corporation will find itself in the embarrassing position of having protected itself legally but having lost a substantial part of its market.

Consider, for instance, the case of two very different organizational responses. When faced with defective products, the
organization that manufactured the Dalkon Shield mounted a
primarily legal defense. This protected the corporation but did
nothing to assuage consumer fears. Eventual result: bankruptcy.
In contrast, consider the behavior of Procter & Gamble (P&G)
when the Rely tampon was shown to be statistically linked to
a life-threatening condition called toxic shock syndrome (Mitroff
and Kilmann, 1984). There was no conclusive proof that the
Rely tampon was solely responsible for toxic shock syndrome,
yet P&G managers were quick to remove the product from the
market. Result: further consumer confidence and trust.

Our interviews also demonstrated that the facilitator's task
is not necessarily best filled by the CEO, unless the CEO has
either had special training or is by nature able to handle enormous stress, listen to and respect diverse viewpoints, and mediate
among various professional concerns (Lagadec, 1987). Similarly,
the CEO is not necessarily the best person to guide the organization through a major crisis or to be the media spokesperson—
and it requires very wise CEOs indeed to recognize this about
themselves and delegate to someone else the authority and
responsibility to take charge during a crisis. Also, as we have
stressed in previous chapters, crisis management issues are too
systemic and complex to be addressed by only one person.

One of the central tasks of the CMU, although it is not
appreciated at the current time, will be the constant monitoring of the key assumptions that underlie the general belief system of the individuals constituting the organization and thus
underlie the crisis plans. Another key task of a CMU is the peri-
odic surveying of employee opinion on crisis potential and crisis management. The questionnaires provided in Resource B
addressing the Onion Model are a first step toward this purpose. They can enable a CMU to compare employee perceptions regarding crisis assessment and crisis-preparedness. These
comparisons will help the CMU construct a meaningful dialogue among employees on why these subjects are perceived
differently. Through these surveys and the early warning signals they provide, the CMU will be able to assess how well the

organization is doing across every level of the Onion Model and to suggest corrective action.

Other tasks are also needed. One is brainstorming, encouraging novel experiments that could help the organization prepare for crises. Complete prevention is not the point of crisis management. The point is to find out what is feasible by asking creative questions. In our field interviews we encountered a very creative idea in a pharmaceutical company. Because of the all-too-real threat of product tampering, company managers were very concerned about improving security through more effective preventive strategies. They began to view their packaging—a bottle—as a house and deliberately considered this question: "If we wanted to keep a burglar out of our house, how would we do it?" They considered each element in turn, viewing the cap of the bottle as the front door of the house and the sides of the bottle as the walls. The team went even further: "Suppose we were dealing with two burglars, one with only a high school education and one with a Ph.D.; what, if anything, would we do differently?" Someone in the group hit on the very creative idea of forming an internal "assassin team" and a "counterassassin team." The assassin team would come up with one way to penetrate the seals of the bottles and the counterassassin team would try to stop them. Both teams learned, to their displeasure but not to their complete surprise, that there was no foolproof way to keep a determined adversary out. They did learn the cost-effectiveness of various preventive actions. Most important of all, they learned how to think the unthinkable.

As this example shows, it is not enough to ask managers and employees to passively determine the potential crises in their organization by listing them on paper and then discussing their findings in a meeting. The complexity of the issues involved, and the inevitable defense mechanisms, make this an extremely limited approach. Rather, the search for potential crises should also involve a determined and organized process. Thus, one of the key tasks of any CMU is to ask itself some very unpleasant questions: "What if intelligent, determined adversaries learned all there was to know about the critical vulnerabilities of our organization? What if they suddenly gained access to our most important, privileged, confidential information? What if they infiltrated our own CMU or safety department and knew the different ways our company could be hurt the most? What could we do?" These critical questions need to be asked, and answered, by a special crisis unit that is both empowered and rewarded by the organization. Unless this unit has formal recognition and support, creativity is chancy. In most organizations, such a unit does not now exist. Quite simply, one must be formed. Crisis management is too important to leave to chance.

Lastly, one of the major tasks for members of the CMU is to organize and supervise training sessions for themselves as well as for the organization's employees. An executive CMU requires a great deal of training if it is to function properly. Ideally, frequent training drills and simulations should be conducted for each major type of crisis. This is not common in today's organizations. It is extremely difficult, if not impossible, to get a team of senior executives to sit still for major training or simulation exercises with their managers and employees.

Structure

We believe that every corporation will eventually appoint a senior executive who will coordinate or at least have major responsibility for crisis management on a nearly full-time basis. To give this matter some perspective, it is helpful to point out that fifty to a hundred years ago, accountants were peripheral employees in their companies. Today, a full-time accountant is a given for every organization. Likewise, we believe that in time, all of the functions related to crisis management will be so thoroughly integrated with the day-to-day management of an organization that it will be virtually meaningless to ask how much time or money is devoted to normal business activities and how much is devoted to crisis management.

At the same time, every organization also needs to have throughout its structure other people, not necessarily on the CMU, who can help in the event of a crisis. No matter how competent it is, no single unit can handle all the tasks and issues that need to be addressed on a day-to-day basis.

When it comes to the issue of centralization versus de-centralization, managers in crisis-prepared organizations must understand that it is not an either-or question. Crisis management needs to be done at the operating-division level and at the headquarters level simultaneously. Those closest to the seat of a potential crisis may know some of the particular factors better, but only headquarters can coordinate in the event of simultaneous multiple crises.

Information

One of the key concerns of a CMU is information — gathering internal and external data about the vulnerability of the organization and communicating effectively in the heat of crisis.

Modern technology has proved to be a mixed blessing. Today's rapid travel and instantaneous communication mean that no organization is an island. In the event of a major crisis, no organization can keep its actions secret. The case of Exxon illustrates this. The senior executive in charge of the cleanup operations wrote a terse memo saying that after a certain date they would cease trying to clean up Prince William Sound no matter how strongly they were ordered to do so — and apparently failed to consider the possibility that such a memo might fall into outside hands. It is the height of folly for any organization to assume that its activities in any phase of crisis management will not be found out. We are not saying that it is all right for an organization to engage in unethical behavior as long as information does not leak to the outside world. This subject is so important that we devote an entire chapter (Chapter Ten) to the ethical basis of crisis management.

The CMU should be responsible for organizing the total communications network and process that crisis management requires. This includes, for example, developing a data base of contacts inside and outside the company; selecting and training spokespersons; developing an adequate communication system; and determining the potential media strategies to be used with different audiences (Fink, 1986; Mindszenthy, Watson, and Koch, 1988). Choosing the appropriate media of communication is particularly important. Crisis-prone organizations tend to concentrate on the content of their information (usually in an attempt to convince their stakeholders that it was not their fault), ignoring the question of process. This is a mistake. Issues about crises are as much existential and emotional as they are technical, and the kinds of media used should be "rich" enough to communicate human emotions as well as technical issues (Weick, 1988).

Effective communication should also be directed inside the organization. It is a mistake to believe that employees should be left in the dark or that they will not find out anything on their own. Obviously, certain critical details, such as entry codes for computer data, should be protected on a strict need-to-know basis, but all employees, no matter what their level, need to know that the organization is prepared for contingencies and that their cooperation is essential if the plans are to work. Employees themselves can see directly that a major product tampering incident or an act of sabotage could cost them their jobs as well as damage their environment.

We interviewed a company in the aeronautics industry that developed a very effective way of sensitizing its employees to product failure. After a near-miss accident of one of its experimental jets, caused partly by manufacturing problems, the company asked the pilot to explain to the manufacturing employees what happened while in the air. For two hours, the pilot described the incident to hundreds of employees — not only the technical part of the incident but also how it felt to be up there, realizing that the plane was about to crash. This dramatic presentation not only helped make quality control less abstract, but also emphasized the employees' personal responsibilities for the life of an individual they all knew and respected.

Lastly, CMU members should decide on the nature of the messages to be communicated to external stakeholders. In the heat of a crisis managers often make the fatal error of trying to protect their own frames of reference, what we have been calling in this book their existential core. Consider this additional example, taken from Tortorella (1987): Suppose your company makes millions of toasters each year. The overwhelming majority of your products operate without harm. However, you also know, because you have collected the statistics, that out of every ten million or so, a hundred are likely to contain defective wiring and start a fire. You also know that out of the hundred, perhaps one is likely to give rise to a fire that could burn down an entire house. You know that through improved quality control you have done everything possible, within cost-effective means, to minimize the number of toasters with defective wiring. You also know, although this would be difficult to justify to the public, that if you were to attempt to reduce this number even further, the cost of doing so would go up astronomically with no substantial guarantee of success. So, even though you do not like it, you and society are going to have to live with some crises.

Notice that this hypothetical situation is very different from the notorious Ford Pinto case. This is not the same as sitting down and calculating the value of a life, as Ford executives did. Rather than spend the money to fix a known design flaw, Ford decided to leave the design unchanged and set aside a fraction of the money saved in a legal defense fund to pay off the claims of car-crash victims (Black and Worthington, 1988). The electric toaster had no apparent design defect: either through normal manufacturing or use, something out of the ordinary happens to make the toaster become defective.

Now suppose the one toaster that is destined to cause a serious fire is bought by an orphanage; in the middle of the night the orphanage burns to the ground, and many children are killed. If you send your chief engineer to explain to the public that your company was not responsible for this disaster, considering that the calculated probability was one in ten million, the public will be outraged. The explanation, which makes sense from an engineering perspective, is an insult to human dignity.

The point is that no single function can be allowed to dominate a CMU. Here a facilitator is critical. Facilitators must be able to span different professional languages and concerns and blend them together in a reasonable and coherent response. They must not prematurely close off gathering or discussing information; at the same time, they must not allow the discussion to drag on into a stalemate. Time and time again, our interviewees commented that facilitators must be able to deal in the "extremely murky, gray area" that haunts most human endeavors.

Rewards

Designing an efficient reward system for crisis management is one of the most difficult tasks. As we saw with NASA, rewarding employees for uncovering product defects also runs the risk that they will *produce* defects to collect the reward, especially if the overall culture of the organization is relatively "sick." There is another problem: reliability is invisible—people do not know how many mistakes they did not make since, by definition, reliability does not provide for different outcomes (Pauchant and Mitroff, in press; Weick, 1987). To make reliability "visible" is especially difficult in organizations where a culture of self-inflated or self-deflated behavior has developed. Self-inflated people notice only dramatic or highly visible actions; self-deflated individuals attempt to fight with all their might their existential boredom. In either case it would be particularly difficult to develop a culture of reliability, which is, by definition, mostly invisible and often boring.

Managers in crisis-prepared organizations have invented a number of ways to increase the visibility of reliability and to reward their employees for sustaining it. Some collect extensive statistics of minor incidents by department, publish them widely inside the organization, and give the best departments both financial and symbolic rewards. Others have developed seminars in crisis management to sensitize their employees to the importance of "trivial" events; others have implemented a *real* quality circle program where employees are publicly rewarded for their suggestions and actions. Overall, managers in crisis-prepared organizations do not reward their employees only for the exceptional. They value and reward the day-to-day practice of staying somewhat anxious about the reliability of a system.

The Influence of Space and Time

While Galbraith's model (1977) of organizational design has provided the basis for the structure of this chapter, we wish to emphasize here two additional variables not explicitly mentioned in his model: the dimensions of space and time. In our current "age of narcissism" (Lasch, 1979), the concepts of gigantism and speed are often idealized: gigantism is sought to achieve security and omnipotence, and speed to reduce as much as possible delays in satisfaction. As we have discussed in another publication (Mitroff and Pauchant, 1990), the assumptions that "bigger is better" and "faster is better" can lead to catastrophes. To paraphrase the late E. F. Schumacher (1973), if small is beautiful, slow is beautiful too.

So far, we have not been able to produce systems that can be efficient and simple at the same time. Perhaps still prisoners of the metaphor of the machine, we have believed that "better" necessarily means bigger, more difficult, more complex. Many others have noted that designing larger and larger systems, in search of economies of scale, is devastating from a human point of view (see, for example, Peters, 1988). There is another motivation for smaller systems: their security.

Generally, size is directly related to complexity, and we know that the overall technical and social complexity of a system constitutes the preponderant context in which crises arise. Two major strategies for reducing the number of crises and their impact are (1) decreasing the system's overall complexity, and (2) increasing human complexity, as in helping people sustain a certain degree of anxiety or multiplying the number of perspectives adopted (Weick, 1987).

In relation to the design of large sociotechnical systems, a number of rules need to be emphasized. First, individuals in charge of the security of the system need, as much as possible, to be in direct sensory contact with the technology. No technology can replace the eyes, nose, ears, fingers, or intuition of a conscientious employee who has worked in the field for years. We have many examples of crises that were triggered in part by the failure of security devices and automatized control mechanisms. Second, attempting to resolve more complex problems with ever more complex technologies is a vicious circle, and some crisis-prepared organizations are trying to reduce the overall complexity of their entire operations. One oil company, for example, made the decision to freeze the acquisition of new information technologies if the task could be done with existing ones; an insurance company de-automated some claims processing, simplifying the process itself rather than complicating the information system. Also, as we have mentioned previously, other managers are calculating a "dependency cost" relative to their advanced technologies. Drawing on their past experience of crises, some organizations have introduced various "buffer mechanisms" to protect their most important tasks: for example, technical changes such as rerouting information systems networks or adding redundancies to their most crucial technologies; contingency plans for a redeployment of personnel; and alternative strategies for the production or distribution of products and services. However, and this is the important point, crisis-prepared organizations attempt to buffer potential threats *without substantially adding* to the overall complexity of their operations. And some organizations, understanding that the complexity of some issues escapes their own control, are attempting to take a wider perspective. For example, managers from different industries in U.S., Canadian, and French companies are regrouping themselves into a number of inter-company and inter-industry CMUs for the purpose of exchanging experiences and ideas (Lagadec, 1991).

   The second concept that influences our notion of organizational design is time — in particular, the notion of speed. Many organizations, under the intense pressure of a global competitive environment, force a tempo of innovation that does not allow time for testing these innovations before they are implemented. As repeated studies in crisis management have documented, the increase in speed of decisions and processes also increases the dangerous tight-coupling characteristics of complex systems. For example, when the stock market crashed in 1987, the international network of information technology *contributed to* the impact of that crisis (Sobel, 1988). As another example, technical innovations in the nuclear industry have been introduced so fast that the operators of these systems have not had time to fully understand some of their dangerous sides (Perrow, 1984). These examples demonstrate the dilemma existing today between the diverse imperatives toward innovation and the difficulties for human systems to test these innovations before implementing them.

A New Conception of Organizational Design

Design issues related to crisis management units echo the design issues of organizations in general; at the same time, a crisis management perspective also modifies fundamentally the overall perspective from which organizations should be designed. Two paradoxes need to be simultaneously addressed in questions of design (see Figure 6.2). The first paradox is the need for a human system to be simultaneously controlled and flexible: control being the need for structure, hierarchy, order, reliability, routine, and stability; flexibility being the need for change, freedom, adaptation, chaos, uncertainty, innovation, movement, and the like. This particular paradox is the one most acknowledged and debated in corporate boardrooms and universities: how to achieve, at the same time, centralization and decentralization, stability and creativity, order and innovation. The executives we interviewed also expressed these particular themes: market uncertainties, the increased rate of technological innova-

Figure 6.2. Two Paradoxes in Organizational Design.

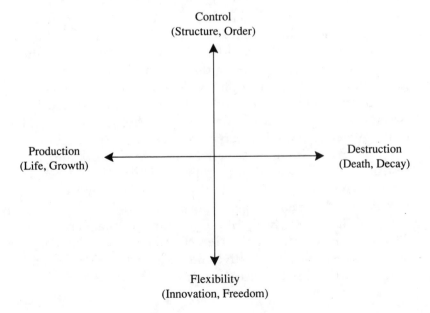

tions, the need to become more competitive, flexible, aggressive, and innovative. These particular themes are also the ones emphasized in management books and consulting advice such as Tom Peters' *Thriving on Chaos* (1988) or Rosabeth Moss Kanter's *When Giants Learn to Dance* (1989). Awareness that both order and chaos are necessary presupposes a view of the organization as a *productive* system that needs to survive in a complex environment. From this perspective, the purpose of organizational design is to find the optimal position between order and flexibility to achieve more productivity.

Notice, however, the second paradox: a crisis management perspective requires that we see an organization as a *destructive* system as well as a productive system. In Figure 6.2 "production" points to progress, life, productivity, growth, development, actualization, achievement; "destruction" includes the notions of crises, disasters, death, decay, injuries, pollution, alienation.

Today's managers and academicians have so much difficulty transcending the first paradox that we can wonder if they will ever address the second. This is to say that Figure 6.2 is not only about organizational design. It also reflects the issue of the fundamental purpose of an organization. Most corporate executives, and in particular those managing crisis-prone organizations, focus on the left side of that figure. They are busy experimenting with the paradox of order and chaos with the objective of becoming more productive and competitive in the global environment. However, we believe that to understand fully the issues embedded in industrial disasters, this debate between order and chaos needs also to pass through the issue of death. A view that would incorporate the existence of crises must both fully recognize the destructive nature of organizations and restructure the view of the world presently used by the people who manage them. It is only through this potentially terrifying recognition that real change is possible.

We have already addressed this fundamental paradox in Chapter One: embracing the Heraclitian perspective that each action carries in itself a creative and a destructive element, and that destruction itself is necessary for a system to be "alive." We are especially indebted to Schumacher (1977) for having pointed out the dimensions included in Figure 6.2. Throughout this book, we have emphasized that the issues surrounding crisis management are not only cognitive, they are also emotional and existential. This is the whole point of Figure 6.2: the paradoxes of order/chaos and life/death cannot be fully understood and dealt with at the cognitive or logical level alone; they also need to be dealt with at the existential level, grounded in personal experience. Problems between order and chaos, between life and death are not convergent; they cannot be dismissed once and for all, once the "best" solution is found. Rather, they are divergent, necessitating a long, painful, and ongoing working through, going beyond logic alone. Integrating these two fundamental paradoxes, and then transcending them, lead to a totally different focus in corporate design and strategy that is crisis-prepared. This focus emerges from a deep understanding of what it is to be human, grounded in personal experience and arising from the attempt to address the two paradoxes. Schumacher, echoing the views of existential philosophers and theologists, has also pointed to this difference (1977, pp. 126–127):

> *Divergent* problems cannot be killed; they cannot be solved in the sense of establishing a "correct formula"; they can, however, be transcended. A pair of opposites — like freedom and order — are opposites at the level of ordinary life, but they cease to be opposites at the higher level, the really human level, where self-awareness plays its proper role. It is then that such higher forces as love and compassion, understanding and empathy, become available, not simply as occasional impulses (which they are at the lower level) but as a regular and reliable resource. . . . How can opposites cease to be opposites when a "higher force" is present? . . . *These are not logical but existential questions.* . . . That opposites are transcended when "higher forces" — like love and compassion — intervene is not a matter to be argued in terms of logic: It has to be experienced

in one's actual existence. . . . It is important for us to become fully aware of these pairs of opposites. Our logical mind does not like them: it generally operates on the either/or or yes/no principle. . . . The pairs of opposites of which freedom and order and growth and decay are the most basic, put tension into the world, a tension that sharpens man's sensitivity and increases his self-awareness. No real understanding is possible without awareness of these pairs of opposites which permeate everything man does. . . . Everywhere society's health depends on the simultaneous pursuit of mutually opposed activities and aims. The adoption of a final solution means a kind of death sentence for man's humanity and spells either cruelty or dissolution, generally both [emphasis added].

Concluding Remarks

The changes we advocate in this chapter require a radical departure from the metaphors that have, so far, guided efforts in organizational design. For this reason, we believe that crisis management must receive active and explicit representation on the boards of directors of all corporations. The board must know the general plans and underlying assumptions that govern not only the general policies of the corporation but those that are specifically devoted to crisis management. This means that the board needs to know which crises the organization has chosen to prepare for, how they have prepared, and for which reasons.

All these changes also must be supplemented by appropriate legislation where possible. We believe that crisis management needs to be mandated by laws, especially in industries with high risk, such as nuclear power and chemical processes. However, new legislation needs to be drafted extremely carefully, for it is not clear that meeting the minimum requirements necessarily leaves an organization or its communities better off. The question of organization design also reaches beyond the corporation itself. It involves other institutions on which all organizations depend. For instance, we believe the time is long overdue for insurance companies to give special incentives to organizations that engage in serious and effective crisis management programs, just as some now do with safer drivers. In short, we have just begun to scratch the surface of the many aspects of organizations that need to be thought about.

Rate Your Organization

As with the previous chapters, you will find in Resource B a questionnaire designed for rating your organization on this layer of the Onion Model. We strongly recommend that you answer this questionnaire and share it with several colleagues.

SEVEN

Preparing for the Worst:
When Crisis Management Is Strategic

> It is an extremely serious matter for a man to find himself too much
> surrounded by apparent securities. A consciousness of security
> kills life. . . . A man can have but one authentic life, the life which
> his vocation demands of him.

— Jose Ortega y Gasset, *In Search of Goethe from Within*

Effective crisis management is no longer just a matter of managing crises. All the concerns and questions we have considered up to this point are equally applicable to the skills and strategies that all organizations need if they are to survive in today's highly competitive global economy. The same basic set of processes are involved in both crisis management and strategic management. Managers in crisis-prepared organizations have learned this fundamental lesson: crisis management concerns the totality of their organization as well as their relation with their environment and is an expression of the organization's fundamental purpose or strategic vision. To say it another way, if an organization is not positioned well with regard to crisis management, then it is probably not well positioned to compete successfully in the new global economy.

Historically, the concept of reliability was an essential part of management in general and strategy in particular. In 1916, one of the "building fathers" of the management field, a man named Henri Fayol, explicitly stated that the first function of management was *prévoyance,* a word that meant on the one hand, "to forecast and foresee," and on the other, "to secure and make reliable" (Fayol, 1916). Fayol certainly saw the importance of this concept, having spent most of his professional life as an engineer and a director in the mining industry, and having personally experienced a large number of disasters.

126

As is the case with other classical management scholars, however, it seems that Fayol's work has been misinterpreted (Aktouf, 1989). His posterity mostly remembers his four last functions of general management: organizing, directing, coordinating, and controlling. Along with Fayol's original intent, the discipline of reliability as a whole has been phased out from the basic training and curriculum used to teach new managers, or relegated to a subdepartment or placed under the umbrella of manufacturing or production. We hope that, in the future, managers in all industries will again embrace Fayol's original view, remembering that these concerns are part of what management is all about.

Crisis Management and Strategic Management

Authors in the field of strategic management have offered a multiplicity of definitions of this term (Chaffee, 1985; Miles and Snow, 1978; Miller and Friesen, 1980; Mintzberg, 1973, 1988; Pauchant and Fortier, 1990). The model of "competitive strategy" introduced by Michael Porter (1980) is perhaps the most in vogue of these. Whatever the definition, the field of strategic management has the following characteristics: a focus on environmental relations, a complex set of stakeholders, the involvement of top management, a concern for the whole organization, the expression of a consistent pattern, and an emergent process. These same concepts are central to crisis management; in addition, a crisis management perspective brings new challenges to the traditional views of strategic management.

A Focus on Environmental Relations

It is now admitted that strategic management concerns itself with the ways a firm uses "strategy to deal with . . . environments" (Chaffee, 1985, p. 89). In particular, drawing from biology and open-system theory, it has been shown that an organization must adapt and "co-align" itself with its environment if it wants to survive and grow. The strategist is viewed as a person "who is wrestling bravely with a universe that he is wise enough to know is too big for him" (Lindblom, 1959, p. 27). In this perspective, environmental monitoring and scanning, the need for adaptation between a firm and its environment, as well as the need for constant innovation and flexibility, are considered paramount in strategic management (Burns and Stalker, 1961; Miles and Snow, 1978; Quinn, 1980; Thompson, 1967).

Crisis management also implies "dealing with environments," but the nature of this relationship is different. First, the environment is not seen as something "out there," an entity distinct from the firm. Managers in crisis-prepared organizations, being less cognitively and emotionally bounded, understand better their fundamental connection with their environment. They can, for example, empathize with the experiences of their customers when using the firm's products. Also, they go beyond the "threat and opportunity" analyses advocated in traditional strategic management, searching for opportunities or potential threats in the environment; they also study how the firm itself can be an opportunity and a threat to its environment. Thus, to paraphrase Lindblom, a strategist embracing a crisis management perspective is "a person living bravely in a universe that he is wise enough and emotionally open enough to know is complex, only partially intelligible, beautiful, sometimes dangerous, and often fragile to the actions implemented by organizations."

A Complex Set of Stakeholders

Traditional economic theory identifies a limited set of stakeholders: customers, stockholders, and employees. "Stakeholder analysis" is a familiar tool for strategic management. Strategic management, with its emphasis on examining competitive and political forces in order to find an optimal niche, has a more complex set of stakeholders (Hambrick, 1980; Porter, 1980): distributors, suppliers, buyers, innovators, regulators, or other companies that can produce substitute products or services.

A crisis management approach also requires a stakeholder analysis, but with some differences. First, the range of stakeholders is broader. Crisis management takes into account members of the general community, minority and disadvantaged groups, even nature itself. In addition, unborn future generations are also given special consideration, as industrial crises can have potentially disastrous effects on these stakeholders. For example, the negative effects of Bhopal or Chernobyl on children yet to be born in those areas have not yet been scientifically determined. Second, a crisis management perspective requires also that we expand the number of criteria or characteristics from which stakeholders are identified in the first place. Strategy tends to emphasize financial, technological, competitive, legal, and political criteria; crisis management adds to this list emotional, ecological, social, ethical, medical, moral, spiritual, aesthetic, psychological, and existential criteria. Most of those considerations are absent from today's competitive strategic management models. In fact, proponents of today's frameworks praise themselves for having removed from their models "all the material on the values of society and the manager" (Kiechel, 1987). Third, studies have shown that the various stakeholders involved in a crisis have different frames of reference or basic assumptions, and that these different assumptions can *contribute to* the development of the crisis (Bowonder and Linstone, 1987; Gephart, Steier, and Lawrence, 1989; Hall, 1976; Pauchant and Mitroff, 1990, in press). For example, in his in-depth study, Shrivastava (1987) has shown that the three major stakeholders involved with the Bhopal disaster — the Indian governmental agencies, Union Carbide, and the victims — had different "domains of reference": the social, political, and "relief" domains (government); the technical, financial, and legal domains (Union Carbide); and the medical, economic, and experiential domains (victims).

One of the fundamental functions of a CMU in the future will be to examine the nature of and the relationship between the different stakeholders' assumptions, including their own. This subject is so important that we discuss it in detail later in this chapter, with concrete examples.

The Involvement of Top Management

The involvement of top management is still considered paramount in strategic management, even though some see this involvement as more democratic, participative, and incremental than in earlier years (Pascale, 1984; Quinn, 1980).

Similarly, the involvement of top managers is absolutely essential for developing a systemic strategy in crisis management and convincing others in the organization to cooperate. Most of the CMUs now existing in organizations are made up of the heads of different departments, crisis management issues being by definition multidisciplinary.

A Concern with the Whole Organization

By definition, the field of strategic management is concerned with the overall direction and purpose of an organization; it theoretically integrates diverse areas to achieve this "meta-management" (Hafsi, 1985), providing a sense of identity.

Similarly, one of the major purposes of crisis management is the attempt to manage the crises that could potentially disturb an entire organization. Managers in crisis-prepared organizations go even further: they are also concerned with the survival or development of their stakeholders and their industry as a whole and the environment.

A Consistent Pattern

The strategy of an organization has been compared to the personality of an individual (Mintzberg, 1988) or labeled the organization's "character" (Selznick, 1957). Continuing this metaphor, consistency is one fundamental characteristic of strategic management, as it is an expression of the overall organizational perspective and sense of identity.

A strategy in crisis management is affected by—and emerges from—the character of its managers, the organizational culture, and its structure. In particular, a self-inflated or self-deflated organizational culture will hinder development of a crisis management strategy through its faulty basic assumptions.

An Emergent Process

In the past, strategies were believed to be mostly planned and articulated by top management; today the consensus recognizes the relative emergence of strategies (Mintzberg, Raisinghani, and Theoret, 1976; Pascale, 1984; Quinn, 1980). In crisis management, too, planning is a continual, ongoing process. Any plans are only as good as the general thought processes that went into them. Also, while strategy can be seen as a plan, a ploy or a position, it is also a pattern of thoughts and actions embedded in a general perspective (Mintzberg, 1988). Many strategic decisions in general and in crisis management in particular are emergent in nature. The true purpose of planning is the understanding that is achieved by systematically thinking through the critical issues one is facing, either currently or in the future (Michael, 1978; Mitroff, 1988). Managers who work in crisis-prone organizations but who fundamentally understand the need for a systemic strategic management can become a major part of the emergent process of crisis management.

Despite some fortunate exceptions, the field of strategic management as a whole has seldom acknowledged the importance of industrial crises. Management professors largely ignore crisis management, which means that annual cohorts of soon-to-be managers will be tempted to develop in their future organizations the restricted views they learned in business school. As Mitroff and Kilmann commented in another book (1984, p. 36), "Going to almost any one of the current business schools . . . is probably the very worst thing one could do in preparation for coping with corporate tragedies." We sincerely hope that a time will come when the discussion of crisis management issues will be a part of all basic curriculum in all business schools.

Challenging Assumptions

Many of the things that happen during a crisis are related fundamentally to the collapse of managers' most important beliefs about themselves, their firm, and their environment. A case we were recently involved with illustrates the process.

One of the major zoos in the country was faced with a potential crisis: they were charged with abusing the elephants under their care. Zoo administrators were concerned about how this charge would affect the zoo's reputation and hence the community donations on which it depended. A few months after the crisis had simmered down, and after the zoo's reputation had been damaged, Mitroff was called in to help these managers see whether there were any critical lessons that could be learned from the experience.

Working together, they did something that few managers ever do: they went back and determined what their belief system was before the crisis and evaluated how the crisis had affected that system. It took several hours, but slowly about thirty major assumptions emerged (see Mason and Mitroff, 1981, and Mitroff, 1988, for the methodology used). Astonishingly, literally every one of these assumptions was proved invalid by the crisis situation. This is a difficult exercise, intellectually and emotionally. People have to admit, to themselves and in front of others, that some of the things they had long believed about their organization or themselves are no longer true — if they ever were. In effect, they have to challenge some of the most fundamental aspects of their view of the world.

At the end of the day, the thirty beliefs were summarized on a flipchart for all to see. It was readily apparent that they fell into three distinct groups or clusters, consisting of about ten assumptions each. An interesting portrait emerged — not only of this organization, but one that applies to many organizations, especially technical ones, even more so those that provide a service to the general public.

The first cluster related to credibility. In one way or another, all ten of the assumptions in this group expressed the fact that this organization truly believed that their scientific standing gave credibility to whatever they said. If they said that they had not abused elephants, then the outside world would believe them. As these managers learned painfully, and some are still in need of learning, the outside world is not composed of scientists. While it is absolutely necessary for the zoo to maintain its high credibility and standing with the scientific community, this is not sufficient to gain the trust and confidence of the general public.

The second set of assumptions all pertain to the belief that their own employees would not sabotage or betray them. And yet, it was the zoo's own employees that released to the press allegations of animal abuse by other employees. The final set of assumptions related to the belief that if a crisis happened, then the zoo's sister organizations would rush to its defense. In the past the zoo had worked with diverse organizations on such projects as the protection of animals, and assumed that in their hour of need these organizations would close ranks. How wrong they had been!

If a major crisis has anything to teach us, it is this: a crisis does not challenge just one or two critical beliefs. Almost any organization can survive if one or two of its fundamental beliefs are challenged. A crisis can threaten literally *every* belief. In fact, this phenomenon is what distinguishes a crisis from an accident.

As a second example of these challenges, especially in relation to high technology, consider the case of Hinsdale. In 1988, a fire in an Illinois Bell facility in Hinsdale, a Chicago suburb, destroyed all telecommunications for five hundred thousand subscribers, some for as long as three weeks. The financial impact (repairs plus business losses) was estimated at between $200 and $300 million.

After the crisis, we were called in to determine what lessons could be learned from it. After conducting interviews in more than thirty companies in many different industries that had been affected by the outage, we found that all respondents had learned a very basic lesson: they had rediscovered the telephone! All these managers had fallen into the same trap: assuming the availability of the telephonic network, which for most companies also affected their computer system. They were not prepared for this crisis. Many had developed other security measures, such as restricting access to their computer network, protecting the building that housed their computers, or enhancing their own network, but in this particular case, none of these variables was at fault: it was the *total telephonic network* that broke down. Telephone technology is essentially invisible, and it is assumed to be available. (One manager commented, "We all know where the dial tone comes from — it's coming from God.") These assumptions *amplified the impact* of the crisis. As one manager explained, "We had taken the telephone for granted. We had backed up our own system, and our network, but not the telephone." Many other respondents made similar observations.

The Exxon *Valdez* crisis reveals other invalid assumptions. From our discussion with several top executives at Exxon, together with information collected from readings and from other managers in the oil industry, it is clear that Exxon was operating under a host of false beliefs: that Exxon and the state of Alaska were prepared for a crisis of large magnitude; that the proper cleanup equipment was in place and in good operating order; that crews had been well trained for such a spill; that the proper procedures for a spill of the magnitude encountered would be followed; that the weather would be benign; that all those involved truly knew their roles and what to do; that the information and communication lines of the company were designed to allow communication across divisions and to get the right information to the right people on time; that the design of oil tankers was appropriate in the case of such crises . . . and so on.

Two Pragmatic Strategies

At this point, you are probably asking, "Well, where do we start? Tell me what to focus on. Are all these concepts important?" The answer to this last question is, unfortunately, yes! As we have seen, the issues in crisis management (like those in strategic management) are, by their nature, systemic, multidisciplinary, complex, ill defined, interrelated, diffuse, and disorderly. The next chapters attempt to answer this very pragmatic question. In Chapter Eight, we present specific crisis management interventions, based on many concrete strategies currently implemented in some of the best crisis-prepared organizations in the United States, Canada, and France. For the moment, we describe two pragmatic strategies to help managers orient their crisis management efforts: the concept of "phases" and of "dual portfolio."

Phases of a Crisis

Studies in crisis and disaster management indicate clearly that the phenomenon of crisis is articulated from different phases or stages (Fink, 1986; Raphael, 1986; Shrivastava, 1987). Specifically, most crises move through five essential phases (see Figure 7.1). The failure to manage any one of these phases well may be responsible for the occurrence of a crisis in the first place and then for its escalation.

In the figure, the boxes labeled "Signal Detection" and "Preparation/Prevention" constitute *proactive types* of crisis management. If done properly and if successful, these activities can prevent many crises from occurring in the first place. "Containment/Damage Limitation" and "Recovery" are the *reactive types* — activities done after a crisis has happened, in an attempt to contain its damage and recover from its effects. In this book we call this "crash management." The box labeled "Learning" points to the *interactive type* of crisis management, which is rarely done in most organizations. It can either be a part of crisis management plans in the absence of a crisis or a result of the experience of a crisis, as seen in the examples of the zoo or Hinsdale. Together these phases constitute the total scorecard by which an organization and its managers will be judged. Some organizations have failed on *every one* of these five phases. Others have done everything possible in each phase, and so have successfully weathered a crisis.

From the commission studies conducted after events such as *Challenger* or the *Valdez,* and also from experts in crisis man-

Figure 7.1. The Three Essential Types of
Crisis Management and Their Five Phases.

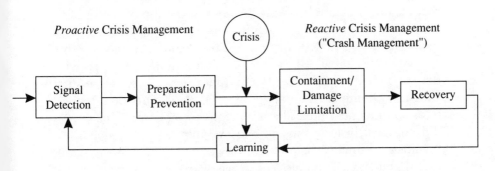

Interactive Crisis Management

agement communication (Lagadec, 1989; Mindszenthy, Watson, and Koch, 1988; Tortorella, 1987), we know that managers of organizations involved in a crisis will be asked five key questions:

1. When did you have an inkling that there was a critical defect or something wrong in your system, organization, product, or service?
2. If you did not know something was wrong, why not?
3. What, if anything, did you do about it?
4. If you did not do anything about it, why not?
5. If you had known beforehand that such a crisis was possible, what could you have done?

Imagine how Johnson & Johnson might answer those questions in relation to the Tylenol crisis; then compare Union Carbide's hypothetical answers on the Bhopal disaster and Exxon's on the *Valdez* crash.

Let us examine each of these phases in greater detail.

Signal Detection. Long before the actual occurrence, a crisis usually sends off a persistent trail of early warning signals, or symptoms, announcing its probable occurrence, what Fink (1986) has called "prodomes." If these signals are not attended to, a major crisis is highly likely. If you have any doubt, look at the report of the presidential commission on the *Challenger* disaster (*Report of the Presidential Commission on the Space Shuttle Challenger Accident,* 1986). At the end of the report is a virtual audit trail of key memos that failed to make it through to the top of the organization and get the serious attention they deserved. In effect these memos warned that if the space shuttle continued to fly, disaster was inevitable. One of the most painful memos starts with the anguished cry, "Help!" It says that the problems connected with the O ring are so dangerous that they must be attended to as soon as possible. The important thing is that this memo did not exist in isolation but was one of a continuing chain of memos announcing the problem. We have found in our research that managers and employees in crisis-prone organizations are very skilled at blocking out the signals of impending crises, whereas those in crisis-prepared organizations have the opposite skill of sensing even very weak signals. The very worst of crisis-prone organizations even deliberately block out all signals. They live by the rationalization that "no news is good news."

Early warning signals do present problems. For one thing, managers are exposed to a tremendous number of signals all the time, and it is extremely difficult to pick out the truly important. For another, different crises send off different kinds of signals, and it is not always possible to tell which kind of crisis a particular signal indicates. A rash of graffiti may be a signal warning of an act of violence by a disgruntled employee, or it may be something much more benign. A sudden increase in equipment failures may be an early warning signal of employee sabotage — or the result of defective materials from a supplier. One important function of a CMU is to monitor the processes of tracking and analyzing these signals.

Preparation and Prevention. To avoid crises, organizations need tested, in-place prevention and preparation mechanisms. This reinforces the importance of early warning signals: it is extremely difficult to prevent something that has not been detected. The purpose of the prevention phase is to probe the organization for signs of weakness *before* a determined adversary does so, and to evaluate whether the total set of relationships within a system has become too complex or too tightly coupled. This prevention effort cannot be passive; one must *actively* probe for weaknesses and potential problems. The pharmaceutical company's internal "assassin teams" described earlier are an example of this active investigation.

The second part of this phase is preparation. In the midst of a crisis, few people can act efficiently and calmly without some training. Preparation involves designing various scenarios and sequences of actions for imagined crises, and testing them fully until all those involved are familiar with their roles.

Containment and Damage Limitation. Unfortunately, it is impossible to prevent crises completely, since destructive tendencies are a natural characteristic of all living systems. So the next phase of crisis management consists of developing damage-limitation mechanisms (what we have previously called "crash management") to prevent the damage from spreading and engulfing other unaffected parts of the organization. Exxon, in the case of the *Valdez,* had to keep the oil spill from spreading (metaphorically speaking) and contaminating additional areas. Notice that this phase of crisis management is relative to the type of accident that has occurred. For example, after the *Challenger* explosion, nothing more could have been done to protect the lives of the astronauts. And, considering that this explosion occurred in front of literally millions of people, it was particularly difficult to reduce the impact on the public.

Recovery. This phase involves developing and implementing tested, in-place, short-term and long-term recovery mechanisms. The emphasis on tested and in-place is crucial — without this kind of forethought and planning, individuals in the throes of a crisis are rarely able to respond in an efficient and conscious manner. The recovery phase has several aspects, the most obvious of which is the attempt to recover what has been lost, which could involve tangible or intangible assets. We have found that organizations in which managers had identified in advance which items, processes, and personnel were absolutely necessary for daily operations were the most effective organizations in implementing this phase. A common mistake made by crisis-prone managers is to focus exclusively on internal operations while not addressing, or addressing too late, the effects a crisis has outside the firm.

Members of a group who work on this phase of recovery often describe the experience as "exhilarating" and have observed that the group is more cohesive than usual, stimulated by the common goal of accomplishing an undeniably crucial task. During our interviews, many VIPs and managers stated that they wished their employees would demonstrate the same motivation for their daily work as they did for their efforts in the recovery phase.

It is especially important to prepare employees against potential cognitive biases. Studies on the effects of crises have demonstrated the effect of these biases. Dutton (1986) has clearly established that the personnel responsible for tracking these issues in organizations did not treat them in the same manner if they considered them to be crises. While we have so far emphasized the *affective* biases or defense mechanisms developed in relation to a threatening event, a complementary set of *cognitive* biases are also operating, such as decreased capacity to deal with complex problems, increased cognitive rigidity, inability to consider long-term issues; tendency to hang on to familiar solutions, faulty belief in invulnerability, and so on. These phenomena could indeed be powerful, considering the amount of stress encountered in crisis situations (Smart and Vertinsky, 1977).

For these reasons, it is extremely difficult, if not impossible, to implement effective crisis recovery mechanisms without testing them prior to the crisis. The Exxon *Valdez* disaster is a perfect illustration of this. If an organization is not productive in anticipating crises, then it is forced into being reactive, patching things up after the damage has been done.

Learning. The last phase of crisis management is continual learning and reassessment to improve what has been done in the past. Interactive learning is vital, but it is particularly painful to accomplish, considering the emotional wounds that a crisis often inflicts on individuals.

As we have stressed in previous chapters, to let oneself learn one must be able to accept anxiety without succumbing to dread. In our interviews, about half of our respondents indicated that they and their colleagues had learned something valuable during their previous crises: one-third acknowledged the necessity of being more proactive before the occurrence of a crisis; another third also stressed the importance of communication, both inside and outside the organization, as a means of preventing a crisis. Despite these admissions, however, managers had rarely acknowledged the kinds of assumptions mentioned in the zoo example ("our credibility would save us," "our employees would not betray us," "our sister organizations would rush to our defense"). Rarer still were comments offered on feeling out of control, uncertain, or vulnerable. It seems that this deeper learning is only accessible to people who are not too emotionally bounded, who are working in organizations that allow such learning to take place, and who have been engaged in processes that allow such root assumptions to surface.

In Chapter Nine we will discuss in some detail how managers can make themselves more "ready to learn" about crisis-preparedness. For the moment, we wish to note that the powerful forces that hinder people from learning may temporarily diminish feelings of anxiety, but are more destructive in the long run. As the psychologist Abraham Maslow noted, after commenting on the rate of turbulence and uncertainty in our modern society, "We need a different kind of human being . . . [people] who are able confidently to face tomorrow not knowing what's going to come. . . .This means a new type of human being. Heraclitian, you might call him. The society which can turn out such people will survive; the societies that cannot . . . will die" (1971, pp. 58–59).

Dual Crisis Management Portfolio

As we saw in Chapter One, crises tend to cluster into groups; so do actions in crisis management (review Figures 1.2 and 1.3). This finding about clustering has an important implication: instead of having to prepare for every conceivable kind of crisis, which would overtax financial, intellectual, and emotional resources, managers can limit their preparations in a systematic manner.

The recommended strategy is simple: every organization should pick at least one crisis in each family to defend itself against. Since all crises within a particular cluster are similar, then preparing for at least one per cluster confers some degree of protection for the others in that cluster. The corollary is that *all* clusters must be addressed, since the clusters are so dissimilar. In other words, what good does it do for an organization to prepare for crisis X if the equally dangerous crisis Y, for which it is not prepared, should happen? Time and time again, we have found that, at best, most organizations protect themselves against one or two crises from just one cluster. For the same systemic reasons, each organization needs to implement, at minimum, one crisis management action from each of the preventive clusters.

In summary, then, managers need to implement in their organization a number of actions, considering simultaneously the five major phases of crisis management, the four crisis clusters, the four crisis management clusters, and the four layers of the Onion Model. Figure 7.2 displays the relationships of these various elements.

But before any such strategy can be developed, managers must first create a crisis management unit to focus its energies in the area. As a first step, we have listed some fundamental questions that need to be answered; see Exhibits 7.1 and 7.2.

Concluding Remarks

As already emphasized, neither a complete theory of crises nor a complete theory of organizational crisis management has been proposed to date (Morin, 1976; 1990b). Nonetheless, the fact that we have presented the underlying structures of both the causes and management of crises indicates that an overall framework for crisis management is beginning to emerge. The contention, therefore, that there is no way to prevent or to manage crises better is no longer valid. We may still be a long way from understanding and managing all the aspects of crises, but now we know for certain that reactive crisis management strategies, or not having a strategy at all, is no longer viable in today's world.

Rate Your Organization

As with the previous chapters, you will find in Resource B a questionnaire designed for rating your organization on this layer of the Onion Model. We strongly recommend that you answer this questionnaire and share it with several colleagues.

Figure 7.2. Toward a Systemic Strategy of Crisis Management.

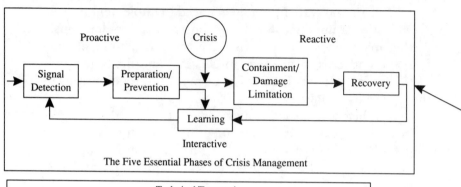

The Five Essential Phases of Crisis Management

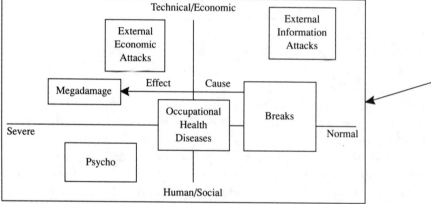

Crisis Portfolio 1: Crisis Clusters

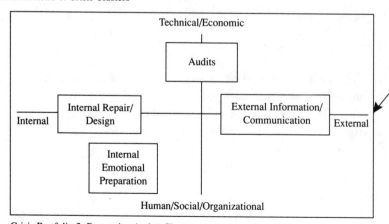

Crisis Portfolio 2: Preventive Action Clusters

Figure 7.2. Toward a Systemic Strategy of Crisis Management, Cont'd.

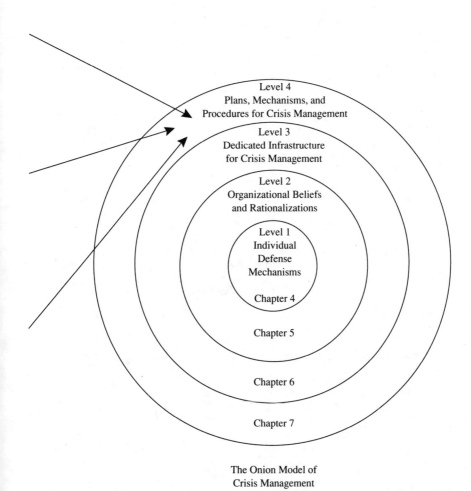

The Onion Model of
Crisis Management

Exhibit 7.1. Critical Issues in Crisis Clusters.

---

1. How many of these potential crises has our organization experienced in the last three years? Why? Why Not? (Because of luck, planning?)
2. How many were foreseen before they occurred?
3. Which ones does our organization attempt to prepare for?
4. How extensive were our organization's preparations? How many people were involved at which levels of the organization?
5. How coordinated were our company's preparations across divisions, functional specialties, etc.?
6. Which crises did/does our organization ignore altogether?
7. What critical assumptions did/does our organization make regarding the crises it could ignore versus not ignore?
8. How valid were/are those assumptions? Why?
9. What needs to change and why in our organization if it is to be better prepared in the future?

Exhibit 7.2. Critical Issues in Preventive Action Clusters.

---

1. How many of those potential preventive actions has our organization adopted in the last three years? Why, why not?
2. What actions has our organization avoided systematically?
3. Which ones does it need to emphasize more? Why?
4. Which ones need to be better integrated? Why?
5. What critical assumptions did/does our organization make regarding the actions it needs to adopt versus those it can safely ignore?
6. How valid were/are those assumptions? Why?
7. What needs to change?
8. How likely is it that our organization will change?
9. What are the consequences for the future crisis potential of our organization if it does not change?

EIGHT

Diagnosing Potential Danger:
Auditing for Crisis-Preparedness

What shall it profit a whole civilization, or culture, if it gains knowledge and power over the material world, but loses any adequate idea of the conscious mind, the human self, at the center of that power?

—William Barrett, *Death of the Soul*

In the four preceding chapters, we have, one by one, examined the layers of the Onion Model: the character of individuals, the organizational culture, structure, and strategy. Table 8.1 summarizes our discussion thus far. It shows in no uncertain terms the major differences between crisis-prone and crisis-prepared organizations.

Profiles of Preparedness

At the end of the previous four chapters, we suggested you answer a questionnaire for evaluating the crisis-preparedness of your organization for each layer of the Onion Model. (For convenience, we have placed these questionnaires in Resource B at the end of this book.) You will recall that each question is to be answered on a range from 1 to 7, and the total response would put the organization in either the safety zone, the question-mark zone, or the danger zone for the layer in question.

    If you were to plot the responses to all four questionnaires on a graph, you would have a visual profile of the organization. (The USC Center for Crisis Management has developed a software package that permits users to do the questionnaire on line, and then evaluates responses and creates the graphs; see Mitroff and Pearson, in press, for a full description of this software program.) In principle there are eighty-one distinct profiles, seven

Table 8.1. Crisis-Prone Versus Crisis-Prepared
Organizations: A Synthesis.

Layers of the Onion Model	Crisis-Prone	Crisis-Prepared
4. Strategy	• Traditional strategic management • Focus on survival and growth • Restricted purpose; fragmented stakeholders • Mostly reactive strategy in crisis management • No special crisis management strategies	• Challenged assumptions • Focus on development and learning • Shared purpose; enlarged view of stakeholders • Reactive, proactive, and interactive strategies • Dual crisis portfolio and "stage strategies"
3. Structure	• No special structure for crisis management • Focus on balancing flexibility and control • No special mechanisms for crisis management • Classical definition of design	• Effective CMUs • Focus on balancing life and death • Special rewards, tasks and training • Challenged concepts of time and space
2. Culture	• Self-inflated/self-deflated cultures • Extreme use of faulty rationalizations (seven times more than crisis-prepared organizations • No awareness of cultural ties • Mostly unconscious, unchallenged	• Culture moving toward positive self-regard • Low use of faulty rationalizations • Awareness of cultural ties • Challenged and accepted
1. Psyche	• Strongly bounded emotionally and cognitively • Constant search for existence/ego satisfaction • High defense mechanisms against anxiety • Self-inflated/self-deflated psyches	• Less bounded; Heraclitian • More concerned about addressing problems • Adequate defense mechanisms embracing anxiety • Psyche moving toward positive self-regard

of which are shown in Figure 8.1. Profiles 1 and 2 are, respectively, the best crisis-prepared and the worst crisis-prone organizations. Profiles 3 through 7 are some of the more distinctive variations that can occur in business organizations.

Profile 3 is an organization that has a good score in three of the four elements: a good set of crisis plans, a good crisis management culture, and a good configuration on individual character. Yet it is seriously deficient in one area: a structure for crisis management. We have labeled this profile "Dangerously Reactive" because, to state the matter bluntly, three out of four is not good enough. Crises are now so complex in their makeup that spur-of-the-moment responses are no longer adequate; explicit prior training and a full structure to guide actions throughout the organization are needed.

There are several possible interpretations for this kind of profile. Perhaps the organization's top management is convinced of the need for a dedicated crisis management structure, but the structure has not yet been implemented. Profile 3 might well be a picture of Johnson & Johnson. The culture of J&J appears to be extremely responsive to both its customers and employees, but at the time of its two Tylenol crises it did not have a crisis management team in place.

Another interpretation of profile 3 is that the three good scores are due to the dedicated efforts of a few individuals. Many organizations have a head of security who is extremely safety minded and anxious to broaden the traditional function of security to include crisis management. Acting mainly on their own, dedicated professionals try everything in their power to prepare the organization, often in spite of itself. It is not possible to tell merely from the particular shape of a profile what is happening within the organization.

Profile 4 reveals a serious contradiction in terms. How can an organization contend that it has the right plans and infrastructure when its underlying culture and the character of its top management are faulty? On the surface these organizations seem to be crisis-prepared, but they are fooling their stakeholders, or themselves, or both. For this reason, we have labeled

Figure 8.1. Crisis-Prone Versus Crisis-Prepared: Seven Typical Profiles.

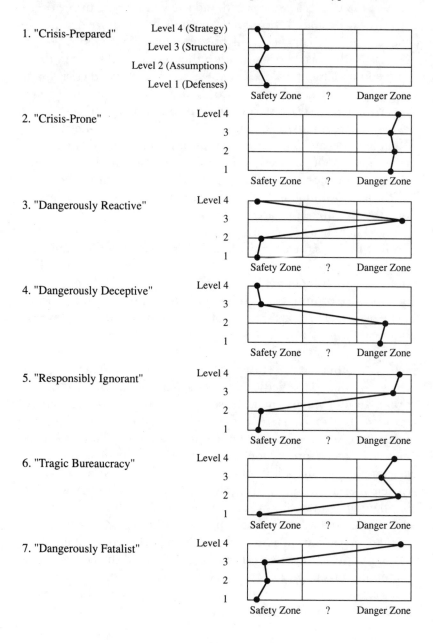

this profile "Dangerously Deceptive." Here again we may encounter a dedicated security professional or some other executive to prepare the organization, often in spite of itself.

Profile 5 is the obverse of profile 4: here the organization's culture and the character configuration of its top management are not dysfunctional and do not embody dangerous rationalizations or defense mechanisms. The organization may merely be ignorant of the need for a proactive stance toward crisis management, or managers may not have yet convinced their stockholders of the need for formalizing a crisis management effort. For these reasons, we have labeled this profile "Responsibly Ignorant." It is far easier to change a faulty set of plans or infrastructure than it is to change a faulty culture and character configuration.

Profile 6 shows an organization that is not prepared on levels 2, 3, or 4, but contends nonetheless that its top management's character configuration is adequate. We have known some organizations with this profile. The top managements were relatively new (either because of recent mergers or acquisitions or because of changes at the top made by the board of directors) but culture, structure, and strategies remained in their old patterns. We have called this profile "Tragic Bureaucracy"; these organizations are stuck in their overall destructiveness, despite attempts by their top management to change this orientation.

Profile 7 is perplexing. The character configuration of its top management, its overall culture, and its structure could be adapted to proactive efforts in crisis management, but this organization refuses to develop proactive actions. We have found this particular pattern in religious organizations, where beliefs in fate were so strong that action plans were primarily oriented to praying or meditating. Prayer and meditation have a place in crisis management (indeed, they express a deep understanding of humility in the face of forces that surpass individuals) but by themselves they are limited. If they are used exclusively, the organization is denied the benefit of other strategic actions that can diminish both the frequency and impact of crises. For this reason, we have labeled this profile "Dangerously Fatalist," while at the same time recognizing part of its fundamental wisdom.

Toward an Ideal Plan in Crisis Management

Table 8.2 is an ideal plan for crisis management, presented in the form of a checklist. As a rule, we do not like checklists, but they can be quite valuable as a starting point. In particular, we use them as a first answer to managers who ask, "But, really, what are the things you are advocating that we are not already doing?" Thus this list and this chapter could also be seen as an argumentative tool for selling crisis management. Toward this goal, we have reproduced this list, formatted as a questionnaire in Resource B.

We derived this list from the best examples we encountered during our interviews in the United States, Canada, and France, pinpointing actions by managers in organizations that, by and large, took crisis management very seriously and had developed innovative approaches to it. We do not suggest that "serious" managers should implement *all* the items in the list. A more realistic view of crisis management leads to a crisis management portfolio, determined by the organization's own needs. However, in the absence of a role model of an organization that is perfectly crisis-prepared, we present this list as an ideal set of actions, to inspire and trigger ideas. Note that the list does not use the terminology of the Onion Model: character, culture, structure, and strategy. Instead, we even regrouped the four elements of the model into a format more readily understandable for managers. The strategic layer has been split into "strategic actions" and "evaluation and diagnosis actions"; the structural layer into "technical and structural actions" and "communication actions"; and we combined the culture and the character layers under the label "psychological and cultural actions."

Strategic Actions

What fundamentally distinguishes crisis-prepared organizations from crisis-prone ones is the overall mood from which they view crisis management. Managers of crisis-prepared organizations do not consider crisis management a cost; they view it as a strategic necessity for ensuring the reliability of their products and

Table 8.2. An Ideal Crisis Management Strategy.

Strategic
 1. Drastic changes in corporate philosophy
 2. Integration of crisis management in corporate excellence program
 3. Integration of crisis management in strategic planning process
 4. Inclusion of outsiders on board, crisis management unit team, and other groups
 5. Training and workshops in crisis management
 6. Crises simulations
 7. Diversification and portfolio strategies

Technical and Structural
 8. Creation of a crisis management unit team
 9. Creation of dedicated budget for crisis management
10. Developing and changing emergency policies and manuals
11. Computerized inventories of plants' employees, products, and capabilities
12. Creation of a strategic emergency room or facilities
13. Reduction of hazardous products, services, and productions
14. Improved overall design and safety of products and production
15. Technological redundancy, such as computer backup
16. Use of outside experts and services in crisis management

Evaluation and Diagnosis
17. Legal and financial audit of threats and liabilities
18. Modifications in insurance coverage
19. Environmental impact audit and respect of regulations
20. Ranking of most critical activities necessary for daily operation
21. Early warning signals detection, scanning, issues management
22. Dedicated research on potential hidden dangers
23. Critical follow-up of past crises

Communication
24. Media training for crisis management
25. Major efforts in public relations
26. Increased information to local communities
27. Increased relationships with intervening groups (police, media)
28. Increased collaboration or lobbying among stakeholders
29. Use of new communication technologies and channels

Psychology and Culture
30. Strong top-management commitment to crisis management
31. Increased relationships with activist groups
32. Improved acceptance of whistleblowers
33. Increased knowledge of criminal behavior
34. Increased visibility of crises' human impact to employees
35. Psychological support to employees
36. Stress management and management of anxiety
37. Symbolic reminding of past crises, dangers, and successes

production systems and for providing competitive advantages. This drastic shift in corporate philosophy (see point 1 in Table 8.2) is difficult to accomplish: it means that executives must learn to consider their firms not only as productive systems but as potentially destructive systems as well. They must be prepared to debate not only issues of success, growth, and excellence but also issues surrounding failure, breakdowns, decay, and death. This does not mean that these executives have to develop a morbid culture, muddling senselessly over failures, disasters, and catastrophes. It only means they need to develop specific capabilities for imagining the worst, in order to manage these events should they occur or, still better, to prevent them in the first place.

This shift in corporate philosophy has a major impact on the definition of "corporate excellence" (see point 2). An executive in the chemical industry stressed, "We not only have the responsibility of bringing to our customers the best products possible at a competitive price. We also need to protect them from their dangerous sides." To support this new view of corporate excellence, crisis-prepared organizations have made substantive changes in their products and their production methods. For example, Johnson & Johnson (J&J) has abandoned making Tylenol in capsule form; others in the food and pharmaceutical industries have developed tamper-proof packaging; a chemical firm has divested itself of its line of aerosol products, in view of their negative impact on the ecology; and DuPont has developed a new generation of safer chemicals.

These organizations have also integrated crisis management into their strategic planning process (see point 3), because they consider crisis management to be strategic in nature. As a bonus, these executives are finding that their crisis management efforts are providing strategic advantages over their competitors. For example, an executive in the insurance industry pointed out that his company had recently won a large government contract over his competitors, in part because of its extensive contingency capabilities in information systems. An executive in the banking industry commented that during a large telephone outage, his company demonstrated its customer focus.

"The crisis gave us the opportunity to really extend our services to our smaller clients. We started with the question 'What can hurt us?' and more recently changed it to 'What can hurt our customers?'"

As a means of challenging their basic assumptions, some firms have included outsiders in their rank (see point 4). A company in the chemical industry has recently included two environmental activists on its board; another in the oil industry has hired key executives with no backgrounds in the industry or in technology in general; other firms have also hired outside consultants as "insultants," to use Peter Drucker's term, in the attempt to challenge some of their basic assumptions. Many companies, understanding that, above all, crisis management requires personal and organizational knowledge, have started formal training and workshops in crisis management, going beyond the traditional issues of security (point 5), and others have initiated crisis simulations (point 6). Some firms have taken these simulations quite seriously: one chemical company hired a former FBI agent to head these efforts; others have used professional actors to simulate the actions of the media, government officials, or terrorists. Still others are simulating the potential responses of the media to the actions implemented by executives. It is obvious that these firms are attempting to go beyond the traditional "fire-drill" approach. These crisis simulations are extremely realistic, and their relevance is strongly supported by top management.

The strategy of diversification (point 7) is widely used in business. Crisis-prepared organizations have expanded this familiar strategy to crisis management. Specifically, they make it a point to implement at least one effort from each of the five categories in Table 8.2.

Technical and Structural Actions

This family of activities is currently the one most developed in organizations. Most firms have started their crisis management efforts either in reaction to a particular crisis — "crash management" — or by focusing on a specific and technical area — "security management." For example, an insurance industry executive explained: "So far, we have focused on obvious stuff, on events that are in front of our eyes. It doesn't take great insight to realize that a bomb can be placed in your computer system."

One of the first tasks implemented by crisis-prepared organizations is to form a crisis management unit (CMU) (point 8). Originally, the CMU's main function was to provide a centralized interdepartmental structure that could make and implement decisions rapidly in the midst of a crisis. However, now CMUs are increasingly being used *before* crises emerge, in an attempt to be proactive. CMUs often comprise managers and executives from different departments, such as legal counsel, governmental and environmental affairs, public relations, security, engineering, human resources, and finance, along with the chief executive or chief operating officer and sometimes the heads of research and development or marketing. Some corporations have even created a whole department, headed by executives with the titles of vice president of crisis management or vice president for safety, health, and the environment.

The effectiveness of the CMU is enhanced by such mechanisms as a dedicated budget for crisis management (point 9); emergency manuals and policies (point 10); a computerized crisis management inventory system (point 11); or specific emergency facilities (point 12). Some firms have decentralized their decisional process so they can take quick action in times of crises: in an insurance company, operations managers were given the full authority to "declare disaster" and switch their information systems to an external firm specializing in computer emergencies, even though each incident involved a set-up fee of $25,000. These firms have also created *good* emergency manuals and policies. They do not resemble the traditional thousand-page emergency manuals that collect dust in so many companies; they are user friendly and are continually updated under the CMU's supervision.

We have also found some firms that have created crisis management data base inventories and computerized decision aids for crisis management. For example, a large food company developed a data base for each of its plants, including information such as key names and contacts, private communication channels, general plant history, number of employees, types of production, potential hazards, detailed product inventory, emergency capabilities developed on the site and in the community, types of health treatments to be administered by types of emergencies, and historical track record of the plant's incidents and improvements. An oil company has started a computerized system to track all technical incidents in its facilities, evaluating their total costs including losses in productivity and environmental costs. A utility company developed a large computerized decision aid for crisis situations, integrating data for each of its operation sites, such as transportation and communication infrastructure, topography and hydrography, service infrastructures, demography, environmental data, emergency plans, capabilities and contacts, and so on. In some organizations CMU decisions are assisted by dedicated emergency facilities similar to military war rooms. An airline company has built two of these facilities, in two strategic locations, equipped with the most advanced information system capabilities and communication technologies.

Finally, other technical efforts in crisis management (see points 13 to 16) include the reduction of hazardous productions, products, and services; the overall improvement of safety; technological redundancy; and the use of outside experts and services in crisis management. The reduction of hazardous productions is linked to changes in the concept of "corporate excellence" (see point 2). The overall improvement of design and safety incorporates the tasks generally implemented by security and safety personnel: screening employees, restricting access areas, inspection and quality control, security forces, special equipment, and restricted computer access. However, the managers of crisis-prepared organizations do not merely *protect* their existing products, services, and production processes; they also *modify* them when necessary, stressing the need for better designs.

Technological redundancies are another method. For example, some banks have developed their own telephonic networks or purchased microwave communications; others have created mobile units in the case of a telecommunication breakdown. Some utility companies, such as Electrécité de France, have created exact doubles of their command centers. To complement their own emergency capabilities, many firms are also using outside experts and services in crisis management. As an indication of this trend, firms offering computer backup and recovery, or companies specializing in environmental emergencies, have recently become a growth industry.

Evaluation and Diagnosis Actions

The third family of crisis management efforts includes diagnostic tools and processes. The first four (points 17 to 20) are already in place in many organizations but to various degrees.

Legal and financial assessments of threats and liabilities (point 17) are standard procedures. Often, crisis-prone organizations focus primarily on these two areas. Sometimes the company's lawyer is the first person contacted in a crisis, even before emergency services! Also, the threat is often undervalued. On the other hand, managers in crisis-prepared organizations have developed specific processes for better evaluating their potential threats.

The modification of insurance coverage (point 18) is also a common strategy. Several issues in this area are currently being debated, such as the precise evaluation of the insurance cost and coverage for environmental disasters or the specific responsibilities of insurance companies in the case of crises spread over time, as in the asbestos case. However, what seems to distinguish the managers of a crisis-prone organization is that they often confuse insurance with crisis management itself. An executive in a transportation company we have evaluated as dangerously crisis-prone said, "Crisis management is like an insurance policy. You only need to buy so much." In essence, this executive made the simplistic assumption that crisis management is a *reactive* strategy to be used only *after* a disaster occurs, and that it is only a cost.

Environmental impact audits (point 19) are conducted by many corporations, since they are required by law in several industries. However, managers of crisis-prepared organizations do not consider them only a matter of law but an opportunity to broaden their concept of "corporate excellence." For example, a manager in the chemical industry stated: "In several areas we go way beyond industry standards in safety and those required by the law. These innovations give us a considerable competitive advantage over our competitors and give us pride in what we are doing." Many organizations have ranked their activities in terms of the importance and criticality to their daily operations (point 20). This criticality is assessed differently by each organization, depending on its specific activities, and is continuously reevaluated by the CMU. Some take the tack of assessing the maximum number of days they can sustain their daily activities without the use of such resources as personnel, cash flow, technologies, inventories, or data; others have identified their most important customers or markets; still others have ranked the critical importance of their various products and services.

The other efforts in this crisis management evaluation family are currently developed only by a few organizations. Early warning signal detection (point 21) seems to be an advanced feature in crisis management. Firms that have developed capabilities in this area understand that most crises and disasters have a history that can be studied with the appropriate process. For example, twenty-nine crises larger than the Exxon *Valdez* disaster took place before that crisis, outside U.S. waters; crises similar to Hinsdale happened previously in Brooklyn, New York City, and Tokyo; the *Challenger* disaster was preceded by a trail of memos that precisely warned of the danger. Some organizations have a professional staff scanning for examples of crises in their industry or in related areas; others have included this activity in their strategic issues management programs; still others have hired specialized staff to track specific issues, such as a director of communication network assisting the chief information officer. In all these cases, findings from this scanning effort are directly communicated to the CMU and are used to orient further crisis management activities.

Even more rarely, a few firms have started a dedicated research program on potential hidden dangers (point 22). These firms are going far beyond traditional strategic analyses of vulnerability, which focus on competitors' moves, market fluctuations, regulatory changes, or technological innovations. They also systematically probe for the dangers hidden in their own products, resources, and processes. We have seen examples of this in previous chapters, in the case of one company's concept of "assassin" and "counterassassin" teams, or of another company's computing the "dependency costs" of its technologies. The critical follow-up and learning from past crises (point 23) is also seldom done. Often, this learning opportunity is provided only when an investigation is mandated by court order, as in the case of the *Challenger*. As was discussed in Chapters Two and Three, reluctance to reflect on past disasters is understandable, as the emotional burden induced by major crises is extremely painful. Also, factors such as legal battles, political maneuvering, or blaming after a crisis make follow-up difficult. At present, only a few crisis-prepared organizations fully understand that crises are not totally negative but that they also provide tremendous opportunities for learning.

Communication Actions

This group concerns how organizations manage their communications and what kind of information is processed between them and their stakeholders. The two first strategies, media training and public relations (points 24 and 25), seem to be the most popular, and the number of consulting firms offering expertise in these areas is increasing. Many companies consider the media strategies used by J&J during the Tylenol crises — high visibility, congruence, honesty, and caring — the model to follow. Too many managers in crisis-prone organizations tend to agree with the public relations director who told us that "a good message can resolve a bad crisis." However, crisis-prepared managers view these efforts as only complementary to all the other actions. Similarly, crisis-prone managers are often *too* concerned with their public image, or confuse the content of their message with the reality of crises. For example, an executive in a chemical company said that a crisis, for his organization, was "to be in the headlines." A public relations director in a gas company defined his job as "making our product invisible." While this strategy is understandable from a public relations point of view, it also has the negative effect of keeping the general public, and the company's executives, ignorant of potential dangers. This goes against the strategy of uncovering hidden dangers (point 22). Crisis-prepared managers provide media training to their top executives, and also offer the same training to managers and supervisors in the field.

Divulging information to local communities (point 26), such as the nature of dangerous products or productions, potential hazards, emergency plans, and so on, is required by law in several industries. In the United States, the "Community Right to Know" act was developed for the chemical industry after it was established that residents of Bhopal believed that the Union Carbide plant there was manufacturing "plant medicine" and thus were unaware of its potential dangers. Many crisis-prepared organizations combine this community program with increased relationships with diverse intervening groups (point 27), such as police, health specialists, laboratories, emergency services, fire departments, and other governmental agencies. In fact, some organizations, such as ESSO-SAF, believe that crisis management exercises cannot be conducted without the explicit participation of these stakeholders.

Overall, it seems that the managers of crisis-prepared organizations collaborate more often with other stakeholders (point 28), such as firms in the same industry, governmental agencies, suppliers, customers, and community members. They understand that secretive attitudes or isolationist tendencies are detrimental to an effective crisis management, and they have recognized that attempting to manage crises through their own internal resources alone simply does not work. Finally, they use different communication technologies and channels for crisis situations (point 29). In the United States, for example, some firms have created a network of toll-free emergency lines. With these lines they can instantaneously track the physical location of the calls received and establish an ongoing "map" of the crisis. Also, while managers in crisis-prone organizations have the tendency to focus on internal communications, that is, communications between members of the organization itself, crisis-prepared managers focus on the dual set of internal *and* external communications, as well as on technical and "human" data.

Psychological and Cultural Actions

This last family of crisis management efforts is currently the least developed in corporations. It is the most subjective and often the most difficult to implement, as it deals with highly emotional issues such as fear, uncertainty, and anxiety. Strong commitment to crisis management by top management, preferably by the chief executive officer (point 30), is essential. Unfortunately, only a few top executives champion these issues currently. We interviewed a number of managers in crisis-prone organizations who wanted to develop stronger crisis management programs, and almost unanimously they emphasized that a fundamental change in the mindset of their top management would be necessary, and that this change would, unfortunately, require the experience of a major crisis. Some typical comments: "In this organization, we will need a lot of black eyes before we start anything" (leisure industry). "Our top management does not believe that bad things can happen to us. Contingency education is not done in industrial and technical companies. It is viewed as a cost, not a profit. However, they do it in the medical profession" (consumer goods industry). "The mindset for senior management is cost reduction and productivity. They believe, 'If others are not doing anything about it, why should we?'" (information system industry). "We cannot keep up with technological innovations. We do not have the people, nor the training, nor the time to keep up. Senior management does not understand these issues. We do live on the edge in some areas" (airline industry). "I'm the only executive defending these issues. We will need a major disaster before anything will change" (chemical industry).

To develop systemic efforts in crisis management requires a fundamental shift in corporate philosophy, understanding that a corporation can become a *destructive* system if some issues are left unmanaged. This is to say that crisis management requires moral, ethical, and political courage as well as the cognitive and existential strength to face and discuss disturbing, anxiety-provoking issues. Toward this aim, some few companies have increased their relationships with activist groups (point 31). For example, a telecommunication firm has developed a network of minority groups, ecologists, consumer groups, and social activists; company managers regularly pool them to understand their views on crucial issues, and report the findings to the CMU. Other companies have integrated representatives of activist groups into their formal structure (point 21). Again, managers of crisis-prepared organizations attempt to avoid an "us–them" mentality.

To improve detection of early warning signals, some crisis-prepared organizations systematically reward whistleblowers who warn of potential threats and dangers that were previously invisible or unacknowledged (point 32). As we talked with these managers, it became evident that they had developed an internal culture where discussing bad news was not only tolerated but also encouraged; it was even formally recorded in employees' evaluation files for future promotions. Other managers have initiated various bonus programs to reward employees for uncovering hidden dangers, malfunctions, or product defects. A few managers are also attempting to increase their knowledge about criminal behavior (point 33). A chemical firm has sponsored seminars for its managers on subjects such as the social and psychological roots of sabotage, the diagnosis of psychopathology in organizations, or the dynamics of terrorism, hiring experts in psychiatry and criminal behaviors. Unfortunately, these subjects are not currently integrated in the basic curriculum of business or engineering schools, and most managers lack basic training in tracking and handling these complex and perplexing behaviors. Some managers in crisis-prepared organizations have also systematically amplified the visibility of the human impact of crises (point 34).

The two next strategies — psychological support of employees and the management of anxiety (points 35 and 36) — involve highly emotionally charged issues. The first focuses more on managing the psychological effect of a crisis *after* it has occurred. To manage these postcrisis traumas, some firms have hired psychotherapists to counsel their employees (strict confidentiality is maintained). After the *Challenger* disaster, NASA opened a crisis hotline for its employees. Some corporations create postcrisis intervention teams, comprising psychotherapists, social workers, and physicians, similar to the ones in communities for managing the effects of large natural disasters such as earthquakes, floods, or fires.

Stress and anxiety management (point 36) is more concerned with managing threatening issues *before* a crisis. This proactive strategy has two elements: (1) preparing managers and employees to function relatively well during a crisis, and (2) helping them surface threatening issues in their day-to-day work. All the studies on decision making under severe stress indicate strong cognitive and affective biases that hinder the effectiveness of decisions. These biases include an overall tendency of overreacting during a crisis; the tendency to wish for complete control and certainty; a bias for scapegoating and blaming; a shortening of time perspective; a chronic tendency to reduce the number of issues under consideration; an overevaluation of positive news and an underestimation of potential problems; the development of a group feeling of invulnerability; and a dangerous tendency to wish to be perceived as the hero or the "savior" of the situation. Managers of crisis-prepared organizations who are conducting crisis management workshops and crisis simulations (see points 5 and 6) are formally working on those issues.

A very few managers are also attempting to manage the anxiety surrounding crisis management in general, addressing how crises can challenge basic assumptions. We have found that this is the single most difficult aspect of crisis management. As we saw in Chapter Three, many executives, managers, and employees in crisis-prone organizations use a variety of defense mechanisms or faulty rationalizations for defending their views of the world against the potential threat that a crisis may pose. We urge the reader to review these rationalizations and to evaluate their strength in his or her own organization. We also suggest that readers reread Chapter Four, which discusses how these psychological and existential defense mechanisms have their origins in individual belief systems. As we have previously stated, managers who have understood the necessity of challenging their basic assumptions have embraced one of the fundamental lessons of existential philosophy: *the need to be "rightly" anxious.* Those few managers who have tried to face and constructively use the feelings of anxiety that a crisis engenders find that this issue is still mostly denied in their organization. As they have told us: "This company does not understand how stress is related to bodies and actions. There has never been a formal workshop on stress management in this company" (consumer goods company). "We're supposed to be winners. Anybody who would suggest any fear or anxiety is seen as a loser" (telecommunications company). "The worst sin you can commit over here is to question our belief about excellence" (chemical company).

The final strategy — symbolically remembering past crises and successes experienced by an organization (point 37) — also concerns this existential domain. A few managers — again a small minority — have found that acknowledging these events is healthier than denying them. As examples, managers in a large food organization wear black armbands on the anniversary of their most important crises; other companies have institutionalized mourning ceremonies and developed symbols for these events, celebrating both their failures and successes.

Concluding Remarks

We did not find any one firm that has developed all the crisis management actions described in this chapter. But managers of crisis-prepared organizations have made sure to implement at least some strategies in each of the five groups, depending on their particular situation. The composite list of thirty-seven strategies should be seen as an ideal crisis management strategic plan, providing a starting point and a basis for comparing the actions presently implemented in your own organization.

Rate Your Organization

As with the previous chapters, you will find in Resource B a questionnaire for evaluating your organization on the criteria discussed in this chapter. We strongly recommend that you answer this questionnaire and share it with several colleagues.

NINE

Inciting Deep Changes:
Treating the Crisis-Prone Organization

[Our age] is an era of radical transition. The old myths and symbols by which we oriented ourselves are gone, anxiety is rampant. . . . The individual is forced to turn inward; he becomes obsessed with the new form of the problem of identity. . . . The next step is apathy. And the step following that is violence. For no human being can stand the perpetually numbing experience of his own powerlessness.

—Rollo May, *Love and Will*

It is time to speak candidly and honestly; anything less will perpetuate the problems we are facing. Many modern organizations and their managers are in trouble. Superficial quick fixes will not help. The problems we face threaten every aspect of our existence. In short, today's managers and their organizations need to change substantially. Considering the extent of the defense mechanisms present in organizations, what is needed is not ordinary organizational change but "organizational deep change," what others have called "quantum change" (Miller and Friesen, 1980). Given the stakes at hand, we have to ask ourselves two questions: why has this need for change not been perceived, and what can be done about it?

At the risk of sounding trivial, we first need to state that *change is difficult.* Self-evident statements are often not fully understood, so the extent of this difficulty is rarely acknowledged. This is a grave error: for individuals and organizations alike, the process of changing is formidable, intricate, enigmatic, long, strenuous, terrifying, challenging, and sometimes tragic. The field of organizational development (OD) has, since its beginning about thirty years ago, produced a great body of knowledge on the theory, process, and technology of change, and many organizations have implemented major change programs. However

164

after a period of great enthusiasm and commitment, these efforts have often fallen short (Bennis, 1989; Mohrman and others, 1989; Zaleznik, 1989).

In this chapter, we use two activities that are complementary to OD—the treatment of individual addictive disorders and treatment of dysfunctional families—to provide some answers to our two questions. While we have chosen to focus on these particular forms of treatment, we also wish to acknowledge that other forms, such as incentives, regulations, and laws, can also provide impetus for change. However, as we have argued throughout the book, resistance to change in regard to crisis management is simply too deep to be profoundly altered by externally imposed means.

Learning from the Treatment of Personality Disorders

Throughout our research in crisis-prone organizations, we found that two personality disorders are especially prevalent: self-inflation and self-deflation. Let us summarize briefly. The self-concepts of both self-inflated and self-deflated people are too weak to handle the minor vicissitudes of life in a healthy way, let alone industrial disasters. Often, even a minor event can become an experience of psychological death. Managers will try to overcome this terrifying feeling with dramatic actions, self-defeating behaviors, or defense mechanisms.

Notice that we are not talking about what is commonly understood as stress, which has to do with *external* phenomena. As we see too often in stress management workshops, "experts" in the field still focus on external factors, such as the kind of lighting in a room, the effect of a deadline, or a mean boss, and suggest different ways to cope, such as relaxation, time management, and so on. When addressing existential questions, however, we need to go beyond the concept of stress, and focus on anxiety, which is a total state of inner turmoil (May, 1950; 1958). Anxiety touches the whole structure of people's experience, their total view of themselves and of the world, the emphasis being placed less on the interaction between individuals and their surroundings, but more on the subjective experiences of individuals themselves. Little wonder that "stress management" workshops are ineffective for dealing with the experience of existential anxiety.

Anxiety is also different from fear. In a sense, fear is object-oriented: one is afraid *of* something. Thus, when we were discussing the example of the tiger in Chapter Four, we used this example at a symbolic level, in which the tiger represents any deeper anxiety-related feelings. Anxiety is not "objectified": one is not anxious *about* something. It is a subjective state, a turmoil in a person's inner experience. To be anxious is to feel threatened from all sides at once, not knowing which direction to defend against (May, 1950). This is not to say that anxiety is not associated with specific threats, such as industrial crises. However — and this is the important point — threats such as industrial disasters do not *cause* as much as they *cue* a state of anxiety that was underlying the inner experience of individuals in the first place, with dramatic results for self-inflated and self-deflated people. These two groups in particular will fiercely deny any attempts to change. To put it bluntly, to let go of their defense mechanisms would be to commit psychological suicide, for they would then have to confront the feelings they tried so hard to escape in the first place.

To state this issue another way, as it is so fundamental for understanding the tragic state in which these individuals find themselves, the threats that trigger feelings of psychological death in one person can seem very minor to another. It could be anything: losing the car key; getting a negative review from the boss; not having one's favorite table in a restaurant; "losing" an argument when defending a marketing strategy; losing 1 percent of market share to a competitor. The problem is not so much in the event itself, but in the effect it can have on the total subjective experience of self-inflated or self-deflated individuals. Imagine, then, the impact on them of such disasters as *Challenger* or Hinsdale.

No one escapes anxiety. To put it another way, the only way to manage anxiety is to confront it. This is the basic message of existential philosophers, psychologists, poets, and novelists. Denial, anger, and all the other defense mechanisms we have discussed cannot reduce anxiety; they are just bandages. The only way to manage anxiety and to move beyond it is to *accept* being anxious, to accept one's relative powerlessness, and to draw from this anxiety the forces that make human beings human. We must not forget that the experience of anxiety, while frightening, is also the source of human creativity. It pushes people to innovate and create, to strive for a better condition, a better world. But accepting the possibility of being anxious is precisely what self-inflated and self-deflated people cannot do. They have lost the battle without having ever fought it. They need "the courage to be" (Tillich, 1952) and "the courage to create" (May, 1975).

The urge to diminish feelings of anxiety is very understandable at the personal level, but the tactics used are often bluntly destructive: consider drugs, alcohol, or compulsive sexual behaviors; consider workaholism, frozen feelings, or self-sabotaging; consider also the different defense mechanisms we have discussed in this book. But no matter how understandable they may be, these behaviors have a tremendously negative impact for individuals, organizations, and the environment. The critical point for our purposes is that deep feelings of anxiety are not only individually based, but are also reinforced by, sometimes created by, the environment surrounding the person, including organizations. To illustrate this, we draw from recent findings on addictive and dysfunctional families.

Learning from the Treatment of Addictive Families

Much has been learned in recent years about the dynamics of dysfunctional family systems. Dysfunctional families suffer from a wide range of severe problems such as alcoholism, child abuse, or drug addiction. Perhaps the most astounding finding is that whatever the particular problem a dysfunctional family suffers from, the problem is in the family system as a whole (Bateson, 1972; Satir, 1967; Whitaker, 1974). A particular person may seem to be the overt carrier of a problem, but the family as a whole perpetuates it. As strange as it sounds, other family members need to maintain the problem because that is the only way they have learned how to function. They become co-conspirators, in that they conspire with the offending member to help maintain the disease or sickness in the family system. If the problem is maintained, then the rest of the family can bond together. By blaming all their problems on one family member (the phenomenon of projection we described in Chapter Four), dysfunctional families avoid having to face the fact that they have serious overall problems.

In recent years, experts in management have begun to extend to organizations what has been learned about families. To some extent, the very same mechanisms that operate in dysfunctional families also operate in dysfunctional organizations (Schaef and Fassel, 1988). The notion of co-conspirators helps explain why so many troubled managers in organizations maintain their troublesome behavior, even though they sometimes freely acknowledge that they need to change. It also helps illuminate the relationship between the behavior of the individual and that of the group, whether that group is a family or an organization. Somehow organizations attract, or shape, employees who have, at an unconscious level, accepted the dysfunctions of the organizational culture. Being a co-conspirator is sometimes a prerequisite for promotion to high office. Little wonder then that dysfunctional managers and their organizations, like dysfunctional individuals and their families, have to approach the very edge of self-destruction before they can change—if even then.

Because this concept of dysfunctional systems helps explain why so many systems remain locked into destructive behavior even up to their point of death, we need to explore their characteristics in greater depth. Only then can we begin truly to see what is required to change.

Characteristics of Dysfunctional Systems

Some of the major characteristics of addictive personalities and addictive family systems, which are nearly the same as characteristics of dysfunctional family systems in general, are indicated in Table 9.1. The major characteristic is denial, by the addict and the other family members as well. The family members thus

Table 9.1. Characteristics of Addictive Family Systems.

---

1. *Denial,* which maintains the dysfunctional system as a closed system
2. *Confusion,* which keeps people from taking responsibility for their actions and for their maintenance of the system itself
3. *Self-centeredness,* as both the addict and the system are in the search of their "fix"
4. *Perfectionism,* or the obsession with being "not good enough"
5. *Dishonesty,* or the use of pathological lies
6. *Scarcity model,* or the tendency to compete with one another for money, time, love, and other basic needs
7. *Illusion of control,* or the search for omnipotence and perfection
8. *Frozen feelings,* or the inability to be in touch with basic feelings, intuition, and other vital sources of information that would allow people to see the system for what it is
9. *Ethical deterioration,* as a result of being constantly immersed in a dysfunctional system
10. *Other characteristics*
    A crisis orientation toward every aspect of life
    Depression
    Abnormal thinking processes
    Extreme dependency
    Extreme defensiveness

Source: Adapted from Schaef and Fassel, 1988.

become a fundamental part of the addict's disease, so that to treat the addict one has to treat the entire family system. Even worse, since everyone is engaged in denial, the entire family constitutes a closed system. The wall of denial prevents the family from taking in valid information from the outside. So the family's very behavior not only keeps it from changing but from learning that it needs to change (Satir, 1967; Schaef and Fassel, 1988).

The strong presence of denial is easy to understand once we appreciate what the system would be required to do if it were to acknowledge its problem and take proper corrective action. All the family members would have to confront the addict and say in the toughest, strongest terms something like this: "We're not going to let you and us out of this room until all of us acknowledge that we have a very serious problem. Because we love you so much, we're not going to participate in your death any longer." To break through the defense system, the family members have to threaten to expel the addict and be prepared to carry the threat through if need be. Because such confrontations are likely to be painful, most members of dysfunctional families will go to almost any length to avoid them. Also, since the family members themselves are likely to suffer from feelings of guilt, shame, and worthlessness (no one ever escapes unscathed from a dysfunctional family system), they are likely to feel that they do not deserve any better. An overwhelming feeling of being trapped pervades dysfunctional families. Given the closed nature of the system, the family is indeed trapped in its own web of self-destructiveness.

It is readily evident that descriptions of these crisis-prone organizations are very similar to descriptions of dysfunctional family systems. We wish to emphasize some of these similarities briefly. Consider item 2 in Table 9.1: confusion. The members of dysfunctional families are so bound up with one another that they have no clear-cut boundaries or separate identities. Similarly, self-inflated or self-deflated managers have tended to surrender themselves to the cultural norms of their organization. Items 3 and 4, self-centeredness and perfectionism, also fit our characterization of self-inflation.

One of the surest ways to recognize a dysfunctional system is to realize that its members cannot see that *they* are the problem. In family systems, members are caught up constantly in maintaining the family lie. In crisis-prone organizations, self-inflated and self-deflated employees continually lie to others and to themselves through the defense mechanisms and faulty rationalizations we have described previously: blaming others, attempting to manipulate the media, or congratulating themselves for their "excellence."

All the characteristics of dysfunctional systems interact strongly with one another; all are deeply intertwined. It is impossible to say which characteristics are causes and which are effects. For example, a tendency toward perfectionism (item 4) will lead people to believe in the scarcity model (item 6) and in the necessity of strict control (item 7). In dysfunctional systems people believe that there is simply not enough of the fundamental elements of life (food, love, money, companionship, trust, honesty, loyalty, dependability) to go around. Thus, if one member of the family secures love or money, somebody else is denied them. This fixed-sum model is much used today in organizations.

As much as we agree with Schaef and Fassel's (1988) description of addictive systems, it should be remembered that addiction itself is a symptom of a larger, deeper disorder. Dysfunctional issues in organizations are much, much deeper and more complex than can be resolved by focusing on one type of addiction. The problem is found in the overall feelings, thoughts, and behaviors that employees develop, and that the corporate culture reinforces, as they attempt to protect themselves from anxiety.

As a last commentary, we note that frozen feelings (item 8) echoes our characterization of bounded emotionality, so present in these organizations and so often expressed in the name of "rationality," "efficiency," and "professionalism." Lack of ethics (item 9) is so important that we devote the entire next chapter to it.

The Cost of Excellence

Signs of self-inflation and self-deflation are everywhere in our society and our corporations *if we have the courage to see them.* These signs are at the origin of widespread trends such as the "search for excellence," the current idealization of charismatic leaders, and the absence of real efforts in crisis management, and they are influencing most of the behaviors of managers and employees alike in our modern organizations, as a few additional examples will show. In an important book, *Quiet Desperation: The Truth About Successful Men,* management consultant Jan Halper (1988) describes what she learned by interviewing more than four thousand U.S. executives, managers, and professionals in Fortune 500 companies. She found that more than 70 percent of her respondents regularly lied to their employees about their poor performance, rather than give constructive criticisms. She also found that 58 percent of middle managers and professionals felt that they had wasted years striving for and achieving their goals, only to find their life empty and meaningless. Similarly, a survey of one hundred thousand U.S. middle managers (Farnham, 1989) indicates that they felt that their top management is listening significantly less to their problems and according them less respect than five years ago. The same trend seems unfortunately similar in Europe, where researchers have documented the negative effects of psychological disorders on work and safety in organizations, as well as the disastrous human and organizational impact of the "search for excellence" (Amado, 1980, 1987; Aubert and de Gaulejac, 1990; Dejours, 1980; Enriquez, 1989; Pagés, Bonetti, de Gaulejac, and Descendre, 1979; Sievers, 1986a, 1986b).

One more example, a finding that is both puzzling and important for understanding the connection between individual personality disorders and the overall dysfunctional culture of crisis-prone organizations. In *Modern Madness: The Emotional Fallout of Success,* psychotherapist Douglas LaBier (1986) reports that many employees who were considered "sick" in their organizations were in reality "normal" from a psychotherapeutic point of view, while employees considered "normal" in their organizations, and even pointed to as role models, actually had serious psychological problems, including irrational passions of power lust, conquest, grandiosity, destructiveness, or craving for humiliation and domination. The point is that many managers, and in particular those in crisis-prone organizations, have institutionalized "sickness" in their culture, thus making it acceptable; furthermore, they put tremendous pressure on "normal" individuals to become "sick" in order to fit in.

The conclusion is clear: the culture of an organization can be a major factor (or, in the language of addictive systems, a major co-conspirator) in the formation and maintenance of addictive, dysfunctional behaviors by the people in that organization. This explains why it is so difficult to get these individuals to change. Dysfunctional behavior is not only reinforced but overtly rewarded. In short, dysfunctional behaviors are a prerequisite for initial membership in the organization and for subsequent promotion. To get managers and employees working for these organizations to change, therefore, involves approaching them as part of a dysfunctional system whose disease is one of their strongest characteristics.

This means abandoning all the simplistic, fragmented, quick-fix approaches to changing individuals in organizations. It means seeing that the gimmicks are themselves co-conspiratorial devices that help to maintain the sickness of the system. For instance, managers who call in one charismatic speaker after another to "motivate the troops" are engaged in perpetuating the problem. Until we can get to the source of the dysfunctions and treat them as major components of the organization, we will have little success in helping individuals to change. But without changes, we are likely to encounter many more industrial crises. Dysfunctional systems cannot, by definition, get better by themselves; over time, they deteriorate. The inevitable outcome of a dysfunctional system is the fragmentation or even death of one or more of its members. It is not what members of the family *do* that leads to disaster; it is how they *are*.

As a concluding note to this description of dysfunctional systems, we urge the reader to read or re-read the play *Death of a Salesman* by Arthur Miller (1949). This play demonstrates so well the characteristics of a dysfunctional family (and, by extension, a dysfunctional organization) that we use it in our crisis management MBA classes and seminars. (In fact, existential literature has proven so effective at addressing corporate anxiety that we are creating a book that presents existential material for use in management training [Pauchant, in press].)

Future Directions for Change

What is the solution? In effect, we need the equivalent of an Alcoholics Anonymous program for organizations! In recent years, Centers for Recovering Families have been formed to treat dysfunctional families. We are convinced that we need equivalent kinds of centers to treat "recovering" managers in organizations, that is, those that wish to change. Of course getting managers to admit openly that they are "sick" and are seeking treatment will not be easy. But the situation is not impossible: in recent years many executives have admitted that they and their colleagues suffer from alcoholism. We hope that the day will come when CEOs will step forward and admit that they and their managers are in trouble and that they have joined together to form a new kind of treatment center for organizations: a Center for Recovering Organizations. We are still far away from developing such a center, but some preliminary insights into the nature of crises and change can provide clues as to how the center would function.

Most experts agree that the process of change, when induced by a crisis, evolves through different stages of resolution. We have summarized the content of these stages in Table 9.2. The levels of change addressed in the table range from the personal to the managerial, and cover such crises as physical death, crisis in existential meaning, severe stress, change in organizational design, and organizational crises. Despite these differences, however, the similarity of the stages of process and resolution is evident. For example, Kübler-Ross (1969) has found that most individuals facing death go through the five stages of denial, rage, bargaining, depression, and acceptance; Fink, Beak, and Taddeo (1971) found that managers confronted with an organizational crisis go through the four stages of shock, defensive retreat, acknowledgment, and change. In effect, these findings allow us to forecast the progress of change.

Most organizations will be in the denial stage when confronted with or even imagining industrial disasters and organizational crises. At the present time, most managers in crisis-prone organizations are still holding on to denial. As a second stage, we can expect tremendous outbursts of anger, guilt, and resentment. Today this stage is mostly visible in some environmental groups, lobbying associations, concerned citizens or customers, some scientific circles and research centers, and some governmental agencies. Through our interviews, we have also met some business executives who expressed these feelings of anger and moral outrage about their own organization but lacked the structural power to make changes.

Still further in the future, we can expect that after a while, more and more executives and managers will attempt to evaluate their situations. When this happens, they will suffer from

Table 9.2. Crises and Stages of Resolution.

Authors	Individual			Organizational		
	Kübler-Ross (1969)	Hanna (1975)	Horowitz (1976)	McWhinney (1980)	Fink, Beak and Taddeo (1971)	Tannenbaum and Hanna (1985)
Source of data	Physical death	Crisis in meaning	Reaction to severe stress	Change in design	Crises	Change, both individual and organizational
Stages	Denial and isolation ("No, not me" stage)		Outcry, panic, fainting		Shock	
			Denial, emotional numbing		Defensive retreat	*Holding on*
	Rage, resentment, envy of others	Attempts to evaluate and understand situation	Intrusiveness, involuntary thoughts and feelings about the event	Retreat, anger, guilt		
	Bargaining with death	Coping, depression				
	Depression	Search for new directions	Working through	Founding, emergence of new ideas	Acknowledgment	*Letting go*
	Acceptance	Resolution	Completion, integration of crisis into life experience	Return, reengagement in life process	Adaptation and change	*Moving on*

deep depression, anguish, and mourning, as they start to realize that their old ways of viewing the world and themselves are inadequate, painfully searching for new "visions," "directions," "values" and "meanings." It is only through this pain, this existential suffering, that resolution, adaptation, and change are possible.

No human being and no organization can jump directly from denial to acceptance and change. This process has to be worked through, one phase at a time, painful though it is. This can be one major function of a Center for Recovering Organizations: to facilitate these phases, helping all members of the organization work through them.

Experts in the field of organizational development are presently disenchanted with the results of most change efforts. Tannenbaum and Hanna, both with considerable experience in the field, have stated this matter most clearly. Their point is so important that we will quote these two experts at some length (1985, p. 99):

> For many years (and, to a considerable extent, even into the present), the primary attention of organizational change facilitators has been on the introduction of change — a diagnosis of the present situation, a decision concerning the goals of the change effort being considered, and a development of strategy and tactics from moving here to there, followed by appropriate implementation in the field. This has been a future orientation — one starting with an assumption of "acceptance," leading to "resolution," a "founding" or rebirth, and "adaptation and change." What has become increasingly clear to us is that *very little, if any, attention has been given to the working through of the potent needs of human systems to hold on to the existing order* — to that which is — and to avoid the powerful feelings that changed circumstances can trigger. The deeply felt experiencing of "shock," "frustration," "loss of meaning," "anger," "need to bargain," "helplessness," and "depression" has been

almost completely ignored (except possibly at a relatively superficial level called "resistance to change"). Thus, the considerable and growing interest in the change process has been one that has not encompassed the totality of that process. It has heavily focused on the *moving on* and has to a large extent neglected or avoided the need to *hold on* [emphasis added].

Change agents such as Tannenbaum and Hanna are our closest approximation of a future Center for Recovering Organizations. Under the auspices of the National Training Laboratories they are conducting weeklong workshops in organizational and individual change using intrapersonal, interpersonal, and group processes. Briefly, they focus on the process of letting go, the preparation for change. They describe their work as a three-step process: (1) consciousness raising, as individuals acknowledge what they are holding on to and note their personal patterns of behavior when becoming anxious; (2) reexperiencing, despite increasing anxiety, the early traumatic experiencese that led to their particular beliefs about themselves, others, or life; and (3) mourning the loss of the old ways of seeing reality.

Clearly, this process of preparing for change and moving on is arduous and long. It requires a certain amount of self-worth, humanistic values such as trust and openness, an experienced and professional staff, psychological support, and realistic patience. It also needs the full support of the top management of the firm; best of all, the CEO and the top executives are invited to participate.

Our future Center for Recovering Organizations will focus not only on the personal patterns of individuals but also on the cultural patterns embedded in the organization. One of the center's primary tasks will be to help the organizations identify these patterns, understand their origins and dynamics, and develop an elaborate program of letting go. One of the fundamental keys for organizational change is to understand how employees use these defensive patterns to reduce their own personal anxiety.

Table 9.3. Organizational Patterns Used for Reducing Anxiety.

Organizational defensive patterns	Mechanisms	Existential effect
Splitting of nurse-patient relationship	• Precise tasks • Increase of the number of patients per nurse • Routinization of activities	• Decrease of closeness with patients in an attempt to decrease anxiety
Depersonalization of individuals	• Patient referred to as "bed number 10" rather than by name • Patient regarded as "sick," not as individual	• Decrease in interpersonal relating
Detachment and denial of feelings	• Extensive moving from job to job • Strict "professionalism"	• Decrease of pain and distress associated with breaking relationships
Attempts to eliminate decisions	• Routinization of tasks • Insistence on "objectivity" • Focus on a few methods	• Reduction of anxiety over making choices
Decrease of responsibilities	• High role ambiguity • Delegation to superiors • Strict use of hierarchy	• Evasion of responsibility
Idealization of training or vocation	• "Nurses are born not made" • Training mostly technical	• Reduction of potential creativity
Avoidance of change	• Holding onto familiar methods • Sabotage of change efforts	• Decrease of uncertainty

Source: Adapted from Menzies, 1960.

For example, Menzies (1960) identified these patterns in an in-depth study of hospitals; we have summarized her findings in Table 9.3. Attempts to reduce the bureaucratic characteristics of the hospitals, such as excessive routinizing of tasks, cumbersome communications, strict use of hierarchical power, high role ambiguity, and so on are bound to fail. The heaviness and rigidity of bureaucracies have a fundamental function often overlooked by most change agents: they allow employees to manage their deep feelings of anxiety. They allow self-deflated individuals to reduce their responsibilities and decrease their need for creative actions; they allow self-inflated individuals to behave like mini-emperors in their little protected worlds. To put the point bluntly, a so-called humanistic effort to reduce bureaucracy by, for example, empowering individuals, increasing responsibility, and reducing rules, has the great risk of being antihumanistic if deep feelings of anxiety are not first acknowledged and worked through. Uncovering these organizational patterns and understanding their deep motivation would be one of the primary tasks of a Center for Recovering Organizations.

Another source of insight for a Center for Recovering Organizations is the guiding principles developed by Alcoholics Anonymous (AA) (Alcoholics Anonymous, 1957; Bateson, 1971; Schwartz, 1990). We have reproduced AA's famous twelve steps in Table 9.4, and we strongly recommend Howard Schwartz's discussion (1990) of the adaptation of the AA model to organizational issues.

We know that many readers will find these steps out of place when it comes to treating managers in organizations, especially considering the spiritual aspects of the AA credo. Nonetheless, we are also convinced that in time an equivalent set of principles will be formulated for organizations. For instance, principle 1 most likely will be reworded to something like: "We admitted we were powerless over the addictive properties of our organizational system that caused many of our members to self-destruct through workaholism, that our lives both on and off the job had become unmanageable." We also believe that some of the more overtly religious aspects will also

Table 9.4. The Twelve Steps of Alcoholics Anonymous.

1. We admitted we were powerless over alcohol, that our lives had become unmanageable.
2. We came to believe that a Power greater than ourselves could restore us to sanity.
3. We made a decision to turn our will and our lives over to the care of God as we understood Him.
4. We made a searching and fearless moral inventory of ourselves.
5. We admitted to God, to ourselves, to another human being the exact nature of our wrongs.
6. We're entirely ready to have God remove all these defects of character.
7. We humbly asked Him to remove our shortcomings.
8. We made a list of all the persons we had harmed, and became willing to make amends to them.
9. We made direct amends to such people wherever possible except when to do so would injure them or others.
10. We continued to take personal inventory and where we were wrong promptly admitted it.
11. We sought through prayer and meditation to prove our conscious contact with God as we understood Him, praying only for the knowledge of His will for us and the power to carry that out.
12. Having had a spiritual awakening as a result of these steps, we try to carry these messages to alcoholics, and to practice these principles in all our affairs.

Source: Alcoholics Anonymous, 1957.

be reworded to something like the following: "We made a decision to turn our organizational will as well as our working lives within and outside our organization over to a moral principle beyond greed, power, or productivity." Indeed, we believe that the formation of a moral creed for the protection of the environment and society in general will become one of the major objectives of all managers. Otherwise, we shall in all likelihood continue to go from one mega-disaster to another. As a sign of this new tendency, many managers are currently attempting to implement in their organizations what is known as the *Valdez* Principles, a set of ten principles created by the Coalition of Environmentally Responsible Economics to help investors make informed decisions about environmental issues (Karrh, 1990). We have summarized these principles in Table 9.5.

Table 9.5. The *Valdez* Principles.

---

1. Protection of the biosphere
2. Sustainable use of natural resources
3. Reduction and disposal of waste
4. Wise use of energy
5. Risk reduction
6. Marketing for safe products and services
7. Damage compensation
8. Disclosure of potential hazards and incidents
9. Environment directors and managers on board of directors
10. Assessment and annual audit

Source: Adapted from Karrh, 1990.

Concluding Remarks: Impetus for Change

The task at hand seems so overwhelming and complex, composed of such intricately interrelated factors that one can easily feel lost trying to determine how to start this deep-change effort. If managers are still in the denial stage (and most are), we need to start not on the changes themselves but on the *preparations* for change, the letting go. This process is best facilitated in a Center for Recovering Organizations. But what will lead these managers to engage in such a process in the first place? There are three main triggers: leadership, grassroots movements, and industrial crises.

Leadership is perhaps the most widely advocated trigger for change. Especially in times of turbulence, leaders have the opportunity to take charge and make changes, providing new visions for the future (Bennis, 1989; Kets de Vries, 1977; Zaleznik, 1989). While this strategy can be powerful, it is not without danger. Self-inflated leaders need to be admired and unquestioningly followed by a self-deflated public. Also, we have a tendency to fall in love with pseudoleaders whose greatest "contribution" is in fact to reinforce the status quo. We need leaders who can go beyond the "don't worry, be happy" defense mechanism. Finally, experts in leadership seem to disagree on its potential for radical change. Some argue that leadership is *the* solution for orienting business organizations in different directions (see, for example, Zaleznik, 1989); others that managers and employees no longer welcome such transformative leadership and have formed an unconscious conspiracy that prevents leaders from taking charge and making changes (Bennis, 1989). If this second view is correct, many managers in organizations have currently cut themselves off from one of the most powerful change mechanisms we know.

The second trigger for change — grassroots movements — is less dramatic or visible and not so well known. Many social advances were originally triggered by such movements, often starting from a small group of individuals (O'Neill, 1989). The present interest in environmental issues is a perfect example of grassroots movements. In a sense, the few crisis-prepared organizations and their managers that we know of represent this movement, and they can become role models for others. Even in crisis-prone organizations, we have met many individuals who implemented some changes in their organizations, quietly and carefully, within the limits of their expertise, resources, and power. Similar grassroots movements can be found in some environmentally concerned groups, research centers, associations concerned about industrial safety, experiments in education conducted in high schools, and so on. Notice the contrast with the leadership trigger. While leadership is, unfortunately, still mostly external to individuals, grassroots movements spring from personal and emotional understanding experienced by the individuals involved. To some extent, these people are beyond the "holding on" stage. Often, they have also experienced some painful personal crises and have been fortified by them.

For us, these grassroots movements represent one of the most hopeful grounds for change. If they could be mobilized and focused, and associate themselves with leaders who have had the same personal experiences, the deep-change process we are advocating could be given a chance. This is to say that organizational change starts above all with a deep personal change of the individuals involved (Grof and Grof, 1990). This is also to say that the most important person who needs to change, and who will be essential in bringing about this change process, is you.

Lastly, one of the most powerful triggers for change is a crisis itself. In our society and our corporations we believe strongly in the idiom "if it ain't broke, don't fix it." Existential philosophers, therapists, and organizational change agents have for a long time acknowledged that a crisis is exactly what is required to shock people out of their convictions and their behavioral patterns, creating an "opportunity space" for creative actions (Hall, 1976; Starbuck and Milliken, 1988). We too found that the most powerful motivation for organizations to implement efforts in crisis management is their repeated direct experience of major crises (see Table 4.1, Chapter Four). However, we obviously cannot actively promote this strategy as an impetus for change, considering the tremendous human, environmental, emotional, and economic costs.

TEN

Crisis Management as an Ethical Activity: Myths and Methods

> A person becomes a person in the encounter with other persons, and in no other way. All functions of our spirit are based on what I call the moral self-realization of the centered self. This is what morality is—not the subjection to laws.
>
> —Paul Tillich, *Existentialism and Psychotherapy*

The purpose of this final chapter is twofold: to summarize briefly the principal issues we have explored in this book, and, at the same time to show that in every case the issues involved are fundamentally ethical. Failure to address crisis management leads invariably to ethical deterioration.

Five Destructive Myths

Our summary will take the form of confronting directly five major myths that can destroy any effective program of crisis management:

1.   Crises are inevitable.
2.   We lack the basic knowledge to understand crises, let alone prevent their occurrence.
3.   Bigger and better technology will prevent future crises.
4.   Extreme preparation for crises leads to a society that is conservative, as crisis management is inherently detrimental to progress.
5.   Emotions have no place in management; they cloud the issues and prevent us from thinking correctly and clearly. We need to be rational about crisis management.

184

Myth 1: "Crises Are Inevitable"

Despite our best efforts at prevention, *some* crises will always occur. Indeed, the destructive characteristic of crises is itself inherent to *all* living systems, including organizations, engendering both the life of these systems and, ultimately, their destruction.

A strict belief in this myth leads to the thesis of inevitability or fatality. The critical word in the first sentence of the preceding paragraph is *some:* some crises are indeed inevitable, but not all. Further, even if some crises are inevitable, this does not mean that we are justified in doing nothing. If we act as if all crises are inevitable, then this has the unfortunate consequence of becoming a self-fulfilling prophesy. The point is that the inevitability thesis is not to be read strictly as a scientific or logical statement but as a moral or ethical imperative. The imperative that ought to apply is: do everything in your power to reduce the factors that make the occurrence of crises inevitable. Failure to act in this manner is precisely how any individual in any organization will be tried in the courts of law, by public opinion, and, ultimately, by themselves. People who have understood this ethical imperative are able to face the Heraclitian and *paradoxical nature of both creation and destruction,* life and death, order and chaos. True crisis management is not only reactive, targeted toward crash management, but also proactive and interactive, stressing the necessity of continuous learning.

Myth 2: "We Lack the Basic Knowledge to Prevent or Understand Crises"

While we lack complete knowledge about crisis management (when have we ever had complete or perfect knowledge about any important subject?), we know enough about the broad, basic factors involved in an effective program of crisis management, and especially their interactions, to undertake proper action if we so desire. The problem is not knowledge, or even financial cost, but the basic will and desire. It is an ethical stance: managers will take proper action because it is inherently right to do so.

Myth 3: "Better Technology Will Prevent Future Crises"

The entire discussion of the Onion Model dispels the notion that crisis management is inherently a matter of technology. Though substantive technical issues are certainly involved, crisis management involves a vast array of complex linkages between political, medical, legal, social, managerial, organizational, moral, ethical, existential, and scientific matters. Indeed, the linkages themselves are more at the basic heart of the issue than the separate effects. As we have argued previously, crisis management is not the same as security management. While crisis management includes security management issues (which are technical in nature), it also goes beyond technical considerations alone.

We have presented numerous faulty rationalizations, and emphasized that they are not to be read merely as informal cognitive policies but rather as their deeper, unstated, moral, existential, or ethical policies. In other words, these rationalizations are often nothing more than moral principles in disguise. For example, the statement, "Our size will prevent us from experiencing a major crisis," when translated into a moral principle, really means, "Whenever an organization is so big and powerful that its size will protect it from a major disaster or crisis, then it has no responsibility toward its employees and the surrounding environment and is justified in expressing no concern toward the environment."

Because the ethical basis of crisis management is so important, it is also important that we expose the ethical basis of some of the concepts that the field of crisis management has inherited without much conscious realization. One of these concepts is borrowed from the field of risk management. A procedure that is commonly used, often casually and informally, to determine which situations an organization should prepare for and which ones can be safely ignored, is probability ranking (Perrow, 1984). It involves estimating, using some procedure or theoretical model, the probabilities of occurrence of a set of negative outcomes, and then ranking them in order from the highest probability down to the lowest. If the potential crisis with the highest probability exceeds some threshold value, then the organization prepares for it. Crises that do not exceed the threshold value are ignored, theoretically with confidence. A more sophisticated version of probability ranking, known as *expected value* or probabilistic consequences, uses essentially the same procedure. In this case, the estimated probability of occurrence of a particular crisis is multiplied by its negative consequences, usually expressed in dollars. The company reasons that if a particular crisis is certain to occur, that is, if its probability of occurrence is 1, then the company would definitely incur the full amount of the negative consequences with certainty. If a particular crisis with negative consequences of $1,000,000 has a probability p of occurring, then *on average* the company can expect to incur a cost of $p \times$ $1,000,000. The concept of multiplying probabilities by their financial consequences is what is known as expected value.

What is wrong with these procedures? Theoretically, nothing; morally, everything. Using these procedures almost always leads to the conclusion that nothing should be done. That decision has produced some of the worst disasters in history. Just a few weeks before the Exxon *Valdez* disaster, preparation for a large spill was discounted because the probability of occurrence was estimated at one in a million.

The trouble with probability procedures is that they become self-fulfilling prophesies. Because some dangerous event has not occurred, it is initially assigned a low probability which is then seen as a vindication of the procedures themselves—a self-perpetuating trap from which there is no escape. Putting everything in probability terms has the almost inevitable result that one prepares for nothing.

There is an even deeper objection: whenever a procedure leads to immoral consequences—failure to prepare for disaster—then choosing that procedure is itself immoral. From a technical point of view the procedures may be "correct," but from a moral perspective, they are not. In organizations, probability procedures may be legitimately used to select from a list of crises the particular one that managers ought to prepare for, but they do not justify the end result of not preparing for *any* worst case.

The only way to avoid getting trapped into a procedure that leads to immoral consequences is not to get into the procedure in the first place.

Myth 4: "Crisis Management Is Inherently Detrimental to Progress"

We decry the argument (see Wildavsky, 1988) that too much safety inhibits progress. Of course it is true that societies that demand zero-risk options before they act will quickly become paralyzed. To avoid *all* risks is really to risk extinction. We do not insist that everything should be, or can be, safe before a society undertakes to build dangerous technologies.

The real point is that managers in crisis-prone organizations, which have a track record of almost reckless disregard of safety, should not be granted approval to engage in experiments with no safeguards whatsoever. One of the most significant factors that characterizes these managers is their sense of inflation or deflation, which reinforces their overall corporate culture. These managers, and their culture, have such deep defects that they are almost guaranteed to precipitate an accident, no matter how careful the procedures for handling dangerous products. No one would contend, or at least we hope not, that known psychopaths should be given license to shoot people at random, as a way of testing and refining automatic rifles. Refusing to permit *all* managers in *all* organizations to undertake dangerous activities is not the same as being anti-progress. Not to make such differentiations is extremely dangerous. Not to see such differentiations is even worse.

Myth 5: "Emotions Have No Place in Crisis Management"

There may well be no universal principles upon which ethics is founded. Unfortunately, most of the "ethical" discussions currently developed in business schools and organizations seem to trivialize the issues by proposing a set of guidelines of what is "right" or "wrong" (Mitchell and Scott, 1990).

In our view, being "ethical" is not so much a matter of discovering a set of fixed rules as it is an ongoing process of uncovering and understanding the underlying principles that guide one's actions. The process, in other words, is all-important. Slowly we are coming to recognize that ethical principles are part of an unfolding conversation with oneself and others (Churchman, 1983). The fundamental nature of ethics is grossly distorted when it is removed from the human context from which it arises. Ethics is part of the fundamental fabric of what it means to be human. And one of the most distinctive things about humans is their ability to converse, to argue, to agree, to agree to disagree.

Seeing ethics as a conversation helps to make clear a number of things:

1. The conversation never terminates, although it can pause and seem to reach some resolutions. When it pauses, it does so for the purpose of taking stock, reflecting, evaluating action.
2. The purpose of the conversation is not to arrive at final, fixed principles, but to keep the process going in the hope of ameliorating the human condition.
3. In principle anyone can enter into the conversation.
4. The parties to the conversation need not be alive or have ever even existed. One can introduce in the conversation Socrates, the devil, or an animal, constructing imaginary conversations in order to further understanding.
5. The only requirement in this process is that all parties contribute something vital to the conversation.
6. To hinder the conversation of any stakeholder or even to exclude certain parties from the conversation, such as future generations, is itself unethical.
7. At a minimum, the conversation must include at least two strongly divergent groups, parties, or voices.

To be able to engage in such a conversation with others is to be truly human. However, it is the in-depth realization of our anxiety and fragility that allows us to enter a true "conversation" with another. Paradoxically, this encounter further pushes us to realize our specificity and aloneness, which pushes us still further to more encounters with others.

No wonder, then, that many individuals will refuse to engage in such "eternal conversations" with themselves and others. To enter such conversations, they would first have to face their basic anxiety; to continue these conversations, they would have to confront their ongoing anxiety, perhaps exacerbated by these encounters. An emotionally bounded person will either refuse all encounters, fearful of being "swallowed up," or surrender to others or to a culture, in the illusion of participating. People with positive self-regard, in contrast, join the eternal ballet of being more themselves by being with others. Because they can integrate the fragility of life and realize the paradoxes between creation and destruction, they are more able to address the phenomenon of crises in ethical terms. They can better understand their own responsibility in confronting crises and the different experiences that others will have.

Conversation Between Two Parties

This last condition — inclusion and respect for different perspectives — is very helpful in gaining a sense of the extreme or polar ends of most ethical conversations. To realize this more clearly, let us observe two characters in such a discussion: Thinking and Feeling. Those who are familiar with the work of the great Swiss psychologist Carl Jung (1971) will of course immediately recognize these two. Thinking is the psychological function that evaluates abstract qualities according to the dictates of formal logic. People who are strongest on thinking (most scientists and engineers) are good at abstracting, theorizing, and generalizing from particular situations to formulate broad principles and scientific models that attempt to describe the universal features of all situations. Feeling is the psychological function that evaluates all life situations, people, or events in terms of their unique worth and inherent likability. Thus, where Thinking attempts to evaluate all things dispassionately according to general standards without reference to the particular person or situation at hand, Feeling always looks for the features of a particular person or situation that make it unique, and hence cannot be subsumed under any general principle. Further, whereas Thinking always seeks to downplay the affect or the emotion of a particular situation, Feeling prefers to heighten it. Obviously neither is preferable in all situations; each has its major strengths and inherent weaknesses.

As an example of a conversation between these two, let us consider the hypothetical situation that is commonly used in value-exploration exercises: five people are candidates for only one kidney machine. The candidates are: a woman with two young children; a teenager; an old man who has lived a full and rewarding life; a criminal with no obvious redeeming values; and a scientist who is on the threshold of making discoveries that will forever change the fate of mankind.

In the exercise, people are typically asked to state a value position and rank the candidates in order of suitability for access to the kidney machine. The point is that, through group discussion, it becomes clear that different people bring differing value standards to such situations. How would our friends Thinking (T) and Feeling (F) approach such an exercise?

For T it is obvious that the solution (in principle, all problems have solutions for T types) begins with finding the proper set of scales with which to rank the candidates; for example, one scale might measure contribution to society. Once the appropriate scales have been determined, each candidate is scored on all the scales, and the single candidate with the best overall score "wins." For T, ethics is reduced to a formula or mechanical procedure. It is not surprising to learn that T types prefer to resolve ethical issues using methods that have the following characteristics (Machol, 1986):

1. They must be "reasonable."
2. They must be widely acceptable to an expert community.
3. They must clearly allow one to weigh the benefits against the costs or "dis-benefits" of any proposed action or procedure.
4. They must permit comparisons of one's deeply held beliefs to beliefs held by others.
5. They must allow one to abstract from a particular situation and talk about properties in their most general sense, for example from the value of any particular life to the statistical value of life in general.

This is one of the fundamental differences between the two: T is driven by the desire to invent formulas to make difficult choices easy and rational — that is, nonemotional. F, on the other hand, believes that in questions of ethics, especially in matters of life and death, the decision *should* be as difficult and as painful as possible. From F's perspective, feeling forces us to acknowledge the pain we cause others by our actions and our inactions. This awareness allows us to change those actions or inactions, and thus become more human, more ethical. For F, feeling is the very essence of ethical choice. In fact, F will often deliberately exaggerate a situation to encourage feeling, just as T will distort the nature of ethical choices by insisting on removing feeling. The manners and styles of both characters are offensive to the other.

At this point F enters the conversation — if indeed F types could be held off this long. F is thoroughly outraged by everything T has said. "You cannot determine questions of life and death using a procedure devoid of all feeling. Feelings are at the heart of what it means to be human, to be alive."

T of course is not content to sit quietly and listen to F's arguments. "What you say is all well and good, but how would you decide? You are only critizing me, leaving me to do the dirty work." To which F has a response: "Instead of accepting a society based on limitations, where we are forced to choose among five unique people, we should be trying to expand society so that all could be saved. And if the level of our knowledge will not permit us to do this now, if we are forced to choose only one of the five to live, the deaths of the others ought to be so painful to us and to the world in general that we are impelled to question the constraints of current society. If we feel this pain, we will be obliged to act to remove these constraints. Why should we accept the limitations of our society?"

To Be Responsible

We now come full circle, back to the concept of responsibility that began this book. To be *ethically responsible* means being responsible not only to oneself, accepting one's own limitations, but also to others, accepting their limitations and perspectives. To be ethically responsible, one must engage in an eternal conversation with others and with self.

At the present time, we do not know which of the two moods expressed in this book — *empathy,* understanding why individuals lie to themselves and others, or *moral outrage* over the lies — will be more instrumental in bringing about change. We believe that both moods are needed. The first recognizes that "slow is beautiful," and that changes in human affairs must be worked through, with kindness and patience. The second emphasizes the need for immediate "deep change," using expediting actions and procedures.

Both moods are an expression of our own character as individual persons. Over the years, we have grown from our "encounter" with each other. It has been our way of attempting to be responsible and authentic to ourselves, to others, and to our profession. It has also been our way of expressing our outrage, our concerns, and our compassion for the people trapped in their web of destructiveness, and for our beautiful and fragile planet. The issues surrounding the field of crisis management are not only about managing crises. Disasters reminds us — and this is perhaps their most positive side — that to manage an organization, to conduct research, or to teach students, we need to be deeply human, facing bravely and responsibly the necessity of both death and life.

Research Procedures

As we mentioned in the preface to the book, much of the material discussed in *Transforming the Crisis-Prone Organization* came from two sources: (1) our personal interviews of over 500 professionals responsible for crisis management in the United States, Canada, and France; and (2) the results of a questionnaire sent to executives in Fortune 1000 companies in the United States. This resource presents some basic information on our research methods.

Personal Interviews

From 1987 to 1991 we conducted 410 interviews with executive managers and professionals located in the United States, 60 interviews with executives in Canada, and 30 interviews with executives in France. These interviewees represented a diversity of industries: food, consulting, oil, telecommunications, manufacturing, governmental agencies, defense, nonprofit sector, insurance, finance, media, leisure, and health care. No single industry represented more than 15 percent of the sample.

Having assured complete anonymity to both the interviewees and their companies, we cannot name specific company or employee names. It should be stressed, however, that our data reflect the circumstances and views of executives and managers working in some of the most visible and well-known companies in the United States, Canada, and France. These companies employ an average of fifty thousand people (10 percent employ more than one hundred thousand; 30 percent employ between ten thousand and one hundred thousand; and 60 percent employ fewer than ten thousand). They generate an average of $6.5 billion in annual revenues (10 percent generate more than $10 billion; 40 percent generate between $1 billion and $10 billion; and 50 percent generate less than $1 billion.

Data Collection

The data were collected by research assistants from USC's Center for Crisis Management (CCM) and from L'École des Hautes Études Commerciales (HEC) in Montreal. Research was also done by the two authors, who personally conducted about half the interviews in this sample.

To build some homogeneity into the data-collection process, we used a questionnaire agenda (Exhibit A.1), which was pretested on fifteen interviewees, for most interviews. The first part of the agenda asks managers to describe their concepts and experiences of crises and crisis management. It then asks them to perform a "stakeholder analysis" (Mason and Mitroff, 1981) and concludes by soliciting opinions on how to improve the company's approach to crisis management.

In the interest of collecting qualitative data on crisis management and of capturing the specific language and experiences of respondents, we were careful to word the questions generally enough to allow for individual expression, but specifically enough to offer a structured content analysis. The interviews were not taped, considering our promise of confidentiality and the sensitivity of the issues involved, but a large volume of notes was taken. The interviews ranged from one hour and a half to three hours in length. When completed, each interview was typed, discussed at length among research assistants, and entered into a relational word data base for ease of retrieval and content analysis.

Interviewees

We drew our pool of interviewees from a variety of sources: conference attendance lists, CCM sponsors, industry listings, and references from previous interviews. Over half of the interviewees were at the senior level of management in their organizations; the majority of these were regarded as crisis management experts or as policy makers who wield significant influence in the company. Great care was taken to ensure that we were interviewing the most knowledgeable and experienced crisis management professionals in each organization.

To double-check our data, in most cases we interviewed a minimum of three persons in each organization, each of whom worked at a different operational level (executive, middle management, and general professional. About half of the respondents were responsible for internal and/or external relations, with titles such as vice president of public relations, director of human resources and industrial relations, vice president of planning, director of media relations, and so on. Another 40 percent held more technically oriented positions, such as controller, director of emergency measures, manager of health and safety, analyst in environmental affairs or specialist in corporate security and emergency planning.

General Results

Considering the number of interviewers and the length of time in which the research occurred (six years), it is difficult to compile accurate, up-to-date statistics. While we do not claim that our study fully represents the situation in all firms, our data are sufficiently diversified and documented to support the strength of the phenomenon that we are addressing in this book. This data indicate that the current state of corporate crisis management can be characterized as follows:

- Fifty percent of the managers interviewed still see crisis management as a mostly technical issue.
- Fewer than one-third of the companies contacted have developed three or more interventions in three different crisis management families or clusters, as defined in Chapter One.
- About 10 percent of these firms can be regarded as crisis-prepared.
- In 1990, only 55 percent of the firms we interviewed had created an official crisis management unit.

- Despite these disconcerting results, about 50 percent of the respondents judged that their company's crisis management plans were sufficient.
- Sixty percent of the respondents defined a crisis as "a negative shift in the demand of our product," "a threat to our company's image," "a stop in our production system," or "a financial loss," thus perpetuating a "closed-system" view of crises.
- Forty percent of these managers considered that a crisis had both internal and external impact.
- Half of the respondents considered crisis management efforts to be reactive in nature, to be applied strictly for the purpose of returning to "business as usual" as soon as possible.

Lastly, when tabulating this data, we found that managers who viewed crisis management as a primary technical and reactive activity used faulty rationalizations, as defined in Chapter Five, seven times more frequently than did managers who embraced a crisis-prepared view.

Exhibit A.1. Crisis Management Questionnaire Agenda.

Question 1:

Industry: _____ Age of the firm: _____

Number of Employees: _____ Annual Sales: _____

Number of Operating Sites: _____ Number of SBU: _____

International Operations: _____

Question 2:

A. Could you help me to understand your responsibilities in your function?

B. Number of years in this function: _____ With the company: _____

Actual Title: _____

Question 3:

A. What are your particular functions in the area of crisis management?

Exhibit A.1. Crisis Management Questionnaire Agenda, Cont'd.

B. How would you define a "crisis"?

C. How would you define "crisis management"?

Question 4:

A. Which crises has your company (or plant) identified as critical?

B. How did your company identify these particular crises?

Question 5:

A. Which crisis management efforts has your company (or plant) identified as critical?

B. How were they decided upon?

Question 6:

A. Could you give me some examples of crises that have occurred within your organization in the past? What did you do?

B. What did you learn from these experiences?

Question 7:

A. Overall, how would you evaluate the crisis management efforts in your company or plant:
    ___ too little
    ___ sufficient
    ___ too much

B. In your company (or plant), is it fairly easy to talk about difficult subjects (things that might be disturbing to you or others)?

C. In your opinion, what kinds of short-term action can your company (or plant) take to avoid crises?

Question 8:

A. What is the official corporate philosophy of your company (or plant)? (A printed document where it is actually stated would be appreciated.)

B. In your opinion, does your company follow this philosophy, or is the statement just "big words"?

Exhibit A.1. Crisis Management Questionnaire Agenda, Cont'd.

Question 9:

How would your top management rate the following corporate purposes?

	Least important					Most important	
	1------2------3------4------5------6------7						
• Bottom line/profits	1	2	3	4	5	6	7
• Community welfare	1	2	3	4	5	6	7
• Quality of work life	1	2	3	4	5	6	7
• Customer satisfaction	1	2	3	4	5	6	7
• Shareholder satisfaction	1	2	3	4	5	6	7
• Welfare of the region	1	2	3	4	5	6	7
• Welfare of the country	1	2	3	4	5	6	7
• Corporate image	1	2	3	4	5	6	7

Question 10:

A. What are the three top crisis stakeholders that your company (plant) focuses on most to make decisions?

B. What is the worst that could happen to them?

1.

2.

3.

Question 11:

In your opinion, how do the following levels of your company (or plant) need to change in order to have a more integrated crisis management effort:

A. Top management level (leadership, politics, company vision)?

B. Social level (organizational culture)?

C. Structural level (administration, human resource procedures, financial policies, and so on)?

Questionnaire Data

In early 1987, with the help of the public affairs office of the National Association of Manufacturers (NAM), we mailed one thousand questionnaires to the public affairs directors of the Fortune 1000 companies. The survey was designed to identify how much experience these companies had with crises in the last three years, to evaluate the types of measures they had developed, and to gauge the general attitudes toward crises. The questionnaire is presented in Exhibit A.2.

We received 114 questionnaires back (11.4 percent response rate) which, considering the sensitivity of the topic, seems acceptable. The sample we compiled seemed highly diversified; however, it is not possible to assure that the sample is totally representative. Potential biases, for example, include the fact that all these firms belong to the same association and that the questionnaires were sent only to public affairs directors.

Respondent organizations employed on the average 13,639 people, ranging from 100 to 100,000, with a standard deviation of 24,277. Also, while the respondents were not required to reveal their identities, of the forty-seven organizations that did so one could recognize some of the most important and visible organizations in the United States. Forty percent of these organizations ranked themselves in the top half of the Fortune 1000 ranking.

Finally, 75 percent of the sample was represented by ten different industries: high technology, heavy manufacturing, agriculture, auto manufacturing, consumer products, food, defense, utilities, health care and chemical development. No individual industry represented more than 10.5 percent of the total sample.

To derive the crisis clusters and the preventive action clusters presented in Chapter One we performed an orthogonal factor analysis of the variables through the SAS program, using varimax rotation to exclude the least consistent structural dimensions. For an item to be included, we insisted on a loading close to .60. Using an eigen value of 1 as a cutoff point, six factors emerged from the data for the crises and five factors

Exhibit A.2. Questionnaire on Corporate Emergencies and Crisis Management.

Title of person completing this form _____

Company name (optional) _____

Fortune 1000 ranking _____ If not applicable, total number of employees _____

Major industry or business _____

Instructions: Below is a list of various potential causes and types of corporate crises. With your major product or business line in mind, please first go down the list and check how many incidents your organization has experienced in the last *three* years. Second, circle your current vulnerability to each. Please be frank and open with your answers; all responses will remain confidential. Thank you.

Type of Potential Crises	Number of incidents in Last 3 Years						Current Vulnerability Compared to 3 Years Ago				
	Zero	1 to 5	6 to 10	More Than 10	Does Not Apply	Don't Know	Much Less	Same	Much More	Does Not Apply	Don't Know
1. Product Defects	☐	☐	☐	☐	☐	☐	1	2	3	4	5
2. Defects in Plants and/or Equipment	☐	☐	☐	☐	☐	☐	1	2	3	4	5
3. Industrial/Environmental Accidents	☐	☐	☐	☐	☐	☐	1	2	3	4	5
4. Computer Breakdowns	☐	☐	☐	☐	☐	☐	1	2	3	4	5
5. Hostile Takeovers	☐	☐	☐	☐	☐	☐	1	2	3	4	5
6. On-Site Product Tampering/Sabotage	☐	☐	☐	☐	☐	☐	1	2	3	4	5

	1	2	3	4	5
7. Off-Site Product Tampering/Sabotage	☐	☐	☐	☐	☐
8. Counterfeiting of Products	☐	☐	☐	☐	☐
9. Rumors, Malicious Slander	☐	☐	☐	☐	☐
10. Bribery/Price Fixing	☐	☐	☐	☐	☐
11. Sexual Harassment	☐	☐	☐	☐	☐
12. Occupational Illness	☐	☐	☐	☐	☐
13. Terrorism	☐	☐	☐	☐	☐
14. Executive Kidnapping	☐	☐	☐	☐	☐
15. Poor Operator Training/Screening	☐	☐	☐	☐	☐
16. Copycat Threats	☐	☐	☐	☐	☐
17. Loss of Proprietary/ Confidential Information	☐	☐	☐	☐	☐
18. Copyright Infringement	☐	☐	☐	☐	☐
19. Boycotts	☐	☐	☐	☐	☐
20. Product Recalls	☐	☐	☐	☐	☐
21. Other (list briefly)	☐	☐	☐	☐	☐

Exhibit A.2. Questionnaire on Corporate Emergencies and Crisis Management, Cont'd.

Instructions: Below is a listing of various actions that organizations can undertake to prevent, cope with, contain, and recover from crises of all kinds. Please rate the extent to which your organization is undertaking each.

Type	Undertaking/Engaging in						
	Not at All				*Extensively*	*Does Not Apply*	*Don't Know*
	1	2	3	4	5	6	7
1. Implemented Preventive Product Packaging	1	2	3	4	5	6	7
2. Implemented Early Warning Systems for Detection of Potential Crises	1	2	3	4	5	6	7
3. Improved Design of Plants/Equipment/ Products	1	2	3	4	5	6	7
4. Improved Systemwide Safety and Security Testing	1	2	3	4	5	6	7
5. Improved Maintenance Schedules and Frequency of Inspection of Plants and Equipment	1	2	3	4	5	6	7
6. Improved Organization Chain of Command	1	2	3	4	5	6	7
7. Brought in Outside Experts to Review Plans and Operations	1	2	3	4	5	6	7
8. Developed Emotional Preparation for Crises by Bringing in Psychological Consultants	1	2	3	4	5	6	7
9. Media Training for Key Executives	1	2	3	4	5	6	7

10. Established a Program of Issues Management	1	2	3	4	5	6	7
11. Developed Behavioral Profiles of Terrorists and Copycat Killers for Better Warning/Protection	1	2	3	4	5	6	7
12. Established Special 800 Numbers for Product Recall or Consumer Fears	1	2	3	4	5	6	7
13. Established Relationships with Government Officials/Agencies at All Levels	1	2	3	4	5	6	7
14. Established "Whistleblower" Programs to Warn of Potential Internal Crises	1	2	3	4	5	6	7
15. Share Crisis Plans Within the Industry	1	2	3	4	5	6	7
16. Reduced Inventories of Hazardous Materials	1	2	3	4	5	6	7
17. Sponsored/Developed Special Legislation	1	2	3	4	5	6	7
18. Legal and Financial Audit of Liabilities	1	2	3	4	5	6	7
19. Environmental Impact Audit	1	2	3	4	5	6	7
20. Established Relationships with Activist Groups	1	2	3	4	5	6	7
21. Conducted Employee Classes on Emergency Preparedness	1	2	3	4	5	6	7
22. Other (list briefly) _____	1	2	3	4	5	6	7

Exhibit A.2. Questionnaire on Corporate Emergencies and Crisis Management, Cont'd.

Instructions: Please indicate the extent of your agreement or disagreement with the items below.

	Agree Strongly 1	2	3	4	5	6	Disagree Strongly 7
1. Every organization should have a permanent crisis management unit or team.	1	2	3	4	5	6	7
2. Most organizations, unless they first experience a major crisis, will not engage in a serious program of crisis management. Why/why not? (Briefly describe) _____	1	2	3	4	5	6	7
3. A company should withdraw its products from the market or shut down its facilities at the first signs that they might cause harm to the public.	1	2	3	4	5	6	7
4. A company should withdraw its products or shut down its facilities only after ordered to do so by federal and state agencies.	1	2	3	4	5	6	7

5. What, if any, are the most important lessons your company has learned regarding crisis management? (Briefly describe) _____

6. Does your organization have a formal crisis management unit (CMU) or team? □ Yes □ No

Are you a member of it? □ Yes □ No

If your organization has a CMU or team, are the following individuals members of it?

Chief Executive Officer □ Yes □ No
Chief Financial Officer □ Yes □ No
Chief Operating Officer □ Yes □ No
Chairman of the Board □ Yes □ No
Director of Engineering/Production □ Yes □ No
Director of Marketing □ Yes □ No
Outsiders □ Yes □ No
Others (please list) _____

Director of Research □ Yes □ No
Chief Legal Counsel □ Yes □ No
Director of Environmental Affairs □ Yes □ No
Director of Security □ Yes □ No
Director of Personnel □ Yes □ No
Director of Safety □ Yes □ No
Director of Public Affairs □ Yes □ No

	Weekly	Monthly	Quarterly	Annually	Only When a Crisis Occurs	Doesn't Apply	Don't Know
	1	2	3	4	5	6	7

7. How often does your CMU team meet?

8. What is the approximate dollar amount of liability claims settled for the past three years?

_____

emerged for the preventive actions. In both cases, the factors were reduced to four factors using two additional analyses.

First, we examined the Cronbach Alpha reliability coefficients for each factor. Second, we performed different Metric Multidimensional Scaling (MDS) through the ALSCAL program on SAS. The measures of proximity used were the Pearson correlation coefficient between the variables. The MDS best-fit two-dimensional solutions seemed adequate according to Kruskal stress coefficients.

Thus, in both cases, the clusters were selected through the use of four stringent criteria:

1. More than 10 percent of the variance had to be explained by each factor.
2. To be included, each item had to load close to .60 on each factor.
3. Each factor had to have a Alpha coefficient of .70. (One factor did not meet this criterion but its Alpha was of reasonable magnitude.)
4. The clustering pattern uncovered from the MDS had to be similar to the clustering patterns established in the factor analyses.

The factor analyses are presented in Tables A.1 and A.2; the MDS results are presented in Figures 1.2 and 1.3. Results were particularly interesting, as they demonstrated the extent of the interdependent relationships between crises, as argued in Chapter One.

As the data indicate, the majority of relationships between crises are positive (see Table A.3 and Figure A.1). For example, environmental accidents are related positively to engineering or technical issues such as plant defects (.55), computer breakdowns (.30), and operator errors (.28). They are also related to a wealth of crises involving social or psychological issues such as sexual harassment (.36), information loss (.35), rumors (.33), off-site tampering (.30), boycotts (.27), on-site tampering (.25), and terrorism (.22). These findings clearly indicate the futility of defining strict cause-and-effect relationships

Table A.1. Varimax Rotated Factor Loadings of Crises (n = 83).[a]

	Factor 1	Factor 2	Factor 3	Factor 4
Reliability (standardized α)	.69	.71	.85	.57
Variance explained by each factor (eigen value)	3.26	2.78	2.65	1.91
Percentage of variance explained	17.20	14.60	14.00	10.00
Cumulative variance	17.20	31.80	45.80	55.80
Counterfeiting of products	.62[b]			
Sexual harassment	.67	.29		
Occupational health diseases	.67			
Loss of confidential information	.74	.31		.27
Copyright infringement	.63		.22	.22
Boycotts	.58		.22	
Product defects		.62		.25
Defects in plants or equipment		.81		
Poor operator training/screening	.33	.66		
Computer breakdowns	.34	.60		
Off-site product tampering	.22		.85	
Terrorism			.74	
Copycat threats			.89	
Bribery				.71
Product recalls	.23			.80
Rumors, malicious slander[c]	.50	.39		
Industrial/environmental accidents	.31	.55	.32	
On-site product tampering		.41	.31	.46
Hostile takeover		-.24	-.26	.51

[a]All loadings $\geq$ .20.
[b]Underlined items represent those that have been included in a factor.
[c]Not included in any factor due to their multiple loadings on different ones.

in the area of crisis management. It is impossible, for example, to determine whether environmental accidents are "caused" by on-site tampering, or whether the accidents themselves are "causing" additional on-site tampering by disturbed employees. The findings also indicate the danger of isolating one factor, such as engineering or financial management, as the definitive source of a crisis. Managers who adhere to this outlook place their organizations in a dreadfully vulnerable position, as this narrow focus does not take into account the complex nature of industrial disasters.

Table A.2. Varimax Rotated Factor Loadings of Preventive Actions (n = 45).[a]

	Factor 1	Factor 2	Factor 3	Factor 4
Reliability (standardized α)	.83	.78	.72	.76
Variance explained by each factor (eigen value)	3.83	3.12	2.76	2.70
Percentage of variance explained	18.20	14.90	13.10	12.90
Cumulative variance	18.20	33.10	46.20	59.10
Early warning systems	.66[b]	.22	.31	.33
Media training	.68		.28	.24
Special 800 number	.66		.34	
Relationships with government	.62	.32		
Sharing of crisis plan within industry	.74			.38
Improved security and safety	.27	.75		
Improved design plants/equipment	.20	.79		
Improved inspection/maintenance		.81		.32
Emotional preparation for crises			.73	
Behavioral profiles of terrorists	.26		.78	
Whistleblower programs			.64	
Relationships with activist groups	.41	.23	.56	
Reduction of hazardous inventories				.72
Development of special legislation			.42	.56
Legal and financial audit of liabilities	.33		.20	.69
Preventive product packaging[c]	.57	.63	.39	
Employee classes	.48	.37	.20	
Improved chain of command		.53		.46
Environmental impact audit	.51			.47
Issues management program	.41		.30	.49
Use of outside experts	.29	.32		.31

[a]All loadings $\geq$ .20.

[b]Underlined items represent those that have been included in a factor.

[c]Not included in any factor due to their multiple loadings on different ones.

Table A.3. Means, Standard Deviation, and Correlations Between Nineteen Types of Crises (n = 85).

	Number of Crises[a]	Standard of Deviation	1	2	3	4	5	6	7	8	9	10	11	12	13	14	15	16	17	18	19
1. Product defect	4.21	3.58	1.0	.20[d]	.50[b]	.19[d]	.09[b]	.17	.22[d]	.34[b]	.22[d]	.02	.07	.28[b]	.21	.14	.21[c]	.002	.13	−.03	.16
2. Environmental accident	3.87	3.30		1.0	.55[b]	.30[b]	.33[b]	.35[b]	.36[b]	.28[b]	.09	.26[b]	.24[c]	.30[b]	.09	.17	.25[c]	.27[b]	.22[c]	−.18[d]	.12
3. Plant defect	3.21	3.27			1.0	.41[b]	.23[b]	.19[d]	.35[b]	.40[b]	.12	.09	.03	.15	−.12	.03	.23[c]	.06	.08	−.08	.02
4. Computer breakdown	2.60	3.29				1.0	.44[b]	.38[b]	.17	.47[b]	.17	.12	.14	.03	.28[b]	−.11	.17	.13	−.07	−.02	−.11
5. Rumors	2.29	3.00					1.0	.39[b]	.41[b]	.38[b]	.06	.28[b]	.23[c]	.36[b]	.21[d]	.13	.25[c]	.25[c]	.07	−.03	.06
6. Information loss	2.18	2.58						1.0	.64[b]	.39[b]	.38[b]	.28[b]	.23[c]	.36[b]	.21[d]	.13	.25[c]	.25[c]	.07	−.03	.29[c]
7. Sexual harassment	1.89	2.51							1.0	.33[b]	.20[c]	.35[c]	.29[c]	.29[c]	.38[b]	.11	.11	.35[b]	.01	−.04	.11
8. Operator errors	1.83	2.81								1.0	.33[b]	.35[b]	.09	−.08	.36[b]	−.06	.04	.04	.24[c]	−.08	.11
9. Recalls	1.73	2.33									1.0	.05	.43[b]	.44[b]	.12	.13	.44[b]	.19[d]	−.03	−.01	.04
10. Occupational illness	1.68	2.74										1.0	.27[c]	.04	.28[c]	.02	−.07	.31[b]	.09	−.08	.04
11. Copyright infringement	1.50	2.46											1.0	.33[b]	.35[b]	.20[d]	.16	.40[b]	.55[b]	−.01	−.06
12. Off-site tampering	1.42	3.00												1.0	.08	.78[b]	.28[c]	.18	−.004	.27[c]	.40[b]
13. Counterfeiting	1.33	2.54													1.0	.02	.07	.06	.58[b]	−.01	.11
14. Copycats	.67	1.50														1.0	.23[c]	.21[d]	.16	−.08	.02
15. On-site tampering	.66	1.24															1.0	−.05	.11	−.18	.04
16. Boycotts	.65	1.94																1.0	.11	.13	.04
17. Terrorism	.62	1.83																	1.0	−.04	.21[c]
18. Hostile takeovers	.44	1.06																		1.0	.18[d]
19. Bribery	.30	1.29																			1.0

[a]: Average number of crises encountered per firm in the last three years.
Reliability: [b]: p(=.01); [c]: p(=.05); [d]: p(=.10).

Figure A.1. Correlations Between Nineteen Types of Crises (n = 85).

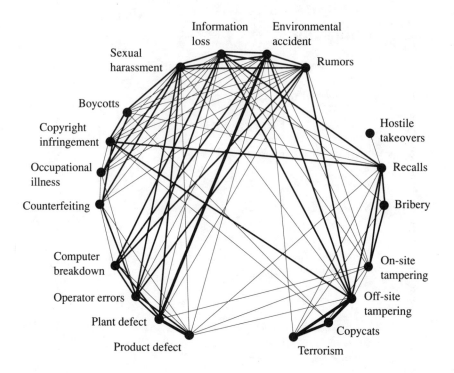

———————— Loose coupling (correlation coefficients between .19 and .29).

———————— Mid-range coupling (correlation coefficients between .30 and .49).

———————— Tight coupling (correlation coefficients >.49).

Evaluating the Crisis-Preparedness of Your Organization

To help you rate your organization's degree of crisis-preparedness, we have developed a questionnaire for each layer of the Onion Model described in this book. These questionnaires will help you determine whether your organization is in the "danger," "question mark," or "safety" zone for each of the four layers of the model, and will provide a useful tool for comparing your company to an ideal crisis-prepared organization.

If possible, distribute copies of these questionnaires to other employees, and compare and discuss your results. If you wish to share your results with us, please send copies of Exhibits B.1 through B.5, along with your official title and a brief description of your firm (including the type of business, number of employees, amount of annual sales revenues, and geographical location of your plant(s)/headquarters) to Professor Thierry C. Pauchant, HEC, University of Montreal, 5255 Decelles Avenue, Montreal, Quebec, H3T IV6, Canada. Tel.: 514-340-6375. We do not claim that these questionnaires are scientific in the traditional sense of the term; they are merely a good starting point for realizing the differences in perception among a company's employees. The executives, managers, and professionals who used these questionnaires generally found them helpful for stimulating thought and discussion about diverse issues in crisis management.

At the end of this resource you will find a graph (Exhibit B.6) on which to plot your responses to the questionnaires and create a visual profile of your organization. The USC Center for Crisis Management has also developed a software package that permits users to complete the questionnaires on line, evaluates the responses, and creates the graphs. A full description of this software is available through the Center for Crisis Management, Graduate School of Business, University of Southern California, Los Angeles, Calif. 90089. Tel.: (310) 740-0154.

**Exhibit B.1. Personality Issues That Affect Crisis Management
(Layer One of the Onion Model).**

Instructions: Please evaluate to what extent most top managers in your organization believe in each statement by circling the appropriate numbers.

	Very true		Neither true nor false			Not true at all	
1. We can handle any crisis.	1	2	3	4	5	6	7
2. If a crisis happens, someone else will rescue us.	1	2	3	4	5	6	7
3. This will not happen to us.	1	2	3	4	5	6	7
4. Nothing good is served by mulling over past crises.	1	2	3	4	5	6	7
5. Our products are not dangerous.	1	2	3	4	5	6	7
6. Our responsibility is, before all, legal and financial.	1	2	3	4	5	6	7
7. Nothing big can hurt us.	1	2	3	4	5	6	7
8. We do enough already.	1	2	3	4	5	6	7
9. Crises are fun. It is our job to manage them.	1	2	3	4	5	6	7
10. We are all professionals and we know what we're doing.	1	2	3	4	5	6	7
11. Prove to me it can hurt us financially.	1	2	3	4	5	6	7
12. Crises happen by fatality; we cannot prepare for them.	1	2	3	4	5	6	7
13. Only bad companies have crises.	1	2	3	4	5	6	7
14. We do not have the time.	1	2	3	4	5	6	7
15. Crises happen by the wrongdoing of a few rotten apples.	1	2	3	4	5	6	7
16. Our job is to keep our stockholders happy by increasing our bottom line.	1	2	3	4	5	6	7

Exhibit B.1. Personality Issues That Affect Crisis Management
(Layer One of the Onion Model), Cont'd.

	Very true		Neither true nor false			Not true at all	
17. We need to focus only on the positive.	1	2	3	4	5	6	7
18. We have other priorities.	1	2	3	4	5	6	7
19. A crisis has always one or two major causes.	1	2	3	4	5	6	7
20. "Don't worry, be happy."	1	2	3	4	5	6	7

Directions for scoring: Total the scores for all the questions. If your total score is above 110, then your organization is in the "safety zone" for this dimension of the Onion Model. If it is between 60 and 99, then your organization is in the "question mark zone." If it is below 59, your organization is in the "danger zone."

Exhibit B.2. Corporate Culture and Crisis Management (Layer Two of the Onion Model).

Instructions: Please evaluate to what extent, in general, most executives, managers, professionals, and employees in your organization believe in each statement by circling the appropriate numbers.

	Very true		Neither true nor false			Not true at all	
1. Our size will protect us.	1	2	3	4	5	6	7
2. Excellent, well-managed companies do not have crises.	1	2	3	4	5	6	7
3. Our special location protects us.	1	2	3	4	5	6	7
4. Certain crises only happen to others.	1	2	3	4	5	6	7
5. Crises do not require special procedures.	1	2	3	4	5	6	7
6. It is enough to react to crises once they have happened.	1	2	3	4	5	6	7
7. Crisis management or crisis prevention is a luxury.	1	2	3	4	5	6	7
8. Employees who bring bad news need to be punished	1	2	3	4	5	6	7
9. Our employees are so dedicated, we can trust them without question.	1	2	3	4	5	6	7
10. Desirable business ends justify taking high-risk means.	1	2	3	4	5	6	7
11. If a major crisis happens, someone else will rescue us.	1	2	3	4	5	6	7
12. The environment is benign; we can buffer ourselves from it.	1	2	3	4	5	6	7
13. Nothing new has really occurred that warrants change.	1	2	3	4	5	6	7
14. Crisis management is someone else's responsibility.	1	2	3	4	5	6	7

Resource B: Evaluating Your Organization 217

Exhibit B.2. Corporate Culture and Crisis Management (Layer Two of the Onion Model), Cont'd.

	Very true		Neither true nor false			Not true at all	
15. It's not a crisis if it does not happen to us or hurt us.	1	2	3	4	5	6	7
16. Accidents are just a cost of doing business.	1	2	3	4	5	6	7
17. Most crises turn out not to be very important.	1	2	3	4	5	6	7
18. Each crisis is so unique, it is impossible to prepare for it.	1	2	3	4	5	6	7
19. Crises are isolated.	1	2	3	4	5	6	7
20. Most crises resolve themselves. Time is our best ally.	1	2	3	4	5	6	7
21. Most if not all crises have a technical solution.	1	2	3	4	5	6	7
22. It's enough to apply technical and financial quck-fixes to problems.	1	2	3	4	5	6	7
23. Crises are solely negative in their impact. We cannot learn from them.	1	2	3	4	5	6	7
24. Crisis management is like an insurance policy. You only need to buy so much.	1	2	3	4	5	6	7
25. In a crisis situation, we just need to refer to the emergency procedures we've laid out.	1	2	3	4	5	6	7
26. We are a team that will function well during a crisis.	1	2	3	4	5	6	7
27. Only executives need to be aware of our crisis plans; why scare our employees or members of the community?	1	2	3	4	5	6	7
28. We are tough enough to react to a crisis in an objective and rational manner.	1	2	3	4	5	6	7

SOURCE: *Transforming the Crisis-Prone Organization,* by Thierry C. Pauchant and Ian I. Mitroff. San Francisco: Jossey-Bass. Copyright ©1992. Permission to reproduce and distribute material (with copyright notice visible) is hereby granted. If material is to be used in a compilation to be sold for profit, please contact publisher for permission.

**Exhibit B.2. Corporate Culture and Crisis Management
(Layer Two of the Onion Model), Cont'd.**

	Very true		Neither true nor false			Not true at all	
29. We know how to manipulate the media.	1	2	3	4	5	6	7
30. The most important thing in crisis management is to protect the good image of the organization through public relations and advertising campaigns.	1	2	3	4	5	6	7
31. The only important thing in crisis management is to make sure that our internal operations stay intact.	1	2	3	4	5	6	7

Directions for scoring: Total the scores for all of the questions. If your total score is above 154, then your organization is in the "safety zone" for this dimension of the Onion Model. If it is between 93 and 154, then your organization is in the "question mark" zone. If it is below 93, your organization is in the "danger zone."

Exhibit B.3. Structural Issues That Affect Crisis Management (Layer Three of the Onion Model).

Instructions: Please answer the following questions by circling the appropriate numbers.

	Not at all		Somewhat in the process			Well-established	
1. Is there a well-established structure for crisis management?	1	2	3	4	5	6	7
2. Is there a well-defined crisis management unit?	1	2	3	4	5	6	7
3. Have the roles of each person on the crisis management unit been clearly identified?	1	2	3	4	5	6	7
4. Have the crisis management unit members practiced their roles and functions?	1	2	3	4	5	6	7
5. Do members of the crisis management unit meet regularly?	1	2	3	4	5	6	7
6. Have they worked out potential sources of conflict among them?	1	2	3	4	5	6	7
7. Is there a clearly identified crisis management unit leader or facilitator?	1	2	3	4	5	6	7
8. Does the crisis management unit interact with other departments?	1	2	3	4	5	6	7
9. Has the crisis management unit given explicit support by your CEO?	1	2	3	4	5	6	7
10. Does the crisis management unit regroup executives and managers from diverse departments?	1	2	3	4	5	6	7
11. Does the crisis management unit include individuals exterior to your organization?	1	2	3	4	5	6	7

SOURCE: *Transforming the Crisis-Prone Organization,* by Thierry C. Pauchant and Ian I. Mitroff. San Francisco: Jossey-Bass. Copyright ©1992. Permission to reproduce and distribute material (with copyright notice visible) is hereby granted. If material is to be used in a compilation to be sold for profit, please contact publisher for permission.

**Exhibit B.3. Structural Issues That Affect Crisis Management
(Layer Three of the Onion Model), Cont'd.**

	Not at all		Somewhat in the process			Well-established	
12. Are "whistleblowers" formally rewarded in your organization?	1	2	3	4	5	6	7
13. Is there a special unit tracking potential warning signals?	1	2	3	4	5	6	7
14. Is there a special unit formally probing for potential crises?	1	2	3	4	5	6	7
15. Is information about crises shared and communicated to the crisis management unit?	1	2	3	4	5	6	7
16. Has a crisis management center or facility been established?	1	2	3	4	5	6	7
17. Have relationships with outside stakeholders been established?	1	2	3	4	5	6	7
18. Is there an explicit communication strategy in crisis management?	1	2	3	4	5	6	7
19. Are backups in communication technologies available?	1	2	3	4	5	6	7
20. Has a crisis management data base been created?	1	2	3	4	5	6	7
21. Are security personnel in direct sensory contact with technologies?	1	2	3	4	5	6	7
22. Have attempts at simplifying procedures and production processes been developed?	1	2	3	4	5	6	7
23. Are workshops and training in crisis management offered?	1	2	3	4	5	6	7
24. Are crisis simulations conducted in your organization?	1	2	3	4	5	6	7

**Exhibit B.3. Structural Issues That Affect Crisis Management
(Layer Three of the Onion Model), Cont'd.**

	Not at all		Somewhat in the process			Well-established	
25. Are media training and workshops offered in your organization?	1	2	3	4	5	6	7
26. Are workshops in "assumptions surfacing" offered?	1	2	3	4	5	6	7
27. Are workshops in criminal behavior offered in your organization?	1	2	3	4	5	6	7
28. Are your employees periodically surveyed about crisis management?	1	2	3	4	5	6	7
29. Are crisis management issues incorporated into production design?	1	2	3	4	5	6	7

Directions for scoring: Total the scores for all the questions. If your total score is above 150, then your organization is in the "safety zone" for this dimension of the Onion Model. If it is between 90 and 150, then your organization is in the "question mark zone." If it is below 90, your organization is in the "danger zone."

SOURCE: *Transforming the Crisis-Prone Organization,* by Thierry C. Pauchant and Ian I. Mitroff. San Francisco: Jossey-Bass. Copyright ©1992. Permission to reproduce and distribute material (with copyright notice visible) is hereby granted. If material is to be used in a compilation to be sold for profit, please contact publisher for permission.

Exhibit B.4. Strategic Issues That Affect Crisis Management (Layer Four of the Onion Model).

Instructions: Please answer the following questions by circling the appropriate numbers.

	Not at all		Somewhat in the process			Well-established	
1. Is crisis management integrated into the overall strategic management process?	1	2	3	4	5	6	7
2. Have specific crisis management policies been formulated?	1	2	3	4	5	6	7
3. Have products and services been modified in the past on the basis of their potential crisis threats?	1	2	3	4	5	6	7
4. Do the crisis management plans reflect the particular "strategic mood" of top management?	1	2	3	4	5	6	7
5. Do plans go beyond technical, economic, and legal considerations?	1	2	3	4	5	6	7
6. Have these plans been formulated on the basis of a critical assessment of strategic assumptions?	1	2	3	4	5	6	7
7. Have stakeholders exterior to the firm been integrated into the strategic management process?	1	2	3	4	5	6	7
8. Are crisis management unit members integrated into the strategic management process?	1	2	3	4	5	6	7
9. Are your CEO and top management actively supporting the crisis management plans?	1	2	3	4	5	6	7
10. Are strategies directed toward the development of the firm and its environment?	1	2	3	4	5	6	7

Exhibit B.4. Strategic Issues That Affect Crisis Management
(Layer Four of the Onion Model), Cont'd.

	Not at all		Somewhat in the process			Well- established	
12. Have the potential threats caused by the organization to its environment been integrated into the crisis management plans?	1	2	3	4	5	6	7
13. Are crisis management plans continuously reviewed and modified?	1	2	3	4	5	6	7
14. Has a crisis portfolio been formally established?	1	2	3	4	5	6	7
15. Has a crisis management portfolio been formally established?	1	2	3	4	5	6	7
16. Are crisis management plans both reactive and proactive?	1	2	3	4	5	6	7
17. Have explicit learning mechanisms been developed?	1	2	3	4	5	6	7
18. Does a special team study previous warning signals inside and outside the organization?	1	2	3	4	5	6	7
19. Are short-term and long-term recovery mechanisms tested and in place?	1	2	3	4	5	6	7
20. Are preventive measures tested and in place?	1	2	3	4	5	6	7

Directions for scoring: Total the scores for all the questions. If your total score is above 110, then your organization is in the "safety zone" for this dimension of the Onion Model. If it is between 60 and 99, then your organization is in the "question mark zone." If it is below 59, your organization is in the "danger zone."

Exhibit B.5. Rating Your Organization Against an
Ideal Crisis-Prepared Profile.

Instructions: Below is a list of activities that would be undertaken and carried out by an ideally crisis-prepared organization. Please evaluate the extent to which your organization is undertaking each of these activities by circling the appropriate numbers.

	Not at all		Somewhat in the process			Well-established	
1. Drastic changes in corporate philosophy	1	2	3	4	5	6	7
2. Integration of crisis management in corporate excellence	1	2	3	4	5	6	7
3. Integration of crisis management in strategic planning process	1	2	3	4	5	6	7
4. Inclusion of outsiders on board, crisis management unit, etc.	1	2	3	4	5	6	7
5. Training and workshops in crisis management	1	2	3	4	5	6	7
6. Crises simulations	1	2	3	4	5	6	7
7. Diversification and portfolio strategies	1	2	3	4	5	6	7
8. Creation of a crisis management unit	1	2	3	4	5	6	7
9. Creation of dedicated budgets for crisis management	1	2	3	4	5	6	7
10. Developing and changing emergency policies and manuals	1	2	3	4	5	6	7
11. Computerized inventories of plants' employees, products, etc.	1	2	3	4	5	6	7
12. Creation of a strategic emergency room or facilities	1	2	3	4	5	6	7
13. Reduction of hazardous products, services, and production	1	2	3	4	5	6	7

Exhibit B.5. Rating Your Organization Against an
Ideal Crisis-Prepared Profile, Cont'd.

	Not at all		Somewhat in the process			Well-established	
14. Improved overall design and safety of products and production	1	2	3	4	5	6	7
15. Technological redundancy, such as computer network backup	1	2	3	4	5	6	7
16. Use of outside experts and services in crisis management	1	2	3	4	5	6	7
17. Legal and financial audit of threats and liabilities	1	2	3	4	5	6	7
18. Modifications in insurance coverage	1	2	3	4	5	6	7
19. Environmental impact audit and respect of regulations	1	2	3	4	5	6	7
20. Ranking most critical activities necessary for daily operations	1	2	3	4	5	6	7
21. Early warning signals detection, scanning, issues management	1	2	3	4	5	6	7
22. Dedicated research on potential hidden dangers	1	2	3	4	5	6	7
23. Critical follow-up of past crises	1	2	3	4	5	6	7
24. Media training for crisis management	1	2	3	4	5	6	7
25. Major public relations efforts	1	2	3	4	5	6	7
26. Increased information to local communities	1	2	3	4	5	6	7
27. Increased relationships with intervening groups (police, media)	1	2	3	4	5	6	7
28. Increased collaboration or lobbying among stakeholders	1	2	3	4	5	6	7

**Exhibit B.5. Rating Your Organization Against an
Ideal Crisis-Prepared Profile, Cont'd.**

	Not at all		Somewhat in the process			Well-established	
29. Use of new communication technologies and channels	1	2	3	4	5	6	7
30. Strong top-management commitment to crisis management	1	2	3	4	5	6	7
31. Increased relationships with activist groups	1	2	3	4	5	6	7
32. Improved acceptance of whistleblowers	1	2	3	4	5	6	7
33. Increased knowledge of criminal behavior	1	2	3	4	5	6	7
34. Increased visibility of crises' human impact to employees	1	2	3	4	5	6	7
35. Psychological support to employees	1	2	3	4	5	6	7
36. Stress management and management of anxiety	1	2	3	4	5	6	7
37. Symbolic reminding of past crises and dangers and successes	1	2	3	4	5	6	7

Directions for scoring: Total the scores for all the questions. If your total score is above 183, then your organization is in the "safety zone." If it is between 77 and 183, then your organization is in the "question mark zone." If it is below 77, your organization is in the "danger zone."

Exhibit B.6. Visual Profile of Answers to Exhibits B.1–B.5.

	Safety Zone	Question Mark Zone	Danger Zone
Layer Four: Strategy			
Layer Three: Structure			
Layer Two: Culture			
Layer One: Psyche			
Idealized: Crisis-Prepared Organization			

Name: _____

Date: _____

References

Aktouf, O. (1989). *Le management entre tradition et renouvellement.* Montréal, Québec: Gaëtan Morin.

Aktouf, O. (1991). Management and theory of organizations in the nineties: Toward a critical radical-humanism. Working paper. Montréal: École des Hautes Études Commerciales, University of Montréal.

Alcoholics Anonymous. (1957). *Alcoholics Anonymous comes of age.* New York: HarperCollins.

Amado, G. (1980). Psychoanalysis and organization. *Sigmund Freud House Bulletin, 4,* 17–20.

Amado, G. (1987). Cohésion organisationelle et illusion collective. In A. Larocque and others (Eds.), *Technologies nouvelles et aspects psychologiques.* Québec: Presses de l'Université du Québec.

American Psychiatric Association. (1987). *Diagnostic and statistical manual of mental disorders* (3rd ed.). Washington, DC.

Ansoff, H. I. (1975). Managing strategic surprise by response to weak signals. *California Management Review, 18,* 21–33.

Argyris, C. (1957). *Personality and organization.* New York: HarperCollins.

Aubert, N., and de Gaulejac, V. (1990). *Le coût de l'excellence.* Paris: Seuil.

Ayres, R. U., and Rohatgi, P. K. (1987). Bhopal: Lessons for technological decision-makers. *Technology in Society, 9,* 19–45.

Barnard, C. (1938). *The function of the executive.* Cambridge, MA: Harvard University Press.

Barrett, W. (1986). *Death of the soul: From Descartes to computers.* New York: Anchor Press.

230   References

Bartol, C., and Bartol, A. (1986). *Criminal behavior: A psychological approach* (2nd ed.). Englewood Cliffs, NJ: Prentice-Hall.

Bateson, G. (1971). The cybernetic of "self": A theory of alcoholism. *Psychiatry, 34,* 1-18.

Bateson, G. (1972). *Steps to an ecology of man.* New York: Ballantine Books.

Baudrillard, J. (1983). *Les strategies fatales.* Paris: Grasset.

Baum, A. (1988, April). Disasters, natural and otherwise. *Psychology Today,* pp. 57-60.

Becker, E. (1973). *The denial of death.* New York: Free Press.

Bellah, R. N., Madsen, R., Sullivan, W. M., Swidler, A., and Tipton, S. M. (1985). *Habits of the heart: Individualism and commitment in American life.* Berkeley: University of California Press.

Bennis, W. G. (1989). *Why leaders can't lead: The unconscious conspiracy continues.* San Francisco: Jossey-Bass.

Bergson, H. (1982). *Matiére et mémoire. Essai sur la relation du corps a l'esprit.* Paris: Presse Universitaire de France.

Bettelheim, B. (1943). Individual and mass behavior in extreme situations. *Journal of Abnormal and Social Psychology, 38,* 417-452.

Billings, R. S., Milburn, T. W., and Schaalman, M. L. (1980). A model of crisis perception: A theoretical and empirical analysis. *Administrative Science Quarterly, 25,* 300-316.

Bion, W. R. (1959). *Experience in groups.* New York: Basic Books.

Black, M., and Worthington, R. (1988). Democracy and disaster: The crisis of (meta) planning in America. *Industrial Crisis Quarterly, 2,* 33-51.

Blake, W. (1958). *A selection of poems and letters.* New York: Penguin Books.

Block, F. (1979). *The origins of international economic disorders.* Berkeley: University of California Press.

Boisjoly, R. (1988, March). Whistleblower [Interview with Roger Boisjoly]. *Life,* pp. 17-22.

Bombardier, D., and Saint-Laurent, C. (1989). *Le mal de l'âme: Essai sur le mal de vivre au temps présent.* Paris: Robert Laffont.

Bowen, M. (1978). *Family therapy in clinical practice.* New York: Aronson.

Bowman, E., and Kunreuther, H. (1988). Post-Bhopal behavior at a chemical company. *Journal of Management Studies, 25,* 387-402.

Bowonder, B., and Linstone, H. A. (1987). Notes on the Bhopal accident: Risk analysis and multiple perspectives. *Technological Forecasting and Social Change, 32,* 183–202.

Brealey, R., and Myers, S. (1981). *Principles of corporate finance.* New York: McGraw-Hill.

Bryson, J. M. (1981). A perspective on planning and crises in the public sector. *Strategic Management Journal, 2,* 181–196.

Burgelman, R. (1983). A process model of internal corporate venturing in the diversified major firm. *Administrative Science Quarterly, 28,* 233–244.

Burns, T., and Stalker, G. M. (1961). *The management of innovation.* London: Tavistock.

Campbell, J. (1949). *The hero with a thousand faces.* Princeton, NJ: Princeton University Press.

Capra, F. (1982). *The turning point. Science, society and the rising of culture.* New York: Bantam Books.

Carson, R. (1962). *Silent spring.* Boston: Houghton-Mifflin.

Chaffee, E. E. (1985). Three models of strategy. *Academy of Management Review, 10,* 89–98.

Chandler, A. D. (1962). *Strategy and structure: Chapters in the history of the industrial enterprise.* Cambridge, MA: MIT Press.

Chanlat, A., and Bédard, R. (1990). La gestion, une affaire de parole. In J. F. Chanlat (Ed.), *L'individu dans l'organization. Les dimensions oubliées* (pp. 79–99). Québec: Presses de l'Université Laval/Paris: Eska.

Chanlat, J. F. (1991). Organizational analysis in French speaking countries: An overview. Working paper. Montreal: École des Hautes Études Commerciales, University of Montréal.

Christensen, S., and Schkabe, L. L. (1988). Financial and functional impacts of computer outages on business. Working paper. Arlington: Center for Research on Information Systems, University of Texas.

Churchman, C. W. (1983). *Thought and wisdom.* Seaside, CA: Intersystems Press.

Clark, J. P., and Hollinger, R. C. (1983). *Theft by employees in work organizations.* Washington, DC: U.S. Department of Justice.

Cohen, H. G. (1980). Prepared comments at the National Conference on Philosophy and Engineering Ethics. Troy, NY: Rensselaer Polytechnic Institute, June 15–20.

Collins, D. E. (1987). *Critical lessons learned from the experience in handling product tampering accidents: The case of Johnson & Johnson.* Presented at the Crisis Management Seminar, Center for Crisis Management, University of Southern California, Los Angeles, CA, September 14–15.

Cooper, R., and Burell, G. (1988). Modernism, postmodernism and organizational analysis: An introduction. *Organization Studies, 9,* 91–112.

Crozier, M. (1963). *Le Phenomène bureaucratique.* Paris: Seuil.

Cummings-Saxon, J., and others (1988). Accidental chemical releases and local emergency response: Analysis using the acute hazardous events data base. *Industrial Crisis Quarterly, 2,* 139–170.

Dejours, C. (1980). *Le travail, usure mentale: Essai de psychopathologie du travail.* Paris: Le Centurion.

Derrida, J. (1973). *Speech and phenomena.* Evanston, IL: Northwestern University Press.

Dostoyevsky, F. M. (1958). *The double: A poem of St. Petersburg* (G. Bird, Trans.). Bloomington: Indiana University Press. (Original work published 1845)

Durkheim, E. (1982). *The Rules of sociological method.* London: Macmillan.

Dutton, J. E. (1986). The processing of crisis and non-crisis strategic issues. *Journal of Management Studies, 23,* 501–517.

El Sawy, O., and Pauchant, T. C. (1988). Templates, triggers and twitches in the tracking of strategic issues. *Strategic Management Journal, 9,* 455–473.

Enriquez, E. (1989). L'individu pris au piege de la structure stratégique. *Connexions, 54,* 145–161.

Eraly, A. (1988). *La structuration de l'entreprise. La rationalité en action.* Brussels: Éditions de l'Université de Bruxelles.

Farnham, A. (1989, December 4). The trust gap. *Fortune,* pp. 56–78.

Fayol, H. (1916). Administration industrielle et générale. Prévoyance, organization, commandement, coordination, contrôle. *Bulletin de la Société de l'Industrie Minérale.* Geneva: International Management Institute.

Fink, S. (1986). *Crisis management: Planning for the inevitable.* New York: AMACOM (A division of the American Management Association).

Fink, S., Beak, J., and Taddeo, K. (1971). Organizational crisis and change. *Journal of Applied Behavioral Science, 7,* 15–37.

Forrester, J. W. (1971). Counterintuitive behavior of social systems. *Technology Review, 73,* 23–45.

Foucault, M. (1984). *Histoire de la sexuality: Le soucis de soi.* Paris: Gallimard.

Frankl, V. E. (1959). *Man's search for meaning: An introduction to logotherapy.* New York: Pocket Books.

Freud, A. (1966). *The ego and the mechanisms of defense* (rev. ed.). New York: International University Press.

Freud, S. (1921). *Group psychology and the analysis of the ego.* London: Hogarth Press.

Freud, S. (1926). *Inhibitions, symptoms and anxiety* (Vol. 20). London: Hogarth Press.

Freud, S. (1961). *Civilization and its discontents* (J. Strachey, Trans.). New York: W. W. Norton.

Friedman, M. (1970, September 3). The social responsibility of business is to increase its profits. *New York Times Magazine,* pp. 13–18.

Fromm, E. (1973). *The anatomy of human destructiveness.* Troy, MO: Holt, Rinehart & Winston.

Galbraith, J. R. (1977). *Organization Design.* Reading, MA: Addison-Wesley.

Garden, A. N. (1979). Getting the best PR from bad situations. *Inc., 1,* 105–106.

Gephart, R. P., Steier, L., and Lawrence, T. (1989). Cultural rationalities in crisis sensemaking: A study of a public inquiry into a major industrial accident. *Industrial Crisis Quarterly, 4,* 27–48.

Gleick, J. (1987). *Chaos: Making of a new science.* New York: Viking.

Goethe, J. W. (1959). *Faust* (P. Wayne, Trans.). New York: Penguin Books. (Original work published 1832)

Grof, C., and Grof, S. (1990). *The stormy search of the self: A guide to personal growth through transformational crisis.* Los Angeles: Jeremy P. Tarcher.

Habermas, J. (1973). *Legitimation crisis.* Boston: Beacon Press.

Hafsi, T. (1985). Du management au métamanagement: Les subtilités du concept de stratégy. *Revue Internationale de Gestion, 10,* 6–14.

Hall, R. I. (1976). A system pathology of an organization: The rise and fall of the old Saturday Evening Post. *Administrative Science Quarterly, 21,* 185–211.

Halper, J. (1988). *Quiet desperation: The truth about successful men.* New York: Warner Books.

Hambrick, D. C. (1980). Operationalizing the concept of business strategy in research. *Academy of Management Review, 5,* 567–575.

Hampden-Turner, C. (1981). *Maps of the mind: Charts and concepts of the mind and its labyrinths.* New York: Collier Books.

Hanna, R. W. (1975). Crisis in meaning: A phenomenological inquiry into the experience of a lack of meaning to life. Unpublished doctoral dissertation, Graduate School of Management, University of California at Los Angeles.

Hardin, G. (1971). Nobody ever dies of overpopulation. *Science, 171,* 524–532.

Harris, L. (1987). *Inside America.* New York: Vintage Books.

Heraclitus of Ephesus (1970). *The cosmic fragments* (G. S. Kirk, Ed.). Cambridge: Cambridge University Press.

Hermann, C. F. (1963). Some consequences of crisis which limit the viability of organizations. *Administrative Science Quarterly, 8,* 61–82.

Hesse, H. (1929). *Steppenwolf* (J. Mileck, Trans.). New York: Bantam.

Hill-Norton, P. (1976, October). Crisis management. *NATO Review, 5.*

Hills, S. L. (Ed.). (1987). *Corporate violence: Injury and death for profit.* Totowa, NJ: Rowman and Littlefield.

Hofstadter, D. R. (1980). *Gödel, Escher, Bach. An eternal golden braid.* New York: Vintage Books.

Horney, K. (1937). *The neurotic personality of our time.* New York: W. W. Norton.

Horowitz, M. J. (1976). Diagnosis and treatment of stress response syndromes: General principles. In H. J. Parad, H. L. Resnik, and L. G. Parad (Eds.), *Emergency and disaster management. A mental health source book.* Bowie, MD: Charles Press.

Jacob, J. P., and Sabelli, F. (1984). Entre malheur et catastrophe: Essai antropologique sur la crise comme représentation. In J. Jacob (Ed.), *Crise et chuchotements* (pp. 13–21). Paris: Presse Universitaire de France.

Janis, I. L. (1989). *Crucial decisions: Leadership in policymaking and crisis management.* New York: Free Press.

Jantsch, E. (1980). *The self-organizing universe: Scientific and human implications of the emerging paradigm of evolution.* New York: Pergamon Press.

Jung, C. G. (1971). *Psychological types* (R. F. Hull, Trans.). Bollingen Series XX. Princeton, NJ: Princeton University Press.

Kanter, R. M. (1989). *When giants learn to dance: Mastering the challenges of strategy, management, and careers in the 1990s.* New York: Simon & Schuster.

Karrh, B. W. (1990). Du Pont and corporate environmentalism. In W. H. Hoffman, R. Frederick, and E. S. Petry, Jr. (Eds.), *The corporation, ethics and the environment* (pp. 69–76). New York: Quorum Books.

Katz, D., and Kahn, R. L. (1978). *The social psychology of organizations* (2nd ed.). New York: Wiley.

Kelly, C. M. (1987). *The destructive achiever. Power and ethics in the American corporation.* Reading, MA: Addison-Wesley.

Kennedy, P. (1988). *The rise and fall of great powers: Economic change and military conflict from 1500 to 2000.* New York: Random House.

Kernberg, O. F. (1979). Regression in organizational leadership. *Psychiatry, 42,* 24–39.

Kets de Vries, M.F.R. (1977). Crisis leadership and the paranoid potential. *Bulletin of the Menninger Clinic, 41,* 349–365.

Kets de Vries, M.F.R. (Ed.). (1984). *The irrational executive. Psychoanalytic explorations in management.* New York: International University Press.

Kets de Vries, M.F.R., and Miller, D. (1985). *The neurotic organization: Diagnosing and changing counterproductive styles of management.* San Francisco: Jossey-Bass.

Kiechel, W., III. (1987, November 9). New debate about Harvard business school. *Fortune,* pp. 34–48.

Kierkegaard, S. (1980). *The concept of anxiety* (S. Thomte, Trans.). Princeton, NJ: Princeton University Press. (Original work published 1844)

Klein, M. (1937). *The psycho-analysis of children* (2nd ed.). London: Hogarth Press.

Koestler, A. (1979). *Janus: A summing up.* New York: Vintage Books.

Kohut, H. (1977). *The restoration of self.* New York: International University Press.

Kohut, H. (1984). *How does analysis cure?* Chicago: University of Chicago Press.

Kohut, H. (1985). *Self-psychology and the humanities: Reflections on a new psychoanalytic approach.* New York: W. W. Norton.

Kübler-Ross, E. (1969). *On death and dying.* New York: Macmillan.

LaBier, D. (1986). *Modern madness: The emotional fallout of success.* Reading, MA: Addison-Wesley.

Lagadec, P. (1981). *La civilization du risque: Catastrophes technologiques et responsibilité sociale.* Paris: Seuil. [Major technological risk: An assessment of industrial disasters. Oxford: Pergamon Press, 1982].

Lagadec, P. (1987). Communication strategies in crisis situations. *Industrial Crisis Quarterly, 1,* 19–26.

Lagadec, P. (1989). *Principles and check list for handling post-accident crises.* Paper presented at the Second International Conference on Industrial and Organizational Crisis Management, New York University, New York City, November 3–4.

Lagadec, P. (1991). *La gestion des crises: Outils de réflexion à l'usage des décideurs.* Paris: McGraw-Hill.

Laing, R. D. (1970). *Knots.* New York: Pantheon Books.

Lao Tzu (1944). *The way of life* (W. Brynner, Ed.). New York: Capricorn Books.

Lasch, C. (1979). *The culture of narcissism: American life in the age of diminishing expectations.* New York: Warner Books.

Lindblom, C. E. (1959). The science of "muddling-through." *Public Administration Review,* 79–88.

Lorenz, E. N., Malkus, W., Spiegel, E. A., and Farmer, J. D. (1963). Deterministic nonperiodic flow. *Journal of the Atmospheric Sciences, 20,* 130–140.

Lystad, M. (Ed.). (1988). *Mental health response to mass emergencies: Theory and practice.* New York: Brunner/Mazel.

McFarlane, A. C. (1985). The etiology of post-traumatic stress disorders following a natural disorder. Unpublished paper.

Department of Psychiatry, Flinders University of South Australia.

Machol, R. E. (1986). How much safety? *Interfaces, 16,* 50–57.

McWhinney, W. (1980). Paedogenesis and other modes of design. In T. G. Cummings (Ed.), *System theory for organization development.* New York: Wiley.

McWhinney, W. (1990). *Of paradigms and system theory.* Working paper. Santa Barbara, CA: The Fielding Institute.

Maier, M. (1988). It was not an accident: An insider's view of the unethical decision-making process that doomed the space shuttle *Challenger.* Videotape of presentation made by Roger Boisjoly at SUNY, Binghamton, February 19.

March, J. G., and Simon, H. A. (1958). *Organizations.* New York: Wiley.

Marcus, A., Bromiley, P., and Goodman, R. (1987). Preventing corporate crises: Stockmarket losses as a deterrent to the protection of hazardous products. *Columbia Journal of World Business, 22,* 33–42.

Maslow, A. H. (1968). *Toward a psychology of being* (2nd ed.). New York: Van Nostrand Reinhold.

Maslow, A. H. (1971). *The farther reaches of human nature.* New York: Viking Press.

Mason, R. O., and Mitroff, I. I. (1981). *Challenging strategic planning assumptions.* New York: Wiley.

Maturana, H. R., and Varela, F. J. (1980). *Autopoiesis and cognition: The realization of the living.* Boston: D. Reidel.

May, R. (1950). *The meaning of anxiety.* New York: Washington Square Press.

May, R. (Ed.). (1958). *Existence: A new dimension in psychiatry and psychology.* New York: Random House.

May, R. (1969). *Love and will.* New York: W. W. Norton.

May, R. (1975). *The courage to create.* New York: W. W. Norton.

Menzies, I. (1960). A case study in the functioning of social systems as a defense against anxiety. *Human Relations, 13,* 95–121.

Merton, R. K. (1957). *Social theory and social structure.* New York: Free Press.

Meyers, G. C. (1986). *When it hits the fan. Managing the nine crises of business.* New York: New American Library.

Michael, D. N. (1978). *On learning to plan and planning to learn: The social psychology of changing toward future-responsive societal learning.* San Francisco: Jossey-Bass.

Miles, R. E., and Snow, C. C. (1978). *Organizational strategy, structure and process.* New York: McGraw-Hill.

Miller, Alice (1981). *Prisoners of childhood. The drama of the gifted child and the search for the self.* New York: Basic Books.

Miller, Alice (1983). *For your own good. Hidden cruelty in child-rearing and the roots of violence.* New York: Farrar, Strauss & Giroux.

Miller, Arthur (1949). *Death of a salesman: Certain private conversations in two acts and a requiem.* New York: Viking Press.

Miller, D. (1988). Organizational pathology and industrial crisis. *Industrial Crisis Quarterly, 2,* 65–74.

Miller, D. (1990). *The Icarus paradox: How exceptional companies bring about their own downfall.* New York: HarperBusiness.

Miller, D., and Friesen, P. (1980). Archetypes of organizational transition. *Administrative Science Quarterly, 25,* 268–299.

Mindszenthy, B. J., Watson, T.A.G., and Koch, W. J. (1988). *No surprise: The crisis communications management system.* Toronto: Bedford House.

Mintzberg, H. (1973). *The nature of managerial work.* New York: HarperCollins.

Mintzberg, H. (1988). Opening up the definition of strategy. In J. B. Quinn, H. Hintzberg, and R. M. James. *The strategy process. Concept, contexts and cases* (pp. 13–20). Englewood Cliffs, NJ; Prentice Hall.

Mintzberg, H., Raisinghani, D., and Theoret, A. (1976). The structure of "unstructured" decision processes. *Administrative Science Quarterly, 26,* 246–275.

Mitchell, T. R., and Scott, W. G. (1990). America's problems and needed reforms: Confronting the ethics of personal advantage. *Academy of Management Executive, 3,* 23–35.

Mitroff, I. I. (1987). *Business NOT as usual: Rethinking our individual, corporate, and industrial strategies for global competition.* San Francisco: Jossey-Bass.

Mitroff, I. I. (1988). *Break-away thinking: How to challenge your business assumptions (and why you should).* New York: Wiley.

Mitroff, I. I., and Bennis, W. G. (1989). *The unreality industry:*

The deliberate manufacturing of falsehood and what it is doing to our lives. New York: Carol Publishing.

Mitroff, I. I., and Kilmann, R. H. (1984). *Corporate tragedies: Product tampering, sabotage, and other catastrophes.* New York: Praeger.

Mitroff, I. I., and Pauchant, T. C. (1990). *We're so big and powerful nothing bad can happen to us: An investigation of America's crisis-prone corporations.* New York: Carol Publishing.

Mitroff, I. I., Pauchant, T. C., Finney, M., and Pearson, C. (1990). Do some organizations cause their own crises? *Industrial Crisis Quarterly, 3,* 269–283.

Mitroff, I. I., Pauchant, T. C., and Shrivastava, P. (1988a). Conceptual and empirical issues in the development of a general theory of crisis management. *Technological Forecasting and Social Change, 33,* 83–107.

Mitroff, I. I., Pauchant, T. C., and Shrivastava, P. (1988b). Forming a crisis portfolio. *Security Management, 33,* 101–108.

Mitroff, I. I., and Pearson, C. (in press). *Critical thinking for messy problems: Concepts, models and software for crisis management.* Los Angeles: Center for Crisis Management, Graduate School of Business, University of Southern California.

Mohrman, A. M., and others (1989). *Large-scale organizational change.* San Francisco: Jossey-Bass.

Morin, E. (1968). Pour une sociologie de la crise. *Connexions, 12,* 2–16.

Morin, E. (1976). Pour une crisologie. *Connexions, 25,* 149–163.

Morin, E. M. (1990a). L'individu, le groupe et l'organization. Working paper. Montreal: École des Hautes Études Commerciales, University of Montreal.

Morin, E. (1990b). *Science avec conscience* (Nouvelle ed.). Paris: Fayard.

Moscovici, S. (Ed.). (1984). *Psychologie sociale.* Paris: Presse Universitaire de France.

Nietzsche, F. (1972). *Ainsi parlait Zaratheustra: Un livre pour tous et pour personne* (G. A. Goldschmidt, Trans.). Paris: Le Livre de Poche. (Original work published 1886)

Nystrom, P. C., and Starbuck, W. H. (1984). To avoid organizational crises, unlearn. *Organizational Dynamics, 12,* 53–65.

O'Connor, J. (1987). *The meaning of crisis: A theoretical introduction.* Oxford: Basil Blackwell.

O'Neill, M. (1989). *The third America: The emergence of the nonprofit sector in the United States.* San Francisco: Jossey-Bass.

Ortega y Gasset, J. (1953). *In search of Goethe from within* (W. R. Trask, Trans.). New York: Harcourt Brace Jovanovich.

Ortega y Gasset, J. (1958). *Man and crisis* (M. Adams, Trans.). New York: W. W. Norton.

Pagés, M. (1984). *La vie affective des groupes. Esquisse d'une théorie de la relation humaine* (2nd ed.). Paris: Dunod.

Pagés, M., Bonetti, M., de Gaulejac, V., and Descendre, D. (1979). *L'emprise de l'organisation.* Paris: Presses Universitaires de France.

Pascale, R. T. (1984). Perspective on strategy: The real story behind Honda's success. *California Management Review, 3,* 47–72.

Pauchant, T. C. (1988a). Crisis management and narcissism: A Kohutian perspective. Unpublished doctoral dissertation, Graduate School of Business Administration, University of Southern California, Los Angeles.

Pauchant, T. C. (1988b). An annotated bibliography in crisis management. Montreal: École des Hautes Études Commerciales, University of Montreal.

Pauchant, T. C. (1989). Le management des crises: D'une mode éphémére à une nécessité stratégique. *Préventique, 27,* 4–13.

Pauchant, T. C. (in press). In search of existence: On the use of the existential tradition in management. In F. Massarik (Ed.), *Advances in organizational development, vol. 2.* New York: Ablex Publishing.

Pauchant, T. C., and Dumas, C. (1991). Abraham Maslow and Heinz Kohut: A comparison. *Journal of Humanistic Psychology, 31,* 49–71.

Pauchant, T. C., and Fortier, I. (1990). Anthropocentric ethics in organizations: Strategic management and the environment: A typology. In P. Shrivastava and R. Lamb (Eds.), *Advances in strategic management* (Vol. 6, pp. 99–114). Greenwich, CT: JAI Press.

Pauchant, T. C., and Mitroff, I. I. (1988). Crisis prone versus crisis avoiding organizations. *Industrial Crisis Quarterly, 2,* 53–63.

Pauchant, T. C., and Mitroff, I. I. (1990). Crisis management: Managing paradox in a chaotic world—the case of Bhopal. *Technological Forecasting and Social Change, 38,* 99–114.

Pauchant, T. C., and Mitroff, I. I. (in press). Management by nosing around: Exposing the dangerous invisibility of technologies. *Journal of Management Inquiry.*

Pauchant, T. C., Mitroff, I. I., and Pearson, C. (1991). Crisis management and strategic management. Similarities, differences and challenges. In P. Shrivastava, A. Huff, and J. Dutton (Eds.), *Advances in strategic management, vol. 8.* Greenwich, CT: JAI Press.

Pauchant, T. C., Mitroff, I. I., Weldon, D. N., and Ventolo, G. F. (1990). The ever expanding scope of industrial crises. A systemic study of the Hinsdale telecommunications outage. *Industrial Crisis Quarterly, 4,* 243–261.

Peck, M. S. (1978). *The road less travelled: A new psychology of love, traditional values and spiritual growth.* New York: Simon & Schuster.

Perrow, C. (1984). *Normal accidents: Living with high-risk technologies.* New York: Basic Books.

Peters, T. (1988). *Thriving on chaos: Handbook for a management revolution.* New York: Knopf.

Peters, T. J., and Waterman, R. H., Jr. (1982). *In search of excellence: Lessons from America's best-run companies.* New York: HarperCollins.

Porter, M. E. (1980). *Competitive strategy, techniques for analyzing industries and competitors.* New York: Free Press.

Prabhu, M. (1988). The role of criminal law in preventing and reducing chemical hazards. *Industrial Crisis Quarterly, 2,* 327–338.

Prigogine, I., and Stengers, I. (1984). *Order out of chaos: Man's new dialogue with nature.* New York: Bantam Books.

Public Citizen (1988). Report on US nuclear safety. Washington, D.C.

Quinn, J. B. (1980). *Strategies for change: Logical incrementalism.* Homewood, IL: Richard D. Irwin.

Raphael, B. (1986). *When disaster strikes: How individuals and communities cope with catastrophe.* New York: Basic Books.

Reilly, A. H. (1987). Are organizations ready for crisis? A managerial scoreboard. *Columbia Journal of World Business, 22,* 79–88.

Report of the presidential commission on the space shuttle Challenger *accident.* (1986). No. 04000000496-3. Washington, DC: Government Printing Office.

Rogers, C. (1980). *A way of being.* Boston: Houghton Mifflin.

Roszak, T. (1986). *The cult of information: The folklore of computers and the true art of thinking.* New York: Pantheon Books.

St. John of the Cross (1959). *Dark night of the soul* (E. A. Peers, Trans.). New York: Doubleday. (Original work published 1577)

Sartre, J.-P. (1947). *Existentialism* (B. Frechtman, Trans.). New York: Philosophical Library.

Sartre, J.-P. (1963). *Search for a method* (H. E. Barnes, Trans.). New York: Knopf.

Satir, V. M. (1967). *Conjoint Family Therapy* (rev. ed.). Palo Alto, CA: Science and Behavior Books.

Schaef, A. W., and Fassel, D. (1988). *The addictive organization.* New York: HarperCollins.

Schein, E. H. (1985). *Organizational culture and leadership: A dynamic view.* San Francisco: Jossey-Bass.

Schumacher, E. F. (1973). *Small is beautiful: Economics as if people mattered.* New York: HarperCollins.

Schumacher, E. F. (1977). *A guide for the perplexed.* New York: HarperCollins.

Schwartz, H. S. (1987). On the psychodynamics of organizational disaster: The case of the space shuttle Challenger. *The Columbia Journal of World Business, 22,* 59–68.

Schwartz, H. S. (1989). Organizational disaster and organizational decay: The case of the National Aeronautics and Space Administration. *Industrial Crisis Quarterly, 3,* 319–334.

Schwartz, H. S. (1990). *Narcissistic process and corporate decay: The theory of organization ideal.* New York: New York University Press.

Sehti, S. P. (1985). The inhuman error: Lessons from Bhopal. *New Management, 3,* 40–44.

Selznick, P. (1957). *Leadership in administration.* New York: HarperCollins.

Shaw, L., and Sichel, H. S. (1971). *Accident proneness: Research in the occurrence, causation, and prevention of road accidents.* New York: Pergamon Press.

Shrivastava, P. (1987). *Bhopal: Anatomy of a crisis.* New York: Ballinger.

Sievers, B. (1986a). Participation as a collusive quarrel over immortality. *Dragon, 1,* 72–82.

Sievers, B. (1986b). Beyond the surrogate of motivation. *Organization Studies, 7,* 335–351.

Sipes, J. D. (1989). Keynote address, Second International Conference on Industrial and Organizational Crisis Management, New York University, New York City, November 3–4.

Slaikeu, K. A. (1984). *Crisis intervention. A handbook for practice and research.* Boston, MA: Allyn and Bacon.

Smart, C. F., and Vertinsky, I. (1977). Designs for crisis decision units. *Administrative Science Quarterly, 22,* 640–657.

Smart, C. F., and Vertinsky, I. (1984). Strategy and the environment: A study of corporate responses to crises. *Strategic Management Journal, 5,* 199–213.

Sobel, R. (1988). *Panic on Wall Street.* New York: Dutton.

Starbuck, W. H., and Milliken, F. J. (1988). Challenger: Fine-tuning the odds until something breaks. *Journal of Management Studies, 25,* 319–340.

Starke, L. (1987). *State of the world 1987: A Worldwatch Institute report on progress toward a sustainable society.* New York: W. W. Norton.

Stevens, W. D. (1989). Keynote address, Second International Conference on Industrial and Organizational Crisis Management, New York University, New York City, November 3–4.

Tannenbaum, R., and Hanna, R. W. (1985). Holding on, letting go, and moving on: A neglected perspective on change. In R. Tannenbaum, N. Margulies, F. Massarik, and Associates (Eds.), *Human system development: New perspectives on people and organizations* (pp. 95–121). San Francisco: Jossey-Bass.

Thompson, J. D. (1967). *Organizations in action.* New York: McGraw-Hill.

Tillich, P. (1952). *The courage to be.* New Haven, CT: Yale University Press.

Tillich, P. (1963, May 17). The ambiguity of perfection. *Time,* pp. 69–72.

Tortorella, A. (1987, August). Crisis Communication. Presented at the Crisis Management Seminar, American Meat Institute, Chicago.

Toynbee, A. (1972). *A study of history.* New York: Weathervane Books.

Tushman, M. L., Newman, W. H., and Romalli, E. (1986). Convergence and upheaval: Managing the steady pace of organizational evolution. *California Management Review, 29,* 29–44.

U.S. Bureau of the Census (1986). *Statistical abstract of the United States: 1987* (107th ed.). Washington, DC: Government Printing Office.

Wansell, G. (1987). *Tycoon: The life of James Goldsmith.* New York: Atheneum.

Watzlawick, P. (1988). *Ultra-solutions: How to fail most successfully.* New York: W. W. Norton.

Weick, K. E. (1979). *The social psychology of organizing* (2nd ed.). New York: Random House.

Weick, K. E. (1987). Organizational culture as a source of high reliability. *California Management Review, 24,* 112–127.

Weick, K. E. (1988). Enacted sensemaking in crisis situations. *Journal of Management Studies, 25,* 305–317.

Weir, D. (1987). *The Bhopal syndrome. Pesticides, environment and health.* San Francisco: Sierra Club Books.

Weisaeth, R. L. (1975). Stress reaction to an industrial disaster. Unpublished paper. Oslo: University of Oslo.

Whitaker, C. A. (1974). Process techniques of family therapy. *Interaction, 1,* 4–19.

Wildavsky, A. (1988). *Searching for safety.* New Brunswick, NJ: Transaction.

Wilkinson, C. B. (1983). Aftermath of a disaster: The collapse of the Hyatt Regency Hotel skywalk. *American Journal of Psychiatry, 140,* 1134–1139.

Zaleznik, A. (1989). *The managerial mystique: Restoring leadership in business.* New York: HarperCollins.

Zaleznik, A., and Kets de Vries, M.F.R. (1975). *Power and the corporate mind.* Boston: Houghton Mifflin.

Index

Index

Linstone, H. A., 34, 129
Location, fallacy of, 86, 89–90
Lorenz, E. N., 27
Louisville, deranged employee in, 95
Love Canal, disaster at, 10
Luck, fallacy of, 86, 98–99
Luxury, fallacy of, 86, 92–94
Lystad, M., 14, 17

M

McDonnell Douglas Company, and DC-10 problems, 14
McFarlane, A. C., 17
Machol, R. E., 191
McNeil Pharmaceuticals, and Tylenol, 90
McWhinney, W., 21, 175
Maier, M., 17, 94
Malkus, W., 27
Management. *See* Crisis management; Strategic management
Manipulation, fallacy of, 86, 101–102
March, J. G., 4, 24, 81
Marcus, A., 34
Maslow, A. H., 53, 140
Mason, R. O., 132, 196
Maturana, H. R., 20
May, R., 8, 18, 19, 21, 53, 61, 63–64, 67, 75, 164, 165, 166, 167
Media: manipulating, 101–102; strategies for choosing, 115–116
Mental health, and personality disorders, 64–73
Menzies, I., 178n, 179
Merton, R. K., 23
Mexico, San Juan Ixhuatepec crisis in, 10
MIC, at Bhopal, 35, 38, 42, 45
Michael, D. N., 131
Milburn, T. W., 11
Miles, R. E., 127, 128
Miller, Alice, 53
Miller, Arthur, 173
Miller, D., 20, 68, 71, 100, 127, 164
Milliken, F. J., 16, 111, 183
Mindszenthy, B. J., 115, 136

Mitzberg, H. D., 127, 130, 131
Mirror, fallacy of, 86, 101–102
Miss America Pageant, vulnerability of, 90
Mitchell, T. R., 188
Mitroff, I. I., 28, 34, 48, 80, 87, 93, 101, 102, 106, 109, 112, 118, 119, 129, 131, 132, 145, 196, 214–227
Mohrman, A. M., 165
Montreal Institute of Technology, mission reversal for, 15–16
Morin, E. M., 19, 20, 21, 141
Moscovici, S., 84
Moss Kanter, R., 106, 122
Myers, S., 93

N

Narcissism: amount of, 69; fallacy of, 86, 98
NASA: and crisis hotline, 162; emotionally-bounded managers in, 63; and mission reversal, 15; psychological trauma at, 16–17; and rationalizations, 87, 94, 97; and responsibility, 5; rewards at, 118; in systemic view, 22, 23–24. *See also Challenger*
National Association of Manufacturers, 28, 109, 201
National Training Laboratories, 177
Negativity, fallacy of, 86, 99–100
Neurosis, and personality types, 66
New York City: telecommunications outages in, 157; and terrorism, 90
Newman, W. H., 12
Nietzsche, F., 20, 70
Nixon, R. M., 101, 102
Nuclear industry: crises-incidents ratio in, 27; systemic impacts on, 14, 15. *See also* Chernobyl
Nystrom, P. C., 12

O

O'Connor, J., 18, 19, 20
O'Neill, M., 182
O Rings: and signal detection, 136; in systemic view, 22, 23, 27, 29